PICTURE THIS

PICTURE THIS

Picture Books
for Young Adults

A Curriculum-Related
Annotated Bibliography

DENISE I. MATULKA

GREENWOOD PRESS
Westport, Connecticut • London

Library of Congress Cataloging-in-Publication Data

Matulka, Denise I.
    Picture this : picture books for young adults : a
curriculum-related annotated bibliography / Denise I. Matulka.
       p.   cm.
    Includes bibliographical references and index.
    ISBN 0–313–30182–4 (alk. paper)
    1. Picture books—Bibliography.   2. Teenagers—United States—
Books and reading.   3. Young adult literature—Bibliography.
I. Title.
Z1033.P52M37   1997
016.0285′5—DC21   97–2234

British Library Cataloguing in Publication Data is available.

Library of Congress Catalog Card Number: 97–2234
ISBN: 0–313–30182–4

First published in 1997

Greenwood Press, 88 Post Road West, Westport, CT 06881
An imprint of Greenwood Publishing Group, Inc.

Printed in the United States of America

The paper used in this book complies with the
Permanent Paper Standard issued by the National
Information Standards Organization (Z39.48–1984).

10 9 8 7 6 5 4 3 2 1

"There is a receptive impressionable quality of mind, whether
in young or old, which we call childlike. A fresh direct vision, a
quickly stimulated imagination, a love of symbolic and typical form,
with a touch of poetic suggestion, a delight in frank and gay color, and a
sensitiveness to the variations of line, and contrasts of form—these are
some of the characteristics of the child, whether they be grown up or not.
Happy are they who remain children in these respects."

—Walter Crane, Nineteenth-Century Children's Illustrator

Contents

Acknowledgments

This reference work is based almost entirely on the holdings at Lincoln City Libraries in Lincoln, Nebraska. I extend gratitude to the librarians and library staff at the Lincoln City Libraries for their invaluable assistance as I selected and researched titles for this resource. In particular, I would like to thank Vicki Wood from the Youth Services Department at Bennett Martin Public Library, who patiently pulled titles from the shelf to verify an illustrator, a publisher, or a publication date. Peter Jorgensen from the Reference Desk at Bennett Martin Public Library verified a multitude of facts, including the origins of W. B. Yeats's retelling of the Irish folktale *Fin M'Coul*, that caterpillars are insects, when Dutch painter Hieronymous Bosch died, and exactly what a person might cook with the spice anise, with unfailing kindness and patience. I would like to note the gracious assistance of Sheila Wall and the Interlibrary Loan staff, who located and secured some rather obscure requests for me that enabled me to continue my research. I am privileged to have access to a magnificent children's literature collection without which this reference work would not have been possible.

Karla Hawkins Wendelin, Ph.D. has had an enormous influence on my writing and my research. Her dedication to the field of education and children's literature is hard to surpass. It was in a children's literature class taught by Karla that I discovered my vocation in life. Her guidance in the early stages of this project was invaluable to me. Her suggestions for organization and titles spurred me on. I hope to one day claim a storehouse of knowledge as vast as hers. All she requested in return was the first autographed copy of any book I published, which I gladly promised her. Thank you, Karla.

Joanne Ferguson, friend and colleague, who believes in me unfailingly and supports me in all my endeavors. She spent many hours reading and critiquing the manuscript, all writers should have such a friend. She is able to make any situation seem hopeful, or at the very least, a learning experience. She consistently sees the contributions I make to the field of children's literature, library youth services, and life in general when others overlook me. Thank you, Joanne.

I wish to express gratitude to the publishers who graciously donated titles. Harcourt Brace Jovanovich shipped me fifty books from their Browndeer and Gulliver Green lines, which are two imprints focusing on history and science. Creative Editions, a company which strives to create literature in an enticing format, sent me three sample titles and a complete full-color, annotated catalog, which was extremely helpful during my research. Lastly, I thank Sierra Club, a publisher with outstanding science titles, which includes Barbara Bash's Tree Tale series. Thank you.

Introduction

WHAT IS A PICTURE BOOK?

Children's literature is the only literary type determined by the age of its audience rather than by any special characteristics that define it. Folktales, fairy tales, tall tales, legends, myths, and poetry are a few literary forms that fall within the realm of children's literature. Unfortunately, by designating titles as "children's literature" a multitude of books are ignored or dismissed because it is assumed only a child will benefit or enjoy the contents within the covers. Interestingly, standard classics such as Daniel Defoe's *Robinson Crusoe* (1719), Jonathan Swift's *Gulliver's Travels* (1726), and Mark Twain's *The Adventures of Huckleberry Finn* (1884) are considered classics of children's literature because generations of children have embraced the stories as their own. Defoe, Swift, and Twain did not write these books for children. In fact, the authors would probably be amused to discover that their novels have been classified and assigned to children.

On the flip side are the fanciful works of Dr. Seuss. Adults can open Mr. Geisel's playful books and instantly be transported back to their youth. Adults everywhere enjoy *The Cat in the Hat* (Random House, 1957) and react as joyfully in the present as they did in the past. *The Cat in the Hat* contains 223 words and introduced a mischievous cat capable of all sorts of mayhem. The open acceptance of the naughtiness of the children, which is encouraged by *The Cat in the Hat*, was a subversive notion in the 1950s. Seuss's *Oh! The Places You'll Go* (Random House, 1990) has become a traditional gift for graduating high school and college students. *Oh! The Places You'll Go* is one of the few children's books to break records on the *New York Times* bestseller list for adults. Dr. Seuss's ability to integrate social issues with humor, creating an instantaneous effect because the message is delivered in a subtle manner, is riveting. *The Sneetches and Other Stories* (Random House, 1961) takes a hard look at discrimination based on appearances. *The Butter Battle Book* (Random House, 1984) is a deceptively simple scrutiny of the insanity of the nuclear arms race. The haunting message of environmental protection is implicit in *The Lorax* (Random House, 1971).

Despite the negative connotation, authors of works for children find that teachers and parents enjoy the books they have written as much as the children, who are the intended audience. Perhaps this explains the popularity of fairy tales and folktales, which have been thought of as a fundamental part of children's literature for more than two hundred years. In between the unquestioning years of childhood and the fond recollections of adulthood are the young adult years of condescension and budding maturity. During these years, teenagers crave wisdom and responsibility but are pulled towards childhood when everything was simple. Rejecting picture books and children's literature epitomizes this struggle.

Within the domain of children's literature are several formats: Novels, easy-readers, biographies, nonfiction, paperback editions, and picture books. Within each of these formats are a gamut of subjects from historical topics to social issues to contemporary fiction.

All picture book formats rely on illustrations and photographs to some extent. The distinct formats supply instruction or delight, or both, depending on the capacity in which they are used. Regardless of purpose, it is always recommended that titles are chosen with purpose in mind; select books that are crafted with thoughtfulness, imagination, and attention to detail. Picture book formats may be organized into the following categories:

1. Alphabet books are often used in an instructional capacity to introduce children to the ABC's. The multitude of ABC books available offer a wide variety of subjects from emotions to traditional animal books. Many titles contain sophisticated word play or intricate illustrations, which require certain experiences or knowledge to appreciate.

2. Concept books are well developed, illustrated titles that explore concepts such as shapes, colors, and time. Other difficult concepts such as principles of grammar and mathematical skills fall into this category.

3. Counting books, like alphabet books, are used in an instructional manner to introduce numbers and simple math concepts. There are many interesting titles to help children understand numbers and counting.

4. Easy readers are transition books for children moving from picture storybooks to chapter books. They are designed to be read with minimal or no assistance from an adult. They have a smaller trim size than standard picture books.

5. Picture storybooks are dependent on a strong relationship between the text and the illustrations to deliver the story. Picture storybook is the designation given to picture books with large amounts of text.

6. Toy books are board books, pull-tab books, flap books, pop-up books, cloth books, and plastic books (bathtub books). They are a wonderful introduction to children's literature.

7. Wordless books are excellent tools for helping children develop oral and written skills since text is usually minimal or absent. Well illustrated wordless books will offer a degree of detail and plot complexity.

Refining the term picture book to illustrated book or books with pictures to sell them to a young adult audiences is unnecessary. An illustrated book has art that supplements the text. A picture book is a union of the text and the illustrations which are of equal importance. Some critics consider picture books with more than 1000 words to be picture storybooks. Picture books can be an individual effort or a collaboration of efforts. Patricia Polacco, Paul Goble, and Gail Gibbons illustrate and write the text for their picture books. Margaret Hodges, Robert D. San Souci, and Jane Yolen are very talented writers, who work with artists with established reputations to create picture books. The unity of a book as a whole remains the central issue in picture books. Pictures books are often referred to as a genre, which is a misnomer because it removes the emphasis from the design and physical attributes. I have elected to consider picture books as a format with a multitude of genres to be found in the pages. No subject is taboo in picture books today: divorce, death, AIDS, racism, war, homosexuality, and religion find their way into picture book plots and illustrations. Outstanding picture books offer illustrations true to the spirit of the story and type that is legible and appropriate to the story. Page layout should move and adjust with the story to allow the plot to move to a successful ending. The Caldecott Medal is awarded each year to an illustrator whose efforts are considered to be the most distinguished for a title published the previous year. Maurice Sendak's *Where The Wild Things Are* (HarperCollins, 1963) won in 1964 and is an ideal example to introduce elements of picture book design to your students. Another title is David Wiener's *Tuesday* (Clarion, 1991), which has sixty-four characters. Try reading *Tuesday* to your class without showing them the pictures. The entire design of *Tuesday* makes the title ideal to introduce the impact of illustration in a story. Chances are they will ask to see the pictures by the time you reach the end of either book. Illustrators are very conscious of colors and choice of medium when determining criteria for each picture book. Outstanding illustrators are known for their distinctive styles or choice of medium. Michael McCurdy and Brian Pinkney are noted for their scratchboard art; Heidi Goennel and Frané Lessac's simple naive paintings are distinctive; Ed Young's luminous impressionistic paintings capture the essence of a story in a very unique way; Jeannie Baker, Susan L. Roth, and Molly Bang are renowned for their masterful collage illustrations. Whatever medium selected, the colors and materials should blend with the story and the theme. An author can use any number of approaches: historical, biographical, or informational, but unity is the goal of any finished picture book.

PICTURE BOOK HISTORY

Children's illustration has evolved in the last 100 years to become a booming business for publishers; yet despite the financial aspects, the true benefactors of the rich traditions of children's illustration is today's child and the picture book. With thousands of new titles published each year, the competition is tough, and only a few stand out among the thousands published.

The nineteenth-century illustrators found an avid audience eager for rich texts accompanied by quality illustrations. For the first time illustrators had the technical means to produce many of the first illustrated books with children in mind. For the first time children were clearly defined as an audience with literary needs distinct from adults. A mass of books designed for children flooded the publishing scene: picture books with nursery rhymes, poetry, limericks, fairy tales, fables, and adventure all appeared suited to appeal to the taste of children.

The 1920s were greatly affected by World War I, the social and economic consequences of the war resulted in a reduction in book publishing, although this did not hinder the interest in developing quality literature for children. One apparent feature of the 1920s was a lack of new and original illustrators for children; the bulk of books were either reprints of Beatrix Potter or nineteenth-century imitators. However, the decade of the 1920s did produce such talent as A.A. Milne collaborating with Ernest Shepard; Wanda Gag, who wrote and illustrated her own books; and Margery Bianco Williams whose *Velveteen Rabbit* with illustrations by William Nicholson is now considered a classic. Nicholson is credited with experimenting with reproduction techniques and the introduction of offset color lithographs.

The depression era 1930s was a productive time in terms of creativity, but artists still felt the effects of a battered economy. The rise of the children's librarian and the special efforts to call attention to the literary needs of children was the boost that kept the market fresh despite limited publication. The 1930s saw the first serious publication of a thorough exploration of children's literature: F.J. Harvey Darton's *Children's Books in England* and the periodical *Junior Bookshelf*, which devoted its pages to children's book reviews. It was also the decade that heralded the first presentation of the Caldecott Award.

World War II was even more devastating economically than World War I, and its effects resulted in a severe shortage of books. In an effort to combat the ravages of war on the book market, Simon and Schuster introduced the Little Golden Books. In England in 1935, Allen Lane had established the Penguin dynasty, which spawned Baby Puffin Books and Puffin Picture Books. The quality of these titles were bleak at best, yet kept the genre of children's books alive and kicking. The 1940s offered the talents of Robert McCloskey, Ludwig Bemelmens, Robert Lawson, Roger Duvoisin, Lois Lenski, and a quirky and very original Theodor Seuss Geisel.

The 1950s heralded a new breed of artists, who looked behind to the past and forward to the future. Post-war years saw a renewal in the interest of the children's library system, which stimulated the demand for quality as well as quantity. The 1950s is also the decade in which Marcia Brown's—winner of the Caldecott Medal three times and Honor recipient six times—career began to blossom. This is also the decade which introduced a master artist, Maurice Sendak.

The picture book, as we know it, took off in the 1960s. An influx of talented artists experimenting with an array of artistic mediums and reproduction techniques allowed the picture book to become a dominant format in children's literature. Artists were discovering the limitless possibilities of the picture book as an artistic outlet, this and recognition of the unity of words and pictures in the development of children, placed the picture book on the pedestal, where it was given serious consideration.

Prior to the 1970s the typical child in a picture storybook was middle-class and white. In the '70s children of color were introduced into picture books, but the portrayal was rife with stereotypes and cultural inaccuracies. Yes, children of different cultures were represented but with white characteristics, which created a need for authenticity and substance. White children also received their fair share misrepresentation, for years they had to bear the "Dick and Jane" stigma. A few writers, such as Ezra Jack Keats, did make attempts to correct this in the 1960s and 1970s. *Whistle for Willie* (Viking, 1964) is a classic that comes under fire for stereotypes perceived by many critics.

The 1980s saw a rising consciousness of racial and sex stereotypes in the children's literature field. In addition, writers began to tackle formerly taboo subjects such as AIDS, presenting poignant, touching messages of a devastating disease that touches the lives of many children. The late '80s and early '90s saw the rise of multicultural literature for children. Prior to 1990 less that one percent of all children's literature published was published by authors of color. The recognition of the importance of depicting authentic, accurate characteristics of race and the role it plays in child development is a landmark of these decades. Children of color are now drawn by authors of color, and escape the bias of stereotyping that has plagued children of color ever since the publication of *The Story of Little Black Sambo* (1899) by Helen Bannerman.

Just over one hundred years ago children had very few books they could call their own. Today, over four thousand titles are published annually; the selection of picture books seems limitless. Modern techniques and production capabilities no longer inhibit the illustrator, and publishers are recognizing the possibilities of children's divisions within publishing houses that hitherto did not cater to young audiences. A wealth of talented illustrators such as Diane Stanley, Floyd Cooper, Jerry Pinkney, and David Wisniewski are taking the picture book from a format to an art form, and the children of the world, despite chronological age, are the ones to reap the benefits. Yet, many critics argue that too much emphasis is placed on art and that showmanship has created a format that is inaccessible to children. This debate is ideal for young adults to gnaw on as they explore the possibilities of picture books.

The history of illustration is a fascinating study all its own. Children's illustration has evolved into an art form, attracting the attention it so richly deserves. In the early nineteenth century publishers enlisted the talents of illustrators to adorn the pages of children's books. The creative hands of Walter Crane, Howard Pyle, N. C. Wyeth, and Randolph Caldecott set in motion a format now known lovingly as picture book, which is enjoyed by children and adults alike. Susan E. Meyer's *A Treasury of the Great Children's Book Illustrators* (Abrams, 1983) is an excellent book for readers interested in an introduction to the artists responsible for creating picture books as a format for children.

PICTURE BOOKS FOR OLDER READERS

Picture books are often viewed as a type of reading that a child begins with and then moves away from. After a child is able to read independently, he or she is introduced to easy readers, chapters books, and novels. The richly illustrated picture books of childhood are left behind. Using the debate of showmanship, I argue that the sophisticated subjects and richly detailed illustrations in flashy picture books are ideal to enhance the education of young adults. Many picture books suffer an unfortunate fate because, while the content is mature, such as with *Kate Shelley: Bound For Legend* (Dial, 1995) by Robert D. San Souci, the picture book format discourages older readers. Other picture book titles that suffer this fate include Ken Mochizuki's *Baseball Saved Us* (Lee & Low, 1993), which looks at the abominable interment camps Japanese Americans were forced to live in during World War II. Elinor Batezat Sisulu's *The Day Gogo Went to Vote: South Africa, April, 1994* (Little, Brown, 1996) celebrates the long struggle of black South Africans, who fought for the right to vote. *The Rime of the Ancient Mariner* (Atheneum, 1992) by Samuel Taylor Coleridge has been illustrated by Ed Young, making the poem accessible for young adults, who might otherwise struggle. *The Ballad of the Harp-Weaver* (Philomel, 1991) by Edna St. Vincent Millay, illustrations by Beth Peck, is from her Pulitzer Prize-winning collection *Harp-Weaver and Other Poems* (Harper, 1923). Using this title with young adults introduces the powerful writing of an early twentieth-century female writer.

COLLECTION DEVELOPMENT

Currently children's and young adult librarians across the country are evaluating their picture book collections, exploring where to shelve the titles preschool children and their parents don't check out. Often picture books about historical figures, religion, and folktales are shelved in the nonfiction section according to the Dewey Decimal system. Picture books stand out against novels and works of nonfiction because of the large size and thin spines that distinguish them. Unfortunately, though the nonfiction section is frequently used for book reports and homework, many of the picture books shelved there are not checked out because teachers and young adults are unaware of the contribution picture book format offers to education. Thus, a large proportion of picture books are never utilized to their full extent.

The public library system in my city has designated "jP" for general picture books and "j" plus a number for nonfiction titles in picture book format. A "j" is used for fiction intended for readers ages six through eighteen. The designation means that sophisticated picture books are nestled among the biographies and encyclopedias in the nonfiction section of the children's department. Shelving the titles with nonfiction signifies that the picture books are for research, but does the format still impede the selection for young adults? I know many libraries separate their young adult collections from children's material by assigning the letters "YA." The appointment of "YA" denotes mature subjects to older readers. Some librarians catalog the picture books for older readers as they would if it were a novel, and then shelve the picture books among the regular young adult collection. The inclusion of picture books with novels or biographies allows for maximum circulation, and also identifies a librarian knowledgeable of her collection. Is it enough to distinguish by call number only? It is amazing, but a simple adjustment in your shelving arrangement or a more drastic reassignment of your call numbers may make all the difference in your circulation figures. However, if titles are not promoted through book talks, reading lists, or book displays, no amount of special shelving or classification will matter. Whatever method of shelving or classification that is employed, knowledgeable librarians will familiarize themselves with the collection and find other means to generate interest in picture books for older readers.

With the thousands of titles published each year, it can be a challenge to expose children and young adults to quality literature. The tendency to allow children to read anything as long as they are reading is a weak notion. Challenge yourself to become familiar with titles children don't gravitate toward and find ways to incite interest. Because a book is not commercially mass-marketed does not mean that it will not appeal to a younger reader. One of the simplest ways to integrate picture book titles into a young adult's reading time is to include them on reading lists. Next time you compile a list of titles about a particular subject, include picture books. When a young adult asks for books about the Civil War include *John Brown: One Man Against Slavery* (Rizzoli, 1993) by Gwen Everett and *Nettie's Trip South* (Macmillan, 1987) by Ann Turner. The bulk of programming dollars are spent on preschool children, reallocate funds and develop programming for young adults. Get caught at the circulation desk reading a picture book. Sharing a picture book with a young adult is an effective means of exposing them to other picture book titles. Responsible book selection includes viewing titles from several angles and keeping in mind audiences of all ages and ethnic backgrounds. Teachers and parents should be prepared for resistance. "That's a book for a baby!" will roll off many young adult's tongues until they experience the benefits of picture books.

The challenge to write, publish, and promote picture book titles that reflect ageless appeal will be an ongoing process shared by authors, illustrators, publishers, librarians, and teachers. Children and parents rely on professionals for guidance; they rely on knowledgeable sources. Using theme and different formats when helping young adults select material allows for a rich and varied reading experience.

ART AND LITERARY DESIGNATIONS

Each annotation includes an assignment of artistic medium, artistic style, and literary form. For the purposes of this resource artistic style is defined as the style of the artwork in each given picture book. I designated the following terms when discussing artistic style: naive, representational, impressionism, expressionism, cartoon style, and folk art. These designations are based my personal interpretation rather than artistic expertise. The notion that art is a matter of interpretation was put to the test when assigning art styles in *Picture This*. In most cases the verso page in picture books contains notes about the medium used for the illustrations and was referred to whenever possible. If the description of artist's method was lengthy, the medium was listed as mixed media. The term "representational" can also be interpreted as "realistic" or "realism." The term folk art was used to describe artwork that conveyed a strong essence of the time or place in conjunction with the story. I consider photographs to be illustrations in the description of picture book as a format. It was decided for the purpose of this resource that photography is a form of illustration, and that the camera is as significant as a paintbrush when illustrating picture books. The literary form designation simply identifies the style of writing in each book (i. e. folktale, tall tale, poetry). Titles classified as fairy tales or legends are as appropriate as titles with the designation of biography or nonfiction.

COMPANION RESOURCES FOR *PICTURE THIS*

Picture This: Picture Books for Young Adults was designed as a resource to help teachers and librarians begin to use picture books with young adults. The 424 annotated titles and over 500 companion titles were selected for their sophisticated content. The appendices, glossary, and indexes were thoughtful additions intended to make integrating picture books into young adult classrooms and libraries easy and fun. I sincerely hope teachers and librarians will find a treasure trove of picture books that will serve a multitude of purposes—whether the group they are working with are young adults, preschoolers, or adults learning to read. Some resources I found particularly insightful were *Beyond Words: Picture Books For Older Readers and Writers* (Heinemann, 1992) by Susan Benedict and Lenore Carlisle, which is a compilation of essays by noted librarians, teachers, students, and illustrators exploring the use of picture books with older readers. *Using Picture Storybooks to Teach Literary Device* (Oryx Press, 1994) by Susan Hall is an annotated bibliography of 300 picture books that demonstrate literary elements such as alliteration, irony, onomatopoeia, parody, and analogy. This is an excellent resource for English and creative writing teachers who want to ignite interest in the art of the English language. *Fairy Tales, Fables, Legends, and Myths: Using Folk Literature in Your Classroom, 2nd ed.* (Teacher's College Press, 1992) by Bette Bosma is an indispensable resource with hundreds of ideas for using folk literature in the classroom. It is important to note that Bosma's emphasis is on the contribution of folk elements in the retellings rather than the illustrations. It is intended to explore adapting the literary form of folk literature into the curriculum. All of the professional resources in Appendix II are excellent selections for professionals interested in exploring picture books and children's literature.

SCOPE AND INTENT OF RESOURCE

The wide array of picture book titles published each year offers something for readers of every age. It is my hope that professionals find this bibliography useful and easy to maneuver. Users unfamiliar with picture book format will find the information in the appendices and glossary especially helpful. Titles from Barbara Bash's Tree Tales series are examples of nonfiction picture books. Authors such as James Cross Giblin and Leonard Everett Fisher produce titles with exquisite illustrations and dependable, accurate information. Titles with spare narrative were included if the illustrations extended the usefulness of the title, adding depth and dimension to the entire book. Frané Lessac's charming Caribbean titles are examples of spare text and strong illustrations. When considering titles, I depended on subject matter as well as illustrations. Gail Gibbon's and Tomie de Paola's cartoon-style illustrations are deceptively simple, but richly detailed and thoroughly researched. Yet each author combines articulate writing and meticulously researched text to produce delightfully readable picture books. Both Gibbon and dePaola manage to bring refreshing light to topics ranging from rainforests to saints. Word count was not a factor when deciding on titles for *Picture This* although most titles have 100 to 3000 words. Accuracy of the information is the key to successful picture book text.

A note about the indexes: There are separate indexes for the annotated titles and the companion titles. Only the titles from the annotated title index are cross referenced in the subject, author, and illustrator indexes; however, by referring to the annotation in which a companion title is referenced, the user will get a good feel for the subject of the companion title.

Finally, I did not include titles I would not recommend personally, so it may be noted that there is little criticism in the annotations. If I liked a book and felt there was a drawback, it was mentioned in passing. It was not my intent to create a critical study of picture books, but rather to build a useful guide to assist librarians, teachers, and parents when selecting and using picture books.

ARRANGEMENT

The titles are arranged into six content areas: The arts, literature and language, mathematics, science and nature, and social sciences and history. The entries are arranged alphabetically by author within each content area. The numerical designations for each entry will guide the user through the appendices and the indexes. Below is a sample entry.

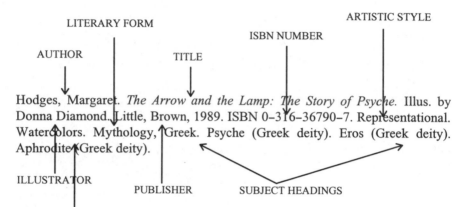

A retelling of the Greek myth of love and the painful consequences of betrayal. Psyche, a beautiful and intelligent girl, with the grace of a deer and the kind heart of an angel, is a threat to Aphrodite, the Greek goddess of love and beauty. Jealous of Psyche, Aphrodite sends her son Eros to ruin any chance of happiness Psyche may have in life. Aphrodite's plan fails when Eros, struck by Psyche's beauty, fails to carry out his mother's commands and spares Psyche. He takes Psyche to his palace and gives her all she desires, exacting one promise in return: That she not look upon his face or from. He warns her to ignore any temptation to discover his identity. But Psyche, with only unseen hands to wait on her and a mysterious husband for company, becomes lonely and wishes for human companionship. At the malicious insistence of her jealous sisters, Psyche betrays Eros and looks upon his sleeping form. To regain her husband, she must complete three tasks set to her by Aphrodite, that include traveling to Hades. The story "Eros and Psyche" can be found in *Metamorphoses, or the Golden Ass*, written in the second century A. D. by Lucius Apuleius. Compare Hodges's version with *Cupid and Psyche* (Morrow, 1996) by M. Charlotte Craft. Explore the tale of "Eros and Psyche" in conjunction with other famous lovers in literature: Tristan and Isolde from the Celtic legend, Arthur and Guinevere from British legend, and the romantic escapades of Don Juan from Spain.

Chapter 1

The Arts

The titles in the arts section include illustrated versions of ballets, biographies of composers, and famous musical pieces. Titles were chosen for both artistic expression and subject content. The titles are most appropriate to use to introduce or enhance the background of the topics taught in music and art classes.

1   Beckett, Sister Wendy. *A Child's Book of Prayer in Art.* Reproductions. Dorling Kindersley, 1995. ISBN 1–56458–875–0. Nonfiction. Religion. Prayer. Christian Art and Symbolism. Art Appreciation. di Bondone, Giotto (1276?–1337?).

A selection of paintings chosen by Sister Wendy Beckett reflecting the importance of values and the power of prayer in daily life. The meaning of respect, love, forgiveness, and family is explored via famous works of art. Each painting appears in its entirety in a reduced format, and details significant to the theme of the paintings are emphasized in vignettes. For example, forgiveness is represented by Giotto di Bondone's *The Kiss of Judas*. Adjacent to the art is commentary by Sister Wendy Beckett, who explores the meaning of each value by examining the details and themes within each painting. The book may be approached from two angles: as a introduction to masterpieces of art or as an examination of the powerful effect of prayer in history. *Lives and Legends of the Saints* (Simon & Schuster, 1995) by Carole Armstrong and *Stories from the Old Testament: Masterwork Paintings Inspired by the Stories* (Simon & Schuster, 1996) are other picture books that explore the powerful effect of religion in art. *The Glorious Impossible* (Simon & Schuster, 1990) by Madeline L'Engle, a narrative story about the life of Jesus Christ, features frescoes by Giotto di Bondone. Other titles featuring reproductions of famous works of art in lieu of original illustrations include *I Spy: An Alphabet in Art* (Greenwillow, 1992) and *I Spy A Fright Train: Transportation in Art* (Greenwillow, 1996), both by Lucy Micklethwait.

2   Burgie, Irving. *Caribbean Carnival: Songs of the West Indies.* Illus. by Frané Lessac. Tambourine, 1992. ISBN 0–688–10780–X. Expressionism. Gouache. Songs. Burgie, Irving (b. 1924). Songwriters. West Indies—Songs and Music. Calypso Music.

A collection of Calypso songs by famed songwriter Irving Burgie. Calypso music is a uniquely West Indian musical expression that is familiar to people around the world. Each song is accompanied by simple guitar and piano arrangements that enable students to explore the lively music of Irving Burgie. Frané Lessac's naive paintings, though simple on the surface, are chock full of details of the colorful and vibrant life of the West Indies. The combined artwork, musical arrangements, and historical significance of this book make *Caribbean Carnival: Songs of the West Indies* a treat. Use with *A Caribbean Dozen: Poems from Caribbean Poets* (Candlewick Press, 1994) edited by John Agard and Grace Nichols, *La Diablesse and the Baby: A Caribbean Folktale* (Annick, 1994) by Richardo Keens-Douglas, *Hue Boy* (Dial, 1993) by Rita Phillips Mitchell, *One White Sail: A Caribbean Counting Book* (Green Tiger Press, 1992) by S. T. Garne to explore the unique expression of Caribbean artists and writers. *Caribbean Canvas* (Lippincott, 1987) by Frané Lessac combines original paintings of island life with West Indian proverbs and poems to create a pictorial journey through the Caribbean islands. *Caribbean Alphabet* (Tambourine, 1989), also by Frané Lessac, is an alphabet book featuring fruits, flowers, and animals native to the Caribbean Islands.

3   Croll, Carolyn. *Redouté: The Man Who Painted Flowers.* Illus. by author. G. P. Putnam's, 1996. ISBN 0–399–22606–0. Naive. Watercolors. Biography. Redouté, Pierre Joseph (1759–1840). Painters. Botanical Illustration.

An attractive biography of nineteenth-century botanical artist Pierre Joseph Redouté. Today, Redouté's paintings hang in palaces and museums all over the world. During his lifetime he was official painter for two majestic women: Empress Josephine and Queen Marie Antoinette of France. Redouté's father told him he could not make a living painting flowers; he encouraged his son to paint saints and heroes. However, the young artist was not concerned with popularity preferring to paint what he loved best, raising flowers as a subject to an art form. His paintings reflect his admiration and thorough understanding of flowers, which Redouté gained through his hours of botanical study. The simple watercolor illustrations are bright and engaging. This book works well to introduce the work of a lesser known artist, the man known as "the Rembrandt of Roses." The methodical approach employed by Redouté is also an example for teachers interested in demonstrating the possibilities of scientific drawing as a learning tool. Other titles about artists include Bijou Le Tord's *A Blue Butterfly: A Story about Claude Monet* (Doubleday, 1995), Amy Littlesugar's *Marie in Fourth Position: The Story of Degas's The Little Dancer* (Philomel, 1996), Sharon Wooding's *The Painter's Cat* (G. P. Putnam's, 1994), and Diane Stanley's *Leonardo da Vinci* (Morrow, 1996).

4   Davol, Marguerite W. *The Heart of the Wood.* Illus. by Sheila Hamanaka. Simon & Schuster, 1992. ISBN 0-671-74778-9. Impressionism. Oils. Cumulative Tales. Trees. Violins. Instruments.

A cumulative tale of the transformation of a tree from its roots in the forest to a musical instrument. A lone woodcutter carries his song into the forest and transfers his music to the tree as he chops it down. A fiddle is fashioned from the wood of the tree and carries the sweet tune of the music with it. The soft paintings by Sheila Hamanaka capture the tranquillity of the forest and the inspiration of the music as it finds its place in the instrument. Throughout the process, the wood never loses its song or its heart. Have students compare this tale with other cumulative tales such as *Bringing Rain to the Kapiti Plain* (Dial, 1981), *Traveling to Tondo: A Tale of the Nkundo* (Knopf, 1991), and *Why Mosquitoes Buzz in People's Ears* (Dial, 1975), three tales by Verna Aardema. Challenge students to create their own cumulative tale about another musical instrument. *The Heart of the Wood* is also a lyrical way to introduce the study of trees. See science and nature section for titles in Barbara Bash's Tree Tales series.

5   Delacre, Lulu. *Las Navidades: Popular Christmas Songs from Latin America.* Illus. by author. Scholastic, 1990. ISBN 0-590-43548-5. Realism. Watercolors. Songs. Latin America. Christmas Music. Bilingual Materials—Spanish.

A bilingual collection of folk music from Latin America with rich illustrations that depict the exuberant Latino holidays. Included are sheet music for each song, sidebars with tidbits of information about significant Latino practices, and recipes of dishes served during the holiday season. The illustrations are richly detailed, capturing the excitement and tradition of Christmas in Latin America. Have students compare these songs with traditional English Christmas songs such as "O' Bethlehem" and "Silent Night." Extend the potential of the book to explore the African American celebration of Kwanzaa and the Jewish celebration of Hanukkah during the Christmas season.

Lulu Delacre is also the author of *Golden Tales* (Scholastic, 1996), a collection of myths and legends from Latin America. Explore other aspects of Latin America culture with these illustrated folktales *The Rooster Who Went to His Uncle's Wedding: A Latin American Folktale* (G. P. Putnam's, 1993) by Ada Alma Flor, *The Race of Toad and Deer* (Orchard, 1995) by Pat Mora, *Pedro Fools the Gringo and Other Tales of a Latin America Trickster* (Holt, 1995) and *I Lost My Arrow in a Kankan* (Lothrop, Lee and Shepard, 1993) by Noni Lichtveld.

6   Downes, Brenda. *Silent Night.* Illus. by author. Knopf, 1995. ISBN 0-679-86959-X. Naive. Embroidery. Songs. Christmas Carols. Christmas.

A collection of traditional Christmas carols complete with lyrics and musical scores. The collection includes such familiar songs such as "Silent Night," "O' Christmas Tree," "O' Come All Ye Faithful," and "Hark! The Herald Angels Sing." The detailed embroidery illustrations are an unusual medium for a picture book but nonetheless capture the innocence and reverence of the night long ago when a savior was born. The birth of Christ is rendered in a series of illustrations that capture specific moments of the first Christmas. With careful planning the title can be integrated into the curriculum without offending members of other religious groups. Proceed with a historical perspective to avoid heated religious debate. *Las Navidades: Popular Christmas Songs from Latin America (*Scholastic, 1990) by Lulu Delacre is one title that explores Christmas songs from another culture. *Deck the Halls* (Simon & Schuster, 1995), with illustrations by Michael Hague and *The 12 Days of Christmas* (G. P. Putnam's, 1986, 1989), with illustrations by Jan Brett are two picture book versions of Christmas carols.

7   Downing, Julie. *Mozart Tonight.* Illus. by author. Bradbury Press, 1991. ISBN 0-02-732881-3. Expressionism. Watercolors. Biography. Mozart, Wolfgang Amadeus (1756-1791). Composers. Classical Music.

An intimate look at a specific period in the life of Wolfgang Amadeus Mozart. Downing's tribute to the musical genius is evident in the engrossing and thoroughly researched narrative. The use of first-person perspective for a figure often shrouded by his music and the intervening centuries is effective. The bulk of the text centers around the creation of "Don Giovanni" and the composer's fears as he brings his masterpiece through inception to production. Inspired to create this book by a trip to Vienna, Julie Downing includes a thorough explanation of her sources, which included actual letters written by the Mozart family. Use this act to demonstrate to students how seemingly innocent events such as a holiday trip can lead to further projects such as the creation of a book. Pair with *Wolferl: The First Six Years in the Life of Wolfgang Amadeus Mozart,*

1756–1692 (Holiday House, 1991) by Lisl Weil for an illustrated introduction to Mozart. *Wolfgang Amadeus Mozart* (Viking, 1990) by Wendy Thompson, from her series Composer's World, is a deeper exploration of Amadeus.

8   Fonteyn, Margot (Reteller). *Swan Lake.* Illus. by Trina Schart Hyman. Harcourt Brace, 1989. ISBN 0-15-200600-1. Expressionism. Acrylics/Pen and Ink. Fiction. Tchaikovsky, Pëtr Ilich (1840–1893). Pëtr Ilich Tchaikovsky's *The Swan Princess.* Ballet.

The story of Swan Lake as told by Dame Margot Fonteyn, famed ballerina, is interesting to read for people who have seen the ballet, and for people who have not but have always wondered about the background of the story. Since ballet is an art form expressed through movement, many viewers become lost and fail to understand the story of love that transcends life. The timeless tale of Odette and Sigfried's love and betrayal at the hands of an evil magician is in the repertoire of most major ballet companies. Famed composer Pëtr Ilich Tchaikovsky is also renowned for his compositions of *Sleeping Beauty* and *The Nutcracker Suite*. Illustrated books of Tchaikovsky's compositions include *Sleeping Beauty: The Ballet Story* (Atheneum, 1994) by Marian Horosko and *The Nutcracker Ballet* (Andrews and McMeel, 1992) retold by Melissa Hayden. Margot Fonteyn has also adapted the story *Coppelia* (Harcourt Brace, 1997), a picture book based on the ballet by Leo Delibes (1836–1891).

9   Handel, George Frederick. *Messiah: The Wordbook for the Oratorio.* Illus. by Barry Moser. HarperCollins, 1992. ISBN 0-06-021779-0. Impressionism. Watercolors. Nonfiction. Handel, George Frederick (1685–1759). Oratorios— Librettos. Composers.

An illustrated version of the libretto for Handel's popular choral work, *Messiah*. Coupled with Barry Moser's breathtaking watercolor paintings, the oratorio takes on a new and exciting dimension. Focus on Barry Moser's illustrations and discuss personal interpretation. Because the entire work is lengthy, excerpts were selected. Selections for the picture book from the oratorio were chosen by Charles Jennens (1700–1773). The entire design of the book is a feast for art and music lovers alike. Use this book to introduce the work of George Frederick Handel. Include the picture book *Handel and the Famous Sword Swallower of Halle* (Philomel, 1990) by Bryna Stevens, an account of Handel's childhood.

10   Hayden, Melissa. *The Nutcracker Ballet.* Illus. by Stephen T. Johnson. Andrews and McMeel, 1992. ISBN 0-8362-4501-6. Representational. Water-

colors. Fiction. Tchaikovsky, Pëtr Ilich (1840–1893). Pëtr Ilich Tchaikovsky's *The Nutcracker Suite*. Ballet.

Performance of the Nutcracker Ballet has become a traditional event of the Christmas season. First staged by famed choreographer George Balanchine in 1954, the ballet is seen by millions of people every year in thousands of productions across the country. The ballet is based on a story by E.T.A. Hoffman and a version by Alexandre Dumas. Have students compare the story versions by both writers with the version by Hayden. Obtain a video production of the ballet and have students compare the warm illustrations by Johnson with a stage production; compare interpretations of the story. *Pëtr Ilich Tchaikovsky* (Viking, 1993) by Wendy Thompson from her Composer's World series is an analytical glimpse at the composer. *Discovers America Tchaikovsky* (Orchard, 1994) by Esther Kalman is a fictional account of the composer's trip to America. Other illustrated versions of his ballets include Margot Fonteyn's *The Swan Princess* (Harcourt Brace, 1989) and Marian Horosko's *Sleeping Beauty: The Ballet Story* (Atheneum, 1994). Tchaikovsky's symphonies played softly in the background will enhance the introduction to the storyline of *The Nutcracker Ballet*.

11   Horosko, Marian. *Sleeping Beauty: The Story of the Ballet*. Illus. by Todd L. W. Doney. Atheneum, 1994. ISBN 0-689-31885-5. Representational. Oils. Fiction. Tchaikovsky, Pëtr Ilich (1840–1893). Pëtr Ilich Tchaikovsky's *The Swan Princess*. Ballet.

The Sleeping Beauty premiered in St. Petersburg, Russia in 1890, capturing the hearts and imagination of people for generations. Aurora and her love for a handsome prince is based on a fairytale from Charles Perrault and has been transferred into many versions, both written and visual. Introduce the classic Perrault version with this title, and then obtain a video of a production of *The Sleeping Beauty* and the Walt Disney version and have students compare the effects of adaptation. The lush oil paintings by Doyle capture the magic and bring the ballet to startling life in a series of breathtaking illustrations. The enchanted sleep of Sleeping Beauty has been illustrated by two renowned artists: Margaret Early's *Sleeping Beauty* (Abrams, 1993) was based on Charles Perrault's (1628–1703) version from his collection *Tales of Mother Goose* (1697); Ruth Sanderson's *Sleeping Beauty* (Knopf, 1986) was inspired by the Brothers Grimm version from *Grimm's Fairy Tales* (1814).

12   Johnson, James Weldon. *Lift Ev'ry Voice and Sing*. Illus. by Elizabeth Catlett. Walker, 1921, 1993. ISBN 0-596-46982-7. Reproductions. Linoleum Cuts. Songs. African Americans. African American Spirituals.

A bold illustrated version of the song widely accepted as the African American national anthem. Written in 1900 to celebrate Abraham Lincoln's birthday, the song has come to signify the struggle for freedom fought by millions of people in America. Each of the bold linoleum cuts, created in the 1940s by Elizabeth Catlett, captures the injustice, sacrifice, and triumphs of the African-American struggle for freedom. This title is ideal to introduce an African American heritage unit in your class. The format is appealing for reading, but the inclusion of sheet music will allow more gregarious students to sing the anthem. Compare with "The Star-Spangled Banner" and open discussion about the origins and importance of anthems in many societies. Peter Spier's *The Star-Spangled Banner* (Doubleday, 1973) offers an ideal companion for *Lift Ev'ry Voice and Sing*.

13   Kalman, Esther. *Tchaikovsky Discovers America.* Illus. by Laura Fernandez and Rick Jacobson. Orchard, 1994. ISBN 0–531–06894–3. Representational. Oils. Fiction. Tchaikovsky, Pëtr Ilich (1840–1893). Composers. Classical Music.

A fictional account of Pëtr Ilich Tchaikovsky's trip to the United States in 1891 to conduct an orchestra at a music hall built by Andrew Carnegie. The trip, taken two years prior to his death, was one of the happiest times in Tchaikovsky's life. The modern conveniences available to Americans and the natural landmarks, such as Niagara Falls, took his breath away. The narrative is told from the vantage point of an eleven-year-old girl, Jenny, who meets the famed composer. Jenny feels she has found a kindred spirit because as a creator, he loves music and ballet as much as Jenny. Other picture book titles about Tchaikovsky's ballets include Margot Fonteyn's *The Swan Princess* (Harcourt Brace, 1989), Marian Horosko's *Sleeping Beauty: The Ballet Story* (Atheneum, 1994) and Melissa Hayden's *The Nutcracker Ballet* (Andrews and McMeel, 1992). *Pëtr Ilich Tchaikovsky* (Viking, 1993) by Wendy Thompson from her Composer's World series is an personal examination of the composer.

14   Le Tord, Bijou. *A Blue Butterfly: A Story about Claude Monet.* Illus. by author. Doubleday, 1995. ISBN 0–385–31102–8. Impressionism. Watercolors. Biography. Monet, Claude (1840–1926). Painters.

A simple story inspired by the paintings of Claude Monet, a nineteenth-century Impressionist artist. Monet used only eight colors in his palette, which Le Tord also used when she created the illustrations in her homage to his exquisite flower paintings. The illustrations reminiscent of Monet's own paintings are soft and delicate. The author includes a partial list of museums in the United States and France that have Monet's paintings in their permanent collections. Pair this title with *Redouté: The Man Who Painted Flowers* (G. P.

Putnam's, 1996) by Carolyn Croll and have students compare the use of flowers as a theme and motivation in paintings. *Linnea in Monet's Garden* (R & S Books, 1985) by Christina Björk is another picture book, which explores the masterpieces of Claude Monet. Springboard into further study of Impressionist artists with *A Blue Butterfly: A Story about Claude Monet.*

15   London, Jonathon. *Hip Cat.* Illus. by Woodleigh Hubbard. Chronicle, 1993. ISBN 0–8118–0315–5. Naive. Gouache. Fiction. Jazz Music. Musicians.

A jazzy story of a hip cat who heads for the city to find his destiny among the great musicians he admires. Working as a waiter to make ends meet, he learns that cool is as cool does and that what matters the most is doing what you do the best, which is the best you can. The brief text and bouncy rhythms make for an ideal read aloud to introduce jazz to students. Woodleigh Hubbard's bold paintings in startling primary colors are as fresh as the text. Pair with *Jazz: My Music, My People* (Knopf, 1994) by Morgan Monceaux and *Charlie Parker Played Be Bop* (Orchard, 1992) by Chris Raschka for an appealing look at music that is uniquely American.

16   Mayer, Marianna. *Turandot.* Illus. by Winslow Pels. Morrow Junior, 1995. ISBN 0–688–09074–5. Expressionism. Oils. Fiction. Puccini, Giacomo (1858–1924). China. Opera.

A passionate tale of the boundless possibilities of love. A spell on Princess Turandot has frozen her heart, and only a suitor capable of answering three riddles will win her hand in marriage and break the spell that keeps her heart captive. For the men who attempt and fail the price is high: a death sentence. Marianna Mayer's adaptation of Giacomo Puccini's famous opera has origins in *A Thousand and One Nights.* The solving of riddles in this tale of love and sacrifice is prevalent theme in literature and music. Have students explore other themes that have spurred other great tales of love. Cinderella tales (see index) are an ideal place to begin searching for themes. Pels's haunting illustrations are dominated by a frosty white overlay that slowly melts away as Turandot's heart thaws and opens to love. The story of Turandot originated in Carlo Gozzi's collection of Asian grotesque tales *Fiabe* (1761–65) and has been transformed into operas by Carl Maria von Weber, Ferruccio Busoni, as well as Giacomo Puccini. Use *Turandot* explore other operas by Giacomo Puccini such as *La Boheme* (1896) and *Madame Butterfly* (1900).

17   McClung, Robert M. *Old Bet and the Start of the American Circus.* Illus. by Laura Kelly. Morrow, 1993. ISBN 0–688–10642–0. Representational. Watercolors/Colored Pencils. Nonfiction. Animals, Circus. Elephants. Circuses.

In 1808 an elephant was a spectacle to behold, and Hackaliah Bailey made the most of his unusual animal. Flocks of people came to Bailey's farm to see the exotic creature with wrinkled gray skin. Before long, Old Bet was so popular that Bailey began to tour neighboring towns. In time Bailey added a bear, a tiger, a lion, a few acrobats, and a clown—the American circus was born! In a rollicking tale based on actual events and accompanied by detailed watercolor paintings of a bygone era, this book explores the start of a very important aspect of American culture. Explore the history of the animal entertainment from its origin to the formation of the modern circuses that children enjoy today. Companion titles include *Circus* (HarperCollins, 1992) by Lois Ehlert, *Seven Blind Mice* (Philomel, 1992) by Ed Young, *Jumbo* (Bradbury, 1992) by Rhoda Blumberg, and *The Elephant's Wrestling Match* (Dutton, 1992) by Judy Sierra.

18   Monceaux, Morgan. *Jazz: My Music, My People.* Illus. by author. Knopf, 1994. ISBN 0-679-85618-8. Naive. Mixed Media. Biography. Jazz Musicians. African Americans—Biographies. Jazz Music.

Illustrated collection of figures who formed and developed the type of music that has come to be known as jazz. The book is broken down into three sections highlighting some of jazz music's most famous contributors. "Early Years" shares the stories of the singers and players who shaped the form. "Swing Years" relates the contributions of the musicians who introduced dance to jazz enthusiasts. The last section highlights the new generation of players and defines bebop and modern jazz. The introduction is written by today's most famous jazz musician, Wynton Marsalis. The original paintings by the author were inspired by the music and intended as a tribute to the diversity of jazz. The bold primary colors that dominate the artwork will appeal to younger readers. *Satchmo's Blues* (Doubleday, 1996) by Alan Schroeder is a fictional biography of jazz great, Louis Armstrong.

19   Nichol, Barbara. *Beethoven Lives Upstairs.* Illus. by Scott Cameron. Orchard, 1993. ISBN 0-531-06828-5. Representational. Oils. Fiction. Beethoven, Ludwig van (1770-1827). Composers. Classical Music.

Young Christophe is embarrassed by the apparent madman who has moved into his house as a boarder. All day long the strange man pounds on pianos without legs and mumbles to himself. Christophe writes letters to his uncle in Salzburg to vent his worries about the lunatic. Through his association with the man, the boy eventually learns that the great musical genius suffers because he can no longer hear the music he so loves to create. This fictionalized account of the hearing loss of famed composer Ludwig van Beethoven is ideal as an introduction to his life and music. The format of the text is inspirational for its unusual point of view. Read this title to students to introduce the tragedy and loss of music in Beethoven's life. The format of this book is an ideal example of creative writing because the narrative is built around the correspondence between Christophe and his uncle. Wendy Thompson's *Ludwig Van Beethoven* (Penguin, 1990) is a detailed account of Beethoven's life and makes a perfect companion for *Beethoven Lives Upstairs*.

20   Price, Leontyne. *Aïda*. Illus. by Leo and Diane Dillon. Harcourt Brace Jovanovich, 1990. ISBN 0-15-200405-X. Acrylics. Fiction. Verdi, Giuseppe (1813-1901). Opera. Egypt.

Opera diva Leontyne Price first performed *Aïda* at the War Memorial Opera House in San Francisco in 1957, making her the obvious choice to retell Giuseppe Verdi's opera of love and war in ancient Ethiopia. Leo and Diane Dillon, two-time winners of the coveted Caldecott Award, use borders and art representative of Egypt and Ethiopia to illustrate the book. Aïda is an Ethiopian princess who disobeys her father by venturing near enemy borders. She is captured by her people's greatest enemy: the Egyptians. A great battle brings the warring armies together. After many bloody battles, the Egyptians win and capture the Ethiopian army, including Aïda's father, the king, who does not reveal his identity. The Egyptian general, Radames, captures the heart of Aïda as well as her people. Tired of bloodshed, he asks that the people of Ethiopia be set free as his reward for victory. Radames also helps the king of Ethiopia escape, but his treachery is discovered and he is sentenced to be buried alive. As he is led to his death and the last block is placed on his grave, Aïda jumps out from hiding to join her lover in his stone grave. Giuseppe Verdi's opera *Aïda* is said to be based on a historical incident uncovered at an archaeological excavation.

21   Ross, Stewart. *Shakespeare and Macbeth: The Story Behind the Play*. Illus. by Tony Karpinski. Viking, 1994. ISBN 0-670-85629-0. Representational. Oils. Biography. Shakespeare, William (1564-1616). *Macbeth* (1605-6). Dramatists, English.

An account of the writing and production of *Macbeth* based on well-known facts. Although some reference is made to Shakespeare's life apart from the writing of *Macbeth*, the text sticks mainly to the creation of his most controversial play. Ross's thorough research combined with lively narration transports the reader effortlessly back to Elizabethan England. Karpinski's complex illustrations capture minute details that enhance the experience of reading the play. A combination of pencil sketches and lush paintings alternately conveys the historical significance of Shakespeare's writing. The title includes a list of Shakespeare's works with dates, important dates in Shakespeare life, and a list of further readings. Prepare students for *Macbeth* with this book, which is sure to pique interest in Shakespeare and his other plays.

22   Schroeder, Alan. *Carolina Shout!* Illus. by Bernie Fuchs. Dial, 1995. ISBN 0-8037-1678-8. Impressionism. Oils. Fiction. United States, South Carolina. Cries. Vendors.

During the early nineteenth century, a young African-American girl describes the music that can be found everywhere—from the clackety-clack of the horses' hooves on the cobblestone streets to the unique and plaintive cries of the vendors along Main Street. In a bygone era, vendors depended on their voices to sell their wares, and each cry was unique to the product and the personality of the vendor. This spirited book is a tribute to a forgotten slice of American history, brought vividly to life through Bernie Fuchs's vivacious oil paintings. In an afterword Alan Schroeder gives a brief history of the "shouts" and "cries" that no longer echo in the streets. Have students create their own "cry" or "shout" to promote an idea or a product important to them and their lives. The title of the book comes from James P. Johnson's piano solo "Carolina Shout!" Alan Schroeder has written two other books that chronicle the contributions of African American musicians: *Ragtime Tumpie* (Little, Brown, 1989), a book about Josephine Baker and *Satchmo's Blues* (Doubleday, 1996), a book about Louis Armstrong.

23   Schroeder, Alan. *Ragtime Tumpie.* Illus. by Bernie Fuchs. Little, Brown, 1989. ISBN 0-316-77497-9. Impressionism. Oils. Fiction. Josephine Baker (1906-1975). Dancers. African Americans—Biography. Women—Biography. African-American Women.

A spirited tale about the youth of Josephine Baker, legendary dancer and entertainer. As child growing up in the streets of St. Louis, Missouri, Tumpie heard all the sweet sounds of the emerging ragtime music. Blaring trumpets hauled her from bed, and strumming banjos lulled her to sleep each night. Bernie Fuchs's exuberant impressionistic paintings capture Ragtime Tumpie's feet as they dance from the streets of St. Louis all the way to the Broadway stage. Each page bursts with the images and sounds of the jazz era in its early years. *Ragtime Tumpie* is suitable as an introduction to outstanding African American women or to explore the unique sound of ragtime music during the turn of the nineteenth century. Pair with *Jazz: My Music, My People* (Knopf, 1994) by Morgan Monceaux and *Lift Ev'ry Voice and Sing* (Walker, 1921, 1993) by James Weldon Johnson to explore African-American influence on music in America.

24   Schroeder, Alan. *Satchmo's Blues*. Illus. by Floyd Cooper. Doubleday, 1996. ISBN 0–385–32046–9. Impressionism. Oils. Biography. Armstrong, Louis (1900–1971). African Americans—Biographies. Musicians. Jazz Music.

A fictional account of Louis Armstrong's childhood based on actual events. Young Louis yearned to play the trumpet like the musicians in the clubs of New Orleans. Each night Louis would peek under the swinging doors and listen to the hot sounds of jazz. Longing to play like Bunk Johnson and other musicians, Louis began to scrimp and save his pennies and nickels until he had enough money buy the trumpet in the window of a pawn shop. Floyd Cooper's luminous paintings capture the spirit and energy of New Orleans in the early days of jazz music. Pair with Morgan Monceaux's *Jazz: My Music, My People* (Knopf, 1994) is an illustrated collection of figures who formed and developed the type of music that has come to be known as jazz. Chris Raschka's *Charlie Parker Played Be Bop* (Orchard, 1992) is a bold, bouncy title about another prominent musician.

25   The Smithsonian Institution. *Celebrate America in Poetry and Art*. Reproductions. Hyperion, 1994. ISBN 1–562–82–665–4. Reproductions. Poetry, American. United States. America in Art. Art Appreciation.

A collection of American poetry that celebrates the last 200 years of America. Each poem is paired with a famous painting from the National Museum of American Art. Students will enjoy exploring the many facets of American life. Teachers will appreciate the unique and unusual examples the authors selected to represent the poems. Best appreciated when explored at a slow pace, the book will be useful in many units of study. A readily available copy on display in the classroom will be examined again and again. Another title with a similar format is *Celebrating America: A Collection of Poems and Images of the American Spirit* (Philomel, 1994) compiled by Laura Whipple.

26   Stanley, Diane. *Leonardo da Vinci*. Morrow, 1996. ISBN 0–688–10438–X. Expressionism. Mixed Media. Biography. da Vinci, Leonardo (1452–1519). Painters. Art Appreciation.

Outstanding illustrated biography of the genius and talent of Leonardo da Vinci. Born during the Renaissance of illegitimate birth, Leonardo rose above his humble station to become a master painter. Leonardo is also the recognized inventor of such things as submarines and a suit to allow breathing under water. His notebooks, written from right to left and in backward script, were astounding discoveries for both the art and science worlds. As with her books about Queen Elizabeth I and Charles Dickens, Diane Stanley once again demonstrates the possibilities of picture book biographies. Her research is thorough covering the history behind his paintings as well as his interest in science and mechanical operations. Use this book to display to students how interesting a report on a famous historical figure can be approached.

27   Stevens, Bryna. *Handel and the Famous Sword Swallower of Halle.* Illus. by Ruth Tietjen Councell. Philomel, 1990. ISBN 0–399–21548–4. Expressionism. Pastels. Biography. Handel, George Frederick (1685–1759). Halle, Germany. Composers.

A fictional account of Handel's childhood as it might have been, based on the few known facts about the composer's early years. His aging father, who supposedly hated music, forbade any music or instruments in the house. His aunt arrives and exposes Handel to music by taking him to church and sneaking a clavichord into the attic. Although facts about Handel's life are sketchy and few, the author managed to create a fascinating tale of one of the greatest composers of classical music. Pair with *Beethoven Lives Upstairs* (Orchard, 1993) by Barbara Nichol and *Tchaikovsky Discovers America* (Orchard, 1994) by Esther Kalman for two other fictionalized tales of famous musical composers.

28   Thompson, Wendy. *Ludwig van Beethoven.* Penguin, 1990. ISBN 0–670–83678–8. Representational. Reproductions/Photographs. Biography. Beethoven, Ludwig van (1770–1827). Composers. Classical Music.

Follows the studies and career of Ludwig van Beethoven from his birth in Bonn, Germany to his celebrated debut in Vienna. Beethoven composed hundreds of pieces of works in his life but is probably most famous for his symphonies. Beethoven began to lose his hearing during his middle age and was completely deaf when he composed his last symphony. The text is filled with musical scores and small pictures of Beethoven and the people important in his life. Pair with *Beethoven Lives Upstairs* (Orchard, 1993) by Barbara Nichol for an illustrated introduction to the life and music of Ludwig van Beethoven. Wendy Thompson's Composer's World series include *Franz Schubert* (Viking, 1991), *Joseph Haydn* (Viking, 1991), *Wolfgang Amadeus Mozart* (Viking, 1990), and *Pëtr Ilich Tchaikovsky* (Viking, 1993).

29   Turner, Robyn Montana. *Rosa Bonheur.* Illus. by Reproductions. Little, Brown, 1991. ISBN 0–316–85648–7. Reproductions. Biography. Bonheur, Rosa (1822–1899). Women—Biography. Painters.

A biography of the nineteenth-century French artist famous for her sensitive paintings of animals and the American West. In an age when women had few hopes to pursue careers, Rosa Bonheur fought for her dreams and won.

The support of her father enabled Rosa to pursue a career as an artist when most women faced limited opportunities and even less chance to pursue a dream. Her stamina and talent became an inspiration for female artists for generations to come. The title is illustrated with reproductions of the artist's work collected from museums all over the world. *Rosa Bonheur* is one title in a series about notable women artists that also includes *Georgia O'Keefe* (Little, Brown, 1992), *Mary Cassett* (Little, Brown, 1994), and *Frida Kahlo* (Little, Brown, 1993).

30   Weil, Lisl. *Wolferl: The First Six Years in the Life of Wolfgang Amadeus Mozart, 1756–1762.* Illus. by author. Holiday House, 1991. ISBN 0–8234–0876–0. Naive. Watercolors. Biography. Mozart, Wolfgang Amadeus (1756–1791). Composers. Classical Music.

A picture book biography of the first six years of the life of Wolfgang Amadeus Mozart. From the age of three, Mozart displayed musical ability and had already composed simple tunes and mastered the clavier. The musical environment he grew up in surely played a part in the development of one of the world's greatest composers. The simple watercolor illustrations are reminiscent of the early picture books by Ludwig Bemelmens and Bernard Waber. Pair with *Mozart Tonight* (Bradbury Press, 1991) by Julie Downing for an illustrated introduction to the music and life of Wolfgang Amadeus Mozart. *Wolfgang Amadeus Mozart* (Viking, 1990) by Wendy Thompson is a thoroughly researched introduction to the genius of Mozart.

31   Willard, Nancy. *Pish Posh, Said Hieronymous Bosch.* Illus. by Leo, Diane, and Lee Dillon. Harcourt Brace, 1991. ISBN 0–15–262210–1. Expressionism. Mixed Media. Poetry. Bosch, Hieronymous (d. 1516). Painters.

An outrageous exploration of the imagination of famed fifteenth-century artist, Hieronymous Bosch. The text was inspired by the bizarre images that grace Hieronymous Bosch's paintings. The Dillons managed to capture the absurdity of the grotesque images that mark the paintings of Bosch and remain as mysterious and elusive to us today as they were to people in the fifteenth century. Nancy Willard has a unique and engaging approach to her biographies, which include fanciful poetry based on thorough research. Other titles by Willard include *A Visit to William Blake's Inn* (Harcourt Brace, 1981), which introduces William Blake's poetry and *A Voyage on the Ludgate Hill* (Harcourt Brace, 1987), a title about the travels of Robert Louis Stevenson.

32   Willard, Nancy. *The Sorcerer's Apprentice.* Illus. by Leo and Diane Dillon. Blue Sky Press/Scholastic, 1993. ISBN 0–590–47329–8. Expressionism.

Watercolors. Poetry. Goethe, Johann Wolfgang von (1749–1832). Magicians. Magic.

A picture book inspired by the seventeenth-century poem "The Magician's Apprentice" by German writer, Johann Wolfgang von Goethe (1749–1832). The common motif found in Goethe's poem has attracted artists and writers ever since it first appeared, including Walt Disney, who adapted it for a segment in the classic animated film *Fantasia*. This innovative version with words by twentieth-century writer Nancy Willard and fantastic images by Leo and Diane Dillon is a unique opportunity for teachers to introduce literary works and the influence classic literature has on modern artists and writers. Nancy Willard has a fresh, appealing approach to her biographies. Nancy Willard also wrote two titles about prominent literary figures *A Visit to William Blake's Inn* (Harcourt Brace, 1981), which introduces William Blake's poetry and *A Voyage on the Ludgate Hill* (Harcourt Brace, 1987), a title about the travels of Robert Louis Stevenson.

33   Wilson, Elizabeth B. *Bibles and Bestiaries: A Guide to Illuminated Manuscripts.* Illus. by Reproductions. Farrar, Straus & Giroux, 1994. ISBN 0-374-30685-0. Nonfiction. Illuminated Manuscripts. Bibles. Bestiaries.

For a thousand years—from the fall of Rome to the dawn of the Renaissance—the images and ideas of the Western world were recorded in glorious manuscripts. Early Arthurian romances, Chaucer's poetry, and the wisdom of the ancient Greeks are just a few of the precious historical words preserved for posterity. The manuscripts, produced through the process of illumination—the art of using silver and gold to illustrate a book—are among the greatest treasures to survive from the Middle Ages. This book, virtually the only one designed for younger readers, captures the beauty and painstaking effort required to produce illuminated manuscripts in stunning full-color reproductions. Young readers used to seeing hundreds of copies of a single book will be mind-boggled by the fact that a single manuscript took years to complete. Everyone who loves reading will enjoy exploring the early history of books. *Gutenberg* (Macmillan, 1993) by Leonard Everett Fisher about the life of Johannes Gutenberg (1397?–1468), the first inventor to use movable type to print a Bible, and *Breaking into Print: Before and After the Invention of the Printing Press* (Little, Brown, 1996) by Stephen Krensky are ideal companion books. *Illuminations* (Bradbury Press, 1989) by Jonathan Hunt is an illustrated alphabet inspired by medieval art.

34   Wooding, Sharon. *The Painter's Cat.* Illus. by author. G. P. Putnam's, 1994. ISBN 0-399-22414-9. Representational. Watercolors. Fiction. Painters. Lotto, Lorenzo (1480?–1556?).

Micio's master spends all of his time painting and charming visitors. Feeling neglected, Micio leaves home because he is tired of being forgotten. He wanders the streets of Venice foraging for a morsel of food and a kind hand to pet him, longing to be home with his master. Eventually his nights sleeping on hard cobblestones under dripping roofs leads him home, where he discovers why his master had been so preoccupied. This fictional story was inspired by the painting *The Annunciation*, which hangs in a small church in Racanati, Italy. The Venetian artist Lorenzo Lotto (1480?-1556?) traveled throughout Italy during his lifetime, and his travels are reflected in his paintings. Sharon Wooding did an exemplary job of integrating Lorenzo Lotto's style into her illustrations, capturing aspects of the historic streets of Venice in each brush stroke. Another book with a fictional story about a famous painting is *The Princess and the Painter* (Farrar, Straus & Giroux, 1994) by Jane Johnson, a title about the creation of Diego Velazques's painting *Las Meninas*.

35   Zadrzynska, Ewa. *The Girl with a Watering Can*. Illus. by Arnold Skolnick. Chameleon, 1990. ISBN 0-915829-64-9. Naive. Reproductions. Fiction. Art Appreciation. Museums.

The Girl with a Watering Can is a fanciful tale of art and mischievous antics. The girl in Auguste Renoir's *The Girl with a Watering Can* (1876) has suffered the pain of a stone lodged in her shoe for many years. Upon removing the stone, the girl discovers that anything is possible, so she jumps from her painting to explore the museum. Her excursion takes the reader through the National Gallery of Art in Washington, D. C., where she trifles with other famous paintings, including Edouard Manet's *Gare Saint-Lazare* (1873) and Henri Rousseau's *The Equatorial Jungle* (1909). This enticing farce will encourage students to look at famous fine art in a new light as they discover the details in famous paintings that make them stand out as masterpieces of art. This book is unique and entertaining for its unusual approach to art. Other titles that use reproductions in lieu of original illustrations include *I Spy: An Alphabet in Art* (Greenwillow, 1992), *I Spy Two Eyes: Numbers in Art* (Greenwillow, 1993), and *I Spy A Fright Train: Transportation in Art* (Greenwillow, 1996), all by Lucy Micklethwait.

Chapter 2

Health

The titles in the health section have young protagonists and are intended for younger children. However, topics concerning illness and handicapped people are often difficult to introduce and even harder to generate discussion about. The titles in this section were selected for their compassionate exploration of delicate subjects. Picture book format allows sensitive topics to be explored and discussed through the storytelling experience.

36   Abeel, Samantha. *Reach for the Moon.* Illus. by Charles R. Murphy. Pfeifer-Hamilton, 1994. ISBN 1–57025–013–8. Impressionism. Watercolors. Poetry. Children's Writing. Physical Handicaps. Authors—Children. Learning Disabilities.

Samantha Abeel always had trouble in her classes. By the time she reached the seventh grade, she had become listless and withdrawn. While other students excelled, her grades dropped, and she displayed a complete lack of interest in school. Samantha was unhappy and suffered silently until she was finally diagnosed as learning-disabled. With the help of two women, her mother and a special teacher, Samantha began a journey of self-discovery that resulted in the creation of this book of poetry. Her moving poetry paired with haunting watercolors celebrates all she has accomplished in her struggle to define herself. Samantha's story is a celebration for anyone who is learning-disabled or loves someone who is. *Reach for the Moon* honors the special intelligence each person has within themselves.

37   Booth, Barbara. *Mandy.* Illus. by Jim La Marche. Lothrop, Lee & Shepard, 1991. ISBN 0–688–10339–1. Representational. Oils. Fiction. Physical Handicaps. Hearing Impaired. Grandmothers.

For Mandy, darkness makes communication difficult; she is unable to read lips or use her hands to sign. She hates the dark and stares out of the window gathering the courage to head into the dark to find her grandmother's lost silver lapel pin. This book, with Jim La Marche's captivating oil paintings, is ideal to help people understand how everyday events and situations pose special challenges for handicapped people. Mandy's bravery will be an inspiration to readers who have a hearing impairment or know someone who does. Pair with *Silent Lotus* (Farrar, Straus & Giroux, 1991) by Jeanne M. Lee and *Handmade Alphabet* (Dial, 1991) by Laura Rankin.

38   Coerr, Eleanor. *Sadako.* Illus. by Ed Young. G. P. Putnam's, 1993. ISBN 0–399–21771–1. Expressionism. Pastels. Historical Fiction. Atomic Bomb. World War II. Hiroshima, Japan. Leukemia. Illness. Physical Handicaps.

It has been ten years since the atomic blast that destroyed Sadako's city and took 200,000 lives, including her Obasan, her grandmother. Her city has been rebuilt, and her people are rebuilding their lives. Suddenly she is stricken with dizzy spells that do not go away. Sadako is taken to the hospital where she learns she has the leukemia—the atomic bomb disease. Her world falls apart until her best friend, Chizuko, reminds Sadako of the legend of the thousand paper cranes. Together they begin to fold a thousand cranes because it is said that a person who does so will be granted a wish. Today a memorial statue of Sadako stands in Hiroshima Peace Park with the words "This is our cry, this is our prayer: Peace in the world" carved into the stone. Each year on Peace Day the children of Hiroshima make paper crane garlands to hang from her memorial. Ed Young traveled to Hiroshima when he was planning the illustrations for this book. Eleanor Coerr based this story on a longer one she wrote, *Sadako and the Thousand Paper Cranes* (Putnam, 1997). Other picture books about the devastating events of the atomic bomb include *Shin's Tricycle* (Walker, 1992) by Tatsuhara Kodama, *My Hiroshima* (Viking, 1987) by Junko Morimoto, and *Hiroshima No Pika* (Lothrop, Lee & Shepard, 1980) by Toshi Maruki.

39   Cowen-Fletcher, Jane. *Mama Zooms.* Illus. by author. Scholastic, 1992. ISBN 0–590–45774–8. Representational. Watercolors. Fiction. Physical Handicaps. Wheelchairs.

An inspiring story of love and courage. Join a little boy and his mother as they share adventures in space and sea. The little boy's mother uses a wheelchair, but this does not stop her from sharing her lively imagination with her son. The touching story of the mother and son was inspired by the author's handicapped sister, who like the mother in the story, does not allow a wheelchair to come between her and her relationship with her son. Soft pastel illustrations celebrate the loving relationship of a mother and son. Initiate discussion of handicap accessible facilities in your school with this gentle tale of courage. Are they adequate? What could be improved? The Americans with Disabilities Act of 1990 (ADA) is a very controversial topic. *Mama Zooms* and other titles with positive presentations of wheelchairs, including *With the Wind* (Orchard, 1991) by Liz Damrell, *My Buddy* (Holt, 1992) by Audrey Osofsky, and *The Storm* (Cobblehill/Dutton, 1995) by Marc Harshman will encourage mature discussion.

40   Fleming, Virginia. *Be Good To Eddie Lee.* Illus. by Floyd Cooper. Philomel, 1993. ISBN 0–399–21993–5. Representational. Watercolors. Fiction. Physical Handicaps. Down's Syndrome. Friendship.

Christy thinks Eddie Lee is a pest! Her mama tells her, "Be good to Eddie Lee." But Christy does not want him following her around all summer. Eddie Lee is different, he has Down's syndrome. An excursion into the woods gives Christy an opportunity to look at Eddie Lee in a different light and she learns to see the world from his eyes. The realistic watercolors are soft and convincing, portraying a special day in the life of a handicapped boy. A positive and affirming view of Down's syndrome in picture book format will invite discussion from students about stereotypes and handicapped people. All students who have a special friend with Down's syndrome will appreciate the loving closure Virginia Fleming brings to this touching story of friendship. Other picture books with characters who see beyond the physical aspects of an individual include *Fat, Fat Rose Marie* (Holt, 1991) by Lisa Passen and *Oregon's Journey* (Bridgewater, 1993) by Rascal.

41   Goldin, Barbara Diamond. *Cakes and Miracles: A Purim Tale.* Illus. by Erika Weihs. Viking, 1991. ISBN 0–670–83047–X. Naive. Oils. Fiction. Visual Impairment. Physical Handicaps. Purim (Jewish holiday). Holidays—Jewish.

Young Hershel, a blind boy, lives a full life despite his handicap. He attends school and plays with the other children in the village. Hershel knows he can do anything he sets his mind to, but his mother and the other villagers continue to treat Hershel with special rules. Tired of being excluded, he is easily distracted by mischief and wreaks havoc in the classroom and in church. Hershel prays to God to give him the ability to help his mother as she prepares the special cakes for the upcoming Purim celebration. In the process he teaches the whole village a lesson. The author included background notes and a recipe for hamantashen, the cakes made especially for Purim. Pair with *Melanie* (Clarion, 1996) by Carol Carrick, a literary fairy tale about a young blind girl who rescues her grandfather from trolls. Both stories depict visually impaired people in strong roles, creating positive images of handicapped individuals. *Cakes and Miracles: A Purim Tale* is also suitable to explore the Jewish holiday of Purim. *Esther's Story* (Morrow, 1996) by Diane Wolkstein is the story of the woman who delivered the Jews from a massacre and the origination of the holiday, Purim.

42   Harshman, Marc. *The Storm.* Illus. by Mark Mohr. Dutton, 1995. ISBN 0–525–65150–0. Representational. Watercolors. Fiction. Wheelchairs. Physical Handicaps.

A story of one boy's courage and determination against tremendous odds. Jonathon is treated differently than the other children. People go out of their way to make sure everything is as easy for Jonathon as possible. What they do not understand is that even though he uses a wheelchair, he is able to do many of the things other people do. It makes Jonathon uncomfortable to be treated differently. When a storm ravages his family's farm, Jonathon proves to the whole town exactly what he is capable of and earns their respect and gains recognition for his bravery. This book is ideal to generate discussion about predisposed notions concerning people with physical handicaps. Mark Mohr's brooding watercolors capture the intensity and anger of a tornado, which parallels the anger and frustration of the small boy.

43   Karim, Roberta. *Mandy Sue Day.* Illus. by Karen Ritz. Clarion, 1994. ISBN 0–395–66155–2. Representational. Watercolors. Fiction. Visual Impairment. Physical Handicaps.

The harvest is in, and Papa and says the children can have the day to spend as they choose. No school! No chores! Mandy Sue Day, a young blind girl, can think of no other way to spend the day than with her horse, Ben. Join Mandy Sue Day and Ben on a leisurely ride and drink in the smells and sounds of the country. The soft watercolor illustrations are realistic and capture the freedom of a spontaneous ride through the countryside on a lazy summer day. Other titles concerned with visual impairments include *Knots on a Counting Rope* (Holt, 1987) by Bill Martin Jr. and John Archambault and *Cakes and Miracles: A Purim Tale* (Viking, 1991) by Barbara Diamond Goldin. Have students close their eyes and read the story out loud, allowing them to experience the horse ride in the same way Mandy Sue Day does.

44   Kroll, Virginia. *Fireflies, Peach Pies, and Lullabies.* Illus. by Nancy Cote. Simon & Schuster, 1995. ISBN 0–689–80291–9. Cartoon Art. Gouache. Fiction. Alzheimer's Disease. Grandmothers. Aging. Elderly Persons. Illness.

Francie's Great-Granny Annabel is forgetful. Sometimes she even forgets Francie's name! As Great-Granny Annabel's sickness gets worse, Francie's mother worries that Francie will forget the loving warm person her Granny is and will recall only the disoriented old woman who mumbles and forgets how do simple everyday tasks. But Francie remembers the peach pies Granny baked and the fireflies she used to help Francie catch before her illness. *Fireflies, Peach Pies, and Lullabies* is a poignant story about the ravaging effects of Alzheimer's disease on elderly people and the ones who love them. Other sensitive portraits of Alzheimer's disease include Ben Shecter's *Great Uncle Alfred Forgets* (HarperCollins, 1996), Audrey O. Leighton's *Window in Time* (NADJA, 1995), Mary Bahr's *The Memory Box* (Whitman, 1992), and Nancy Whitelaw's *A Beautiful Pearl* (Whitman, 1991).

45   Krull, Kathleen. *Wilma Unlimited: How Wilma Rudolph Became the World's Fastest Woman* Illus. by David Diaz. Harcourt Brace, 1996. ISBN 0–15–201–267–2. Expressionism. Watercolors. Biography. Rudolph, Wilma (1940–1994). Polio. Illness. African-Americans—Biography. African-American Women. Athletes. Women—Biography.

Inspiring biography about one of America's most-admired female athletes. A childhood bout with polio leaves Wilma with a paralyzed leg and no hope of walking again. A determined child, Wilma does not give up when the doctor's prognosis is bleak. Facing her illness straight on, she sets her mind on a full recovery. Sheer will and hard work allow Wilma to overcome an illness that has taken thousands of children's lives. Despite the unsightly metal brace, Wilma walks proudly to and from school each day knowing that one day she will walk without it. The bold expressionistic illustrations by David Diaz capture the strength and determination required to make the leap from sickness to an Olympic Gold Medal. The combined effort of Kathleen Krull and David Diaz is a fine example of what is possible in the field of biographies in picture book format.

46   Lee, Jeanne M. *Silent Lotus.* Illus. by author. Farrar, Straus & Giroux, 1991. ISBN 0374–36911–9. Watercolors. Naive. Fiction. Hearing Impairment. Cambodia. Ballet.

Lotus, a young girl who cannot hear or speak, is comfortable in the tranquil world created by the natural forces of earth and water. Her silence brands her an outcast, and she longs to run and play with the village children.

But Lotus, who is as good as she is lovely, is shunned by the village children, who are wary of her inability to talk. Her mother sees her unhappiness and journeys with the child to the city in hope of a miracle that will bring her child the happiness and joy other children enjoy. In the city Lotus sees the king's dancers and finds her voice as she begins to move with natural grace despite her inability to hear the music. This is a reaffirming tale about the different ways people find their voices and a celebration of the different ways people express themselves. The watercolor illustrations were inspired by the twelfth-century temple at Angkor Wat and the 1,000-year-old Cambodian court ballets. Other picture books about Cambodian culture include *The Two Brothers* (Lothrop, Lee & Shepard, 1995) by Minfong Ho, *The Tale of the Spiteful Spirits* (Bedrick/Blackie, 1991), and *Judge Rabbit and the Tree Spirit* (Children's Book Press, 1991) by Lina Mao Wall.

47   Leighton, Audrey. *A Window of Time.* Illus. by Rhonda Kyrias. NADJA, 1995. ISBN 0-9636335-1-1. Impressionism. Watercolors. Fiction. Alzheimer's disease. Elderly Persons. Aging. Illness.

An elderly man suffering the first stages of Alzheimer's disease often confuses his past with his present. The child character of Shawn is developed with sensitivity and is a model for people unsure around or embarrassed by persons who suffer from Alzheimer's disease. Imagining that his grandson is his dead brother, the grandfather speaks of his childhood, recreating his youth. These images dominate the illustrations in a stunning series of soft watercolor paintings. Use this book with *Fireflies, Peach Pies, and Lullabies* by Virginia Kroll (Simon & Schuster, 1995), *The Memory Box* (Whitman, 1992) by Mary Bahr, and *A Beautiful Pearl* (Whitman, 1991) by Nancy Whitelaw for a tempered introduction to a serious ailment that affects thousands of elderly people every year.

48   Martin Jr., Bill, and John Archambault. *Knots on a Counting Rope.* Illus. by Ted Rand. Holt, 1987. ISBN 0-8050-0571-4. Representational. Watercolors. Fiction. Visual Impairments. Indians of North America.

On a cool, dark night a young boy begs his grandfather to tell the special story of his birth and the special events of that evening. This night sky is sprinkled with stars and the calm quiet holds rein across the desert; but on the night the boy was born, a fierce storm raged across the sand. Soft watercolors mark the events in the boy's life, such as his birth and the great horse race no one thought he could win. As the grandfather counts the years with knots on his counting rope, he tells his grandson the miraculous story of his life. Pair with *The Wind* (Orchard, 1991) by Liz Damrell and *Mandy Sue Day* (Clarion, 1994) by Roberta Karim, two stories that feature horses and handicapped children.

Knots on a Counting Rope is a controversial book for many Native Americans because of the stereotypes in the illustrations. Use Paul Goble's celebrated picture books, which are renowned for their authenticity, and compare with *Knots on a Counting Rope.*

49   Moran, George. *Imagine Me on a Sit-Ski!* Illus. by Nadine Bernard West-cott. Whitman, 1995. ISBN 0–8075–3618. Cartoon Art. Watercolors. Fiction. Physical Handicaps. Cerebral Palsy.

Billy has cerebral palsy. He cannot walk and has limited use of his arms, but this does not stop Billy from living a full life. With the use of adaptive equipment, Billy is able to go to school and even learn to ski! *Imagine Me on a Sit-Ski!* is a heart-warming story of a little boy who challenges his physical disabilities instead of surrendering to a life of limited activity. Many students attend classes with handicapped children who have been mainstreamed into regular schools. Use this book in a read-aloud capacity to explore student concerns and feelings about this issue.

50   Newman, Lesléa. *Too Far Away to Touch.* Illus. by Catherine Stock. Clarion, 1995. ISBN 0–395–68968–6. Representational. Watercolors. Fiction. AIDS. Death. Illness.

Sensitive story of the effects of AIDS in the life of a small girl. Uncle Leonard is Zoe's favorite relative, and she looks forward to the time they spend together. On a trip to the planetarium, Uncle Leonard coughs and has to rest a lot. " 'It's part of being sick,' he says." To commemorate the trip and their relationship, Uncle Leonard pastes glow-in-the-dark stars to Zoe's bedroom ceiling. The stars represent his love for Zoe and the possibility of his death from AIDS. He reassures Zoe that although he may die, he will always be "too far away to touch, but close enough to see." Lesléa Newman's moving text and Stock's heartrending illustrations combine to create a successful picture book format about a deadly disease. The topic is handled in an affirming way to enhance the positive aspects of relationships torn apart by AIDS.

51   Osofsky, Audrey. *My Buddy.* Illus. by Ted Rand. Holt, 1992. ISBN 0–8050–1747–X. Watercolors. Fiction. Physical Handicaps. Muscular Dystrophy. Wheelchairs.

A touching story about a boy with muscular dystrophy and his loving relationship with a golden retriever trained to be his service dog. The child is unable to perform many simple tasks because of his handicap, and the lively watercolors show a strong, determined boy facing challenges along with his friend and companion. *My Buddy* is the story of a child being mainstreamed into a regular school, who must learn to cope in a new environment. Use this title to help students understand the special fears many handicapped people feel when placed in "regular" situations.

52   Rankin, Laura. *The Handmade Alphabet.* Illus. by author. Dial, 1991. ISBN 0-8037-0975-7. Representational. Colored Pencil. Fiction. Alphabet Book. Physical Handicaps. Sign Language. Hearing Impaired.

Presenting the manual alphabet in American Sign Language, *The Handmade Alphabet* is an exquisite picture book that celebrates the beauty and expression of sign language. Each colored pencil illustration blends objects that represent letters of the alphabet with a hand signing the letter with which the object begins. The hand signing "j" is scooping a taste of jam from a jar, and fog surrounds the hand signing "f." Use this title along with *Mandy* (Lothrop, Lee & Shepard, 1991) by Barbara Booth and *Silent Lotus* (Farrar, Straus & Giroux, 1991) by Jeanne M. Lee, two titles that have hearing impaired characters. Introduce the alphabet used in American Sign Language and have students learn to sign simple words or perhaps their own names. Invite a storyteller who knows sign language and have him or her sign one of the suggested companion titles while you read the story aloud.

53   Russo, Marisabina. *Alex Is My Friend.* Illus. by author. Greenwillow, 1992. ISBN 0-688-10419-3. Gouache. Fiction. Physical Handicaps. Dwarfs.

A moving story about a boy's realization that his friend, who is one year older than he, has stopped growing. Since they were toddlers, Alex and Ben have played together and shared everything. One day Ben notices that Alex is not like him. The perception of the small child is convincing despite the naive paintings that pull from the realism of the story. The relationship between the two boys is jovial and grows over time. The story is clearly written from a six-year-old child's perspective, but it is an ideal title to open discussion about physical differences with young adults. Use with *Be Good to Eddie Lee* (Philomel, 1993) by Virginia Fleming, another tale about a friendship that succeeds despite the physical differences of the children.

54   Shecter, Ben. *Great Uncle Alfred Forgets.* Illus. by author. HarperCollins, 1996. ISBN 0-06-026218-4. Expressionism. Mixed Media. Fiction. Alzheimer's Disease. Elderly Persons. Aging. Illness.

A touching portrait of a young girl's recognition of her Uncle Albert's increasing memory lapses. One minute he recognizes Emily, and the next asks her who she is and what she wants from him. The soft illustrations capture the confusion and eventual understanding Emily experiences as she struggles to understand the changes in her Uncle Albert's behavior and identifies his memory loss as Alzheimer's disease. The title invites discussion about a serious disease that touches the lives of almost every American. This title is also appropriate to discuss the place of senior citizens in society and the way younger generations are often abrupt and impatient with the elderly population. Pair with *Window in Time* (NADJA, 1995) by Audrey O. Leighton and *Fireflies, Peach Pies, and Lullabies* (Simon & Schuster, 1995) by Virginia Kroll.

Chapter 3

Literature and Language

The literature and language section includes many types of literature, including fairy tales, folktales, tall tales, poetry, and illustrated versions of many famous literary works. The titles were selected for their literary form rather than for their subject (i.e., folktales, pourquoi tales, and fairy tales). Also included are titles that allow students to explore language and language use in the accessible picture book format. Please note that many of the folktales are appropriate to use in history and social studies classes because of the diverse ethnic groups represented. *Fairy Tales, Fables, Legends, and Myths: Using Folk Literature in Your Classroom, second ed.* (Teachers College Press, 1992) by Bette Bosma and *Using Picture Storybooks to Teach Literary Devices* (Oryx Press, 1994) by Susan Hall are two resources English teachers will find indispensable when incorporating picture books into the curriculum.

55   Aardema, Verna. *Bringing Rain to the Kapiti Plain.* Illus. by Beatriz Vidal. Dial, 1981. ISBN 0-8037-0809-2. Naive. Gouache. Folktales, Kenya. Africa, Kenya. Nandi (African People). Cumulative Tales.

A Nandi tale told in the tradition of "This Is the House That Jack Built" explains how Ki-pat, a shepherd, brings rain to the drought-stricken Kapiti Plain to relieve his herd of heat and thirst. This tale was discovered in Kenya, Africa over seventy years ago and has been altered over time to the refrain of "The House That Jack Built" because it reminded its discoverer of his favorite nursery rhyme as a child. Verna Aardema's version is culturally accurate and respectful of Nandi heritage. Beatriz Vidal's simple naive paintings are overflowing with exquisite detail of African culture. This story is ideal for comparison with other cumulative tales. Other popular cumulative tales include "Henny Penny," "I Know an Old Lady Who Swallowed a Fly," and "Chicken Little." Challenge students to write their own cumulative tale using this book as an example. Picture books with cumulative refrain include *Traveling to Tondo: A Tale of the Nkundo of Zaire* (Knopf, 1991) by Verna Aardema and *The Gingerbread Man* (Holiday House, 1991) by Eric Kimmel.

56   Aardema, Verna. *Rabbit Makes a Monkey of Lion*. Illus. by Jerry Pinkney. Dial, 1989. ISBN 0–8037–0297–3. Representational. Watercolors. Folktales, Africa. Africa. Animal Stories.

Based on a tale from West Africa. Rabbit is awakened by Honey Guide singing of a place where sweet honey can be found. Rabbit enlists the aid of Bush-rat and Turtle to figure out a way to get the delicious honey from the calabash tree. When Lion discovers their trespass, he vows to eat them for dinner! Rabbit must quickly think of a way avoid becoming Lion's dinner and at the same time get plenty of honey to fill her tummy. As with all of Verna Aardema's titles, this story succeeds due to her strong writing and skillful narration. Soft watercolor illustrations by Jerry Pinkney make this book a treat. Have students explore the origins of animal tales and the role they play in African and Native American cultures. Extend the book by comparing this tale with the Brer Rabbit tales from the southern United States. Jerry Pinkney and Julius Lester collaborated on several Brer Rabbit titles, including *Further Tales of Uncle Remus* (Dial, 1990) and *The Last Tales of Uncle Remus* (Dial, 1994). Robin Bernard's *Juma and the Honey Guide* (Silver Press, 1996) is a fictional story from Africa in the same tradition as *Rabbit Makes a Monkey of Lion*.

57   Aardema, Verna. *Sebgugugu the Glutton*. Illus. by Nancy L. Clouse. Eerdmans/African World Press, 1993. ISBN 0–86543–377–1. Expressionism. Collage. Folktales, Rwanda. Africa, Rwanda. Bantu Languages.

Sebgugugu is a greedy man who always wants more than he has. After he mistakes the cries of a bird for instructions from the gods to kill his only cow and the family's source of milk, Sebgugugu and his family must travel to distant lands for survival. The deity Imana intervenes, providing for Sebgugugu and his family, but each time he provides, Sebgugugu's greed always surpasses his need. Time after time Sebgugugu fails to give thanks for the offering from the god. In the end, Sebgugugu learns a lesson about greed and hard work in this tale from Rwanda. Nancy Clouse's eclectic collage illustrations add dimension to this tale about an emotion that tempts all people. The greed and the rash behavior of Sebgugugu are themes prevalent in literature. Focus on the theme of greed and its consequence in *Sebgugugu the Glutton* and discuss accountability.

58   Aardema, Verna. *Why Mosquitoes Buzz in People's Ears.* Illus. by Leo and Diane Dillon. Dial, 1975. ISBN 0–8037–6089–2. Expressionism. Mixed Media. Folktales, Africa. Africa. Rumors. Pourquoi Tales.

A mysterious series of events causes all the animals to behave unusually, ending in the death of Baby Owlet. Mother Owl is so sad that she will not hoo hoo hoo to wake the sun. King Lion and the council summon each member of the animal kingdom hoping to get to the bottom of the death. After a grueling examination, King Lion discovers that a small insect is at the bottom of the tragedy. *Why Mosquitoes Buzz in People's Ears* is a pourquoi tale about the irritating noise mosquitoes make. The illustrations in this book won the coveted Caldecott Medal for Leo and Diane Dillon in 1976. This title is a model example of the pourquoi tales prevalent in African and Native American cultures. Explore the purpose of pourquoi tales as a literary form with this book, and encourage students to locate other picture book versions of pourquoi tales. Some are *The Legend of the Cranberry: A Paleo-Indian Tale* (Simon & Schuster, 1993) by Ellin Greene, *Just So Stories* (HarperCollins, 1991) by Rudyard Kipling, and *The Great Ball Game: A Muskogee Story* (Dial, 1993) by Joseph Bruchac.

59   Agard, John, and Grace Nichols (eds.). *A Caribbean Dozen: Poems from Caribbean Poets.* Illus. by Cathy Felstad. Candlewick Press, 1994. ISBN 1–56402–339–7. Naive. Mixed Media. Poetry, Caribbean. Caribbean. Island Cultures. Poets, Caribbean.

Growing up on an island is not like growing up anywhere else. This brightly illustrated collection of poems by over a dozen celebrated Caribbean writers is an exciting poetry collection. Each poem is bouncy and rhythmic, making each reminiscent of the reggae and calypso music styles that originate from the Caribbean area. The poems are unique because of the cultural cadences that mark the words and phrases. The collection is full of unusual information about island cultures and the uniqueness of growing up on a Caribbean island. Compare the poetry of Caribbean writers with American poets whose writing celebrates a sense of place. Robert Frost's poetry is ideal for comparison.

60   Andersen, Hans Christian (Retold by Amy Ehrlich). *The Snow Queen.* Illus. by Susan Jeffers. Dial, 1982. ISBN 0–8037–888011–7. Representational. Pen and Ink. Fairy Tales (literary). Andersen, Hans Christian (1805–1875). Illustrated Classics.

A retelling of Hans Christian Andersen's beloved fairy tale of the endurance of love and the bond that joins two hearts. Two friends, Kai and Gerda, are cruelly separated when a shard from the devil's mirror pierces Kai's heart. The Snow Queen, desiring a companion, steals Kai from his home and friends. Kai, whose heart is frozen because of the sliver of mirror embedded in his chest, turns his back on his world and slowly adapts to the icy, frozen world of the Snow Queen. Gerda, saddened by the loss of her friend, leaves her home and searches around the world for Kai. Compare the literary fairy tales of Andersen with the traditional fairy tales of the Brothers Grimm. Obtain a copy of Andersen's original story and compare it with the retelling by Ehrlich. Other versions of Hans Christian Anderson's literary fairy tales include *The Ugly Duckling* (G. P. Putnam's, 1990) with illustrations by Troy Howell, *Thumbelina* (G. P. Putnam's, 1991) with illustrations by Wayne Anderson, *The Little Mermaid* (Harcourt Brace, 1989) with illustrations by Katie Thamer Treherne, and *The Tinderbox* (Little, Brown, 1990) with illustrations by Barry Moser.

61   Andersen, Hans Christian (Retold by Tor Seidler). *The Steadfast Tin Soldier*. Illus. by Fred Marcellino. HarperCollins, 1992. ISBN 0–06–205001–X. Expressionism. Watercolors. Fairy Tales (literary). Andersen, Hans Christian (1805–1875). Illustrated Classics.

A retelling of Hans Christian Andersen's beloved fairy tale about a special Christmas gift. A little boy receives many wonderful presents for Christmas, but his favorite gift is the set of tin soldiers resplendent in red and blue uniforms, rifles propped on their shoulders. The Steadfast Tin Soldier, who has only one leg, is destined for great adventures. After the boy goes to bed, the toys begin to play. What follows is the Steadfast Tin Soldier's adventures as he searches the city to find a way home to the boy and to the beautiful ballerina who has captured his heart. Hans Christian Andersen (1805–1875) is renowned for his literary fairy tales and wrote four collections of original fairy tales. *The Steadfast Tin Soldier* first appeared in 1835. Compare the literary fairy tales of Andersen with the traditional fairy tales of the Brothers Grimm. Oscar Wilde was famed for his contributions to the literary fairy tale form. Compare elements in the tales of Oscar Wilde and Hans Christian Andersen. Compare illustration as a vehicle to tell a story by comparing this version of *The Steadfast Tin Soldier* with the illustrated versions by Rachel Isadora (G. P. Putnam's, 1996) and P. J. Lynch (Harcourt Brace, 1992).

62   Base, Graeme. *Animalia*. Illus. by author. Abrams, 1986. ISBN 0–8109–1868–4. Surrealism. Watercolors. Fiction. Alphabet Books. Visual Perception. Animals.

Graeme Base's *Animalia* is one of the most exciting and challenging alphabet books ever published. Each letter in the book is represented by an animal and a silly alliterative sentence. Surrounding the animals are hidden pictures that also begin with the letter. For example, "Ingenious iguanas improvising an intricate impromptu on impossibly impractical instruments." Embedded around the central image are obvious objects like iceberg, ice cream cone, and iron. There are also challenging words such as "insignia" and "isosceles triangle." Proper nouns are represented in the flags from Italy, Ireland, and Israel. The author also used abstract nouns like "idea" and "inside." There are words that begin with the letter "i" with no picture like "India" and "igloo." Older students will have to rely on their perception and will have fun challenging each other to see who finds the most words. Student's with developed vocabulary will discover that one iguana is lying on an island clutching an ingot of gold. The text in this book is an excellent example of alliteration, and will challenge students to develop vocabulary.

63   Beneduce, Ann Keay (Reteller). *Gulliver's Adventures in Lilliput.* Illus. by Gennady Spirin. Philomel, 1993. ISBN 0–399–22021–6. Expressionism. Watercolors. Literature (Adaptations). Swift, Jonathan (1667–1745). Illustrated Classics.

An exquisitely condensed adaptation of Gulliver's journey to the island of Lilliput. Jonathon Swift's *Gulliver's Travels* (1726) was one of the earliest fantasy novels, and this book will encourage students visit the library to check out Swift's novel. Spirin's richly detailed paintings capture the tiny Lilliputians, making the paintings worthy of prolonged examination. Spirin's achievement is his ability to scale the proportions of the Lilliputians against the towering frame of Gulliver. The illustrations are historically accurate and can also serve as a study of the eighteenth century. The combination of Beneduce's retelling paired with the magnificent illustrations by Gennady Spirin will capture a new generations of readers. Challenge students to read Jonathan Swift's unabridged version of *Gulliver's Travels.* Another picture book version *Gulliver's Travels* is *Gulliver in Lilliput* (Holiday House, 1995) by Kimberly Bulcken Root. Compare Kimberly Bulcken Root's illustrations with those of Gennady Spirin. Other picture book versions of famous works of literature include *The Tyger* (Harcourt Brace, 1993) by William Blake, *Catskill Eagle: Chapter 96 from* Moby-Dick (Philomel, 1991) by Herman Melville, *The Highwayman* (Harcourt Brace, 1990) by Alfred Noyes, and *The Lady of Shalott* (Oxford University Press, 1986) by Alfred Tennyson.

64   Beneduce, Ann Keay (Reteller). *The Tempest by William Shakespeare.* Illus. by Gennady Spirin. Philomel, 1996. ISBN 0–399–22764–4. Expressionism. Watercolors. Plays (Adaptations). Shakespeare, William (1564–1616). Dramatists, English. Illustrated Classics.

Ann Keay Beneduce has adapted Shakespeare's last play, *The Tempest,* for younger readers. *The Tempest* is the tale of Prospero, a once influential man who was exiled to an abandoned island by his treacherous brother. Prospero vindicates the injustice when a storm—a tempest—blows his brother's ship off course and to Prospero's island. Beneduce's prose retelling is an excellent adaptation of Shakespeare's writing, which is often confusing for younger readers. Gennady Spirin's luminous illustrations are an invitation to one of Shakespeare's most celebrated plays. The details integrated into the illustrations are worthy of extended examination. Have students read the adaptation by Beneduce and Spirin and then read Shakespeare's play. Comparison between the prose version and Shakespeare's play will be interesting for students to explore. *William Shakespeare's A Midsummer's Night Dream* (Dial, 1996) by Bruce Coville is another adaptation of William Shakespeare's plays. Have students compare Bruce Coville's retelling and Ann Keay Beneduce's retelling for style.

65   Bernhard, Emery. *The Tree That Rains*. Illus. by Durga Bernhard. Holiday House, 1994. ISBN 0–8234–1108–7. Naive. Gouache. Folktales, Huichol Indians. Indians of Central America. Indians of Mexico. Floods. Huichol Indians.

Watakame works hard in the fields from sunrise to sunset. One day he chops down a fig tree. He returns the next day to find the tree standing again. To his further amazement, Great-Grandmother Earth appears to warn Watakame of a great flood that will wash away the fields and the people because they have forgotten the gods. Great-Grandmother Earth helps Watakame survive the flood and begin a new life. This myth continues to be recited each year by the Huichol Indians at the Harvest Festival of New Corn and Squash to celebrate Watakame and his part in the new creation of the world. Durga Bernhard's bright gouache illustrations add depth to Emery Bernhard's spare prose. Compare this flood story with the Christian story of Noah and the Ark to explore the common threads of flood stories in different cultures. *Noah* (Philomel, 1994) by Patricia Lee Gauch and *Noah's Ark: Words From the Book of Genesis* (Dutton, 1990) by Jane Ray are illustrated versions of the Christian story of Noah.

66   Bierhorst, John. *The Woman Who Fell from the Sky: The Iroquois Story of Creation*. Illus. by Robert Andrew Parker. William Morrow & Company, 1993. ISBN 0–688–10680–3. Impressionism. Gouache/Pen and Ink. Legends, Iroquois Indians. Indians of North America. Creation Stories. Iroquois Indians.

A creation story from the Iroquois Indian tribe. When a woman hears her two children under her heart, she uses her powers of creation to form the earth. With a toss of her hand, she spread stars across the night sky and creates the soil, plants, animals, rivers, and the seasons. She falls from sky country to earth with her sons, Sapling and Flint, and completes the cycle of creation. This

Iroquois Indian creation myth celebrates the flowering of life on earth and the placement of earth in the pattern of the universe. The credible text by Bierhorst is a fine example of cultural authenticity in folktales. Creation stories are powerful myths deeply imbedded in many cultures. Springboard into a study of creations myths with this book. Some other creation titles are *How the Sea Began* (Clarion, 1993) by George Crespo, *Owl Eyes* (Lothrop, Lee & Shepard, 1994) by Frieda Gates, *The Origin of Life on Earth: An African Creation Myth* (Sights Productions, 1991) by David L. Anderson, and *The Story of Creation: Words from Genesis* (Dutton, 1993) by Jane Ray.

67   Bruchac, Joseph. *Thirteen Moons on Turtle's Back: A Native American Year of Moons.* Illus. by Thomas Locker. Philomel, 1992. ISBN 0–399–22141–7. Representational. Oils. Poetry, Native Americans. Indians of North America. Seasons—Folklore. Turtles—Folklore. Moon—Folklore.

The thirteen moons of the year play significant roles in many Native American cultures, among them the budding moon of the Huron Indians and the moose-calling moon of the Micmac tribe. Each moon story is energized by the turtle, who is said to carry the mystery and wonder of the moon in the shell of its back. The natural world of Native American lore is a place of power and enchantment, where stories are formed from the mysteries of the earth, helping humans live in harmony with nature. *Thirteen Moons on Turtle's Back* is a collection of poems accompanied by lush oil paintings that celebrate the majesty of the moon and her thirteen cycles. An author's note explains the origins of the turtle's shell in the legends. Use this book to introduce a poetry unit with emphasis on theme. Companion moon tales include *Moon Mother* (HarperCollins, 1993) by Ed Young, *Moon Rope: Un Lazo a la Luna: A Peruvian Folktale* (Harcourt Brace, 1992) by Lois Ehlert, and *Moontellers* (Northland, 1995) by Lynn Moroney.

68   Carey, Valerie. *Quail Song.* Illus. by Ivan Barnett. G. P. Putnam's, 1990. ISBN 0–399–21936–6. Naive. Cut Paper. Legends, Pueblo Indians. Indians of North America—Southwest.

Quail perches during harvest time and sings his song: "Ki-ruu, ki-ruu. tsi-ka, tsi-ka." Coyote hears Quail's song and threatens, "Teach me your song or I will swallow you up!" Quail acquiesces, but his song is no ordinary song and Coyote may end up swallowing more than he bargained for. Folk art illustrations and sing-song text make this retelling of a traditional Pueblo Indian tale of a clever quail who outwits a persistent coyote a pleasure to read. The cut paper illustrations are simple but succinct. Carey's voice is authentic and true to the southwestern area that inspired the retelling. The text is a good example of onomatopoeia. Examine onomatopoeia as a literary device and brainstorm a list of words with your students. Companion Pueblo Indian legends include *Crow and Hawk* (Harcourt Brace, 1995) by Michael Rosen and *Dragonfly's Tale* (Clarion, 1991) by Kristina Rodanas.

69   Cassedy, Sylvia, and Kunihiro Suetake (Translators). *Red Dragonfly on My Shoulder.* Illus. by Molly Bang. HarperCollins, 1992. ISBN 0–06–022625–0. Impressionism. Collage. Haiku. Haiku. Poetry, Japanese. Poetry—Animals.

Haiku is the simplest form of poetry. *Red Dragonfly on My Shoulder* is a wonderful introduction to the powerful imagery of haiku. This collection includes thirteen translated haiku poems that are small masterpieces of famous Japanese poets. Although haiku is commonly associated with nature, this collection has animals as a theme. Collage and assemblage illustrations made from everyday items make the pictures as interesting to explore as the haiku. Use the imagery in this book to help students create their own haiku poems. The collage illustrations by Bang will inspire students to consider illustrating their own haiku. *Grass Sandals: The Travels of Basho* (Atheneum, 1997) by Dawnine Spivak with illustrations by Demi is a fictional account of a seventeenth-century Japanese poet, Basho.

70   Chekhov, Anton (Translated by Ronald Meyer). *Kashanka.* Illus. by Gennady Spirin. Gulliver/Harcourt Brace, 1995. ISBN 0–15–200539–0. Representational. Watercolors. Literature, Russian. Chekhov, Anton (1860–1904). Illustrated Classics.

An adaptation of a translation from Russian of Anton Chekov's beloved dog story. Kashtanka has lived with the cabinetmaker, Luka, for many years. One evening he is separated from his master in a snowstorm and wanders the streets lonely and bewildered. Kashtanka is befriended by a circus clown and joins other trained animals who live in the clown's home. Soon Kashtanka is able to perform many tricks and is ready for his first circus performance. On the evening of his debut, from the audience Luka recognizes his lost pet. Luka calls out, and Kashtanka must decide between his new life and the one he left behind. Have students compare this illustrated version with Chekhov's original short story. Discuss the positive or negative effects of adaptation. Pose the question of poetic license with your class. *Firebird* (G. P. Putnam's, 1994) by Rachel Isadora, an adaptation of Igor Stravinsky's ballet, *The Firebird*, and *Peter and the Wolf* (Morrow, 1991) by Michèle Lemieux, an adaptation of Sergei Prokofiev's musical tale, are ideal for comparing adaptations of famous Russian works.

71   Climo, Shirley. *Atalanta's Race: A Greek Myth.* Illus. by Alexander Koshkin. Clarion, 1995. ISBN 0–395–67322–4. Folk Art. Mixed Media. Mythology, Greek. Atalanta (legendary character). Olympic Games. Gender Roles.

Retelling of the myth of a Greek princess, first recorded by Roman poet Ovid in the first-century A.D. Atalanta is abandoned by her father and left for dead in a forest because she was born a female. Rescued by bears and raised by a woodsman, Atalanta learns to run as swiftly as the wind and to hunt with a sure and compassionate hand. She travels through Greece with her quiver and arrows winning honors wherever she goes for her skill as an athlete. She promises to one day "wear a winner's crown of laurel," proving that not only males are gifted with speed and strength. Use *Atalanta's Race* and other illustrated Greek myths the next time you assign *The Iliad.* Some other Greek myths in picture book format include *Wings* (Harcourt Brace, 1991) by Jane Yolen, *Persephone and the Pomegranate: A Myth from Greece* by (Dial, 1993) Kris Waldherr, and *Cyclops* (Holiday House, 1991) by Leonard Everett Fisher. Warwick Hutton also created a series of illustrated Greek myths that includes *Persephone* (Margaret K. McElderry, 1994), *Perseus* (Margaret K. McElderry, 1993), *Theseus and the Minotaur* (Margaret K. McElderry, 1989), and *The Trojan Horse* (Margaret K. McElderry, 1992).

72   Climo, Shirley. *The Egyptian Cinderella.* Illus. by Ruth Heller. Harper Trophy, 1989. ISBN 0–690–04824–6. Expressionism. Watercolors. Fairy Tales, Egypt. Egypt. Cinderella Tales.

An Egyptian Cinderella tale first recorded by Roman historian Strabo in the first century B.C. In Greece, a long time ago, lived a girl called Rhodopis [ra-doh-pes]. Poor Rhodopis is a slave with no family. Her only joy is a pair of rose red slippers, a gift from her master. One day a falcon swoops from the sky and spirits away one of her precious slippers. The falcon drops the slipper into the lap of the pharaoh, who promises to marry the girl whose foot fits the slipper. A slave girl named Rhodopis really existed and wed a pharaoh; as for the red slippers, anything is possible in a fairy tale. Source notes are included. Ruth Heller's jewel-tone paintings are glorious, and the research required to produce such artwork is evident in the watercolor illustrations. Cinderella tales are the oldest recorded fairy tales in the world. Over 500 versions exist. Use other Cinderella tales listed in the index for comparison.

73   Climo, Shirley. *The Korean Cinderella.* Illus. by Ruth Heller. Harper-Collins, 1993. ISBN 0–06–020432–X. Expressionism. Watercolors. Fairy Tales, Korea. Cinderella Tales. Korea.

Pear Blossom, named for the pear tree planted in honor of her birth, is cruelly treated by her stepmother, Omoni. Omoni, irritated by Pear Blossom's gentle nature, works the girl to exhaustion from dawn to dusk. Pear Blossom never complains, but this only angers Omoni, who strives to increase Pear Blossom's discomfort by making her complete three tasks not humanly possible to complete. With the aid of magical intervention, Pear Blossom is able to complete the tasks and in the process gains a nobleman for a husband. This Cinderella tale is based on three Korean versions. The illustrations are richly detailed, showing thoroughly researched elements of the Korean influence, adding dimension to the story. Have students locate other versions of Cinderella tales to compare them with this version. *Kongi and Potgi: A Cinderella Story from Korea* (Dial, 1996) by Oki S. Han is another Korean version of the Cinderella tale. Other Asian versions of the Cinderella tale include *Yeh-Shen: A Cinderella Tale from China* (Philomel, 1982) by Louie Ah-Ling and *Wishbones: A Folktale from China* (Bradbury, 1993) by Barbara Ker Wilson. Note the motif of the magic agent and how it differs from the European versions of Cinderella.

74   Climo, Shirley. *Stolen Thunder.* Illus. by Alexander Koshkin. Clarion, 1994. ISBN 0–395–64368–6. Folk Art. Mixed Media. Myths, Norse. Thor (Norse deity). Norse Mythology.

A myth from the mists of Norse legend. Thor, god of thunder, swings his hammer, and all creatures tremble. No one, not even the frost giants, challenge Thor and his mighty hammer. When his hammer is stolen and held ransom by Thyrm, king of the frost giants, in exchange for the hand of Freya, the goddess of love, Thor, along with Loki the Trickster, must race to the ends of the earth to stop the wedding and regain Thor's hammer. The richly detailed illustrations by Alexander Koskin compliment Shirley Climo's complex and graceful retelling of the Norse myth. The combined efforts of Climo and Koshkin produce a classic tale of love and will make readers eager for more Norse legends in picture book format. The days of the Christian week—for example, Thursday, which is named after Thor—are from Norse legend. Explore the history of the naming of the days of the week with this title. *And Sunday Makes Seven* (Whitman, 1990) by Robert Baden is Costa Rican folktale about the days of the week. Extend and explore folklore about months with two Czechoslovakian titles *Marushka and the Month Brothers* (North-South, 1996) by Anna Vojtech and *The Month Brothers: A Slavic Tale* (Morrow, 1993) by Samuel Marshak. *Odin's Family: Myths of the Vikings* (Orchard, 1996) Neil Philip and *Favorite Norse Myths* (Scholastic, 1996) by Mary Pope Osborne are two anthologies of Norse mythology.

75   Coleridge, Samuel Taylor. *The Rime of the Ancient Mariner.* Illus. by Ed Young. Atheneum, 1992. ISBN 0–689–31613–5. Impressionism. Pastels.

Poetry, English. Coleridge, Samuel Taylor (1772–1834). Illustrated Classics. Poets, English.

An illustrated version of "The Rime of the Ancient Mariner" by the famed English poet Samuel Taylor Coleridge by Caldecott-winning illustrator Ed Young. Mr. Young's soft pastels bring the haunting poem to stunning life. "The Rime of the Ancient Mariner," Coleridge's best-known poem, explores a sailor's reminiscence of the terrible fate that befell his crew after the mariner shoots an albatross. The text is arranged as it is in most anthologies, with the entire poem reproduced in this memorable edition. Use this book in place of any other edition of this poem. Students will enjoy discussing the complexities the illustrations add to the poem. Brainstorm a list of other poems that would be suitable for illustration.

76   Cooper, Floyd. *Coming Home: From the Life of Langston Hughes.* Illus. by author. Philomel, 1994. ISBN 0–399–22682–6. Representational. Watercolors. Biography. Hughes, Langston (1902–1967). Poets, American. African Americans—Biography.

Langston Hughes, one of the greatest African-American poets of the twentieth century, was an influential writer during the Harlem Renaissance in New York City during the 1920s. He lived all over the United States and was always with family, but the one thing he longed for was a home. Inspired by influential black Americans like Booker T. Washington, jazz musicians, and the black soldiers who fought in World War I, he grew up to write about the people he met and the places he visited during his lifetime. When Langston Hughes began to write about his experiences, he found his home. Floyd Cooper's loving illustrations and sensitive portrait will inspire students to explore Hughes's writing. The Harlem Renaissance was a pivotal time in literary history. Expose students to other African-American writers who were prolific at that time. *Langston Hughes* (Creative Education, 1994) by S. L. Barry provides more detailed information in picture book format and is an ideal companion title. *Free to Dream: The Making of a Poet* (Lothrop, Lee & Shepard, 1996) by Audrey Osofsky is a rich biography about Langston Hughes with a design that will be hard to surpass. *The Harlem Renaissance* (Millbrook Press, 1996) by Jim Haskins explores the careers of prominent figures who shaped the literary movement in black America.

77   Cooper, Susan. *The Selkie Girl.* Illus. by Warwick Hutton. Margaret K. McElderry, 1986. ISBN 0–689–50390–3. Cartoon Art. Watercolors. Folktales, Scotland. Seals—Folklore.

A young fisherman sees three lovely girls combing their hair on a rock and immediately falls in love with the fair one. When the girls see him, they dive into the sea, taking the form of seals. Donallan walks home with his heart heavy with love, wondering how to make the lass his. Along the way he meets an old man from the village who knows the secret of these selkies, who come from the sea on the seventh day of the highest tides to take human form. The old man warns him that "a wild creature will always go back to the wild in the end." Mythical creatures from the lore of Scotland and Ireland, Selkies are half human, half seal. Donallan learns the secret of the selkie power to transform, and he captures his true love. Explore other Scottish folktales or compare the selkie myth with mermaid tales. Transformation of humans into animal form is a common theme in literature, explore this motif with *The Selkie Girl*. *The Seal Prince* (Dial, 1995) by Sheila MacGill-Callahan is another Scottish folktale with a similar transformation theme.

78   Crespo, George. *How the Sea Began.* Illus. by author. Clarion, 1993. ISBN 0–395–63033–9. Expressionism. Oils. Folktales, West Indies. Indians. Ocean— Folklore. Creation Stories.

Long ago there was no sea, only land that stretched forever into the distance with only four mountains to break the view. One mountain, Boriquén, was a village where a boy named Yayael, a great hunter, provided meat for the tribe. One day as he was hunting, Yayael looked to the sky and saw the fury of Guabancex, a terrible goddess of wind and water. What follows is the tale of how land came to be surrounded by water and how the mountain of Boriquén became the island of Puerto Rico. This Taino creation myth relates the origins of Puerto Rico, Cuba, Jamaica, and Haiti—the four mountains surrounded by land. An author's note covers in detail the origins of the myth and a pronunciation guide. Compare with other creation myths for consistencies. Jane Yolen's *Encounter* (Harcourt Brace, 1992) examines Taino culture through the exploration of Christopher Columbus and Nina Jaffe's *The Golden Flower: A Taino Myth* (Simon & Schuster, 1996) is a folktale from Puerto Rico, pair these books with *How the Sea Began* to explore a culture that no longer exists.

79   cummings, e. e. *Little Tree.* Illus. by Deborah Kogan Ray. Crown, 1987. ISBN 0–517–56598–6. Representational. Colored Pencils. Poetry, American. Cummings, Edward Estlin (1894–1962). Christmas Trees. Illustrated Classics. Poets, American.

An illustrated version of e. e. cummings celebrated Christmas poem. Deborah Kogan Ray's soft colored pencil illustrations capture the magic of Christmas time in a series pictures perfectly suited to each line of the poem. This picture book makes a perfect introduction to e. e. cummings large body of poetry. Pair with Barry Skip's title from the Voices in Poetry series *e.e. cummings* (Creative Education, 1994) for a biographical exploration of the poet.

80   Day, Nancy Raines. *The Lion's Whiskers.* Illus. by Ann Grifalconi. Scholastic, 1995. ISBN 0–590–45803–5. Expressionism. Collage. Folktales, Ethiopia. Amhara (African People).

Fanaye has long passed the age of childbirth but still longs for a son. One day at the river, Fanaye meets a widowed man with a son. She marries the man and sets about to please her new family. However, everything Fanaye does displeases the boy. She seeks counsel from a medicine man, who sends her on a perilous quest that will earn her the love of her stepson. Nancy Raines Day's narrative is strong and compelling. Grifalconi, celebrated for her stylish picture books, surpasses herself with the unique collage illustrations in this book. Compare this folktale with the motifs found in Cinderella tales, and discuss the role of step-parents in literature. *Fire on the Mountain* (Simon & Schuster, 1994) by Jane Kurtz is another folktale from Ethiopia.

81   dePaola, Tomie. *Fin M'Coul.* Illus. by author. Holiday House, 1981. ISBN 0–8034–0384–X. Cartoon Art. Watercolors. Folktales, Ireland. Fin M'Coul (legendary character). Giants—Folklore. Ireland.

When Ireland was still fresh with magic, it was common to see giants stomping across the hills and valleys. Fin M'Coul was among the big folk who called the Emerald Isle's glens and woods home. Fin and his lovely wife, Oonagh, live on top of Knockmany Hill and are very happy except for their annoyance with giant Cucullin, the strongest creature in the land, who wants to flatten Fin to prove his might. Oonagh, tired of Cucullin and his threats, uses her Irish cleverness to devise a plan to teach the mean and boastful Cucullin a lesson and rid their lives of his overbearing presence forever. Stories about Fin M'Coul have been handed down through generations of Irish families, with the most famous being Fin's help in building the Giant's Causeway between Ireland and Scotland. Tomie de Paola's details in the borders of the illustrations were inspired by Irish jewelry and metal work. Tomie de Paola used W. B. Yeats's spelling of the giant's name from his retelling of the Irish folktale "The Legend of Knockmany." *Fairy Tales of Ireland* (Delacorte, 1990) by W. B. Yeats with illustrations by P. J. Lynch is an accessible collection. Other picture books of Irish folktales include *Saint Patrick and the Peddler* (Orchard, 1993) by Margaret Hodges, *Billy Beg and His Bull* (Holiday House, 1994) by Ellin Greene, and *Jaime O'Rourke and the Big Potato: An Irish Folktale* (G. P. Putnam's, 1992) by Tomie dePaola.

82   dePaola, Tomie. *Strega Nona.* Illus. by author. Simon & Schuster, 1975. ISBN 0–671–66283–X. Cartoon Art. Watercolors. Folktales, Italy. Witches—Folklore. Italy.

Based on an old Italian tale. Strega Nona, grandmother witch, is the village healer, and her cottage is where neighbors from the small Italian village turn when they are ill or in need of a potion to cure a broken heart. Strega Nona's magical tools also include a pot that is always full of pasta, which she trusts to the care of Big Anthony. When Strega Nona leaves for a visit with Strega Amelia, she warns Big Anthony not to tempt the magic of the pot. But Anthony, hungry after a day tending the garden, utters the spell to fill the pot and finds that magic belongs in the hands of people who know how to use it. Strega Nona is a legendary witch figure from Italy. Because of the popularity of this book, Tomie de Paola has written and illustrated other Strega Nona books. He thoroughly researches his topics and includes source notes. His text is peppered with Italian phrases, which students could study to experience a prime example of bilingual prose. Explore the legend of Strega Nona and that of another good witch from Italy: Befana, the Christmas witch. Discuss the connotation of the word "witch" as an old crone or hag figure in literature.

83   Denise, Christopher. *The Fool of the World and the Flying Ship.* Illus. by author. Philomel, 1994. ISBN 0–399–31972–2. Expressionism. Acrylics. Folktales, Russia.

When the tsar announces that he will award the hand of his daughter to the mouse who can build a flying ship, Fool jumps at the chance. A flying ship? His family try to dissuade him, but Fool is determined, and with a wave of his hand he heads from home to take the first steps of his strange journey. Along the way he meets many interesting creatures who are as odd as he is. Together Fool and his friends prove that determination and diversity can be as resourceful as intelligence. There are several variations of this Russian tale; this version was based on the tales of Pëtr Nikolaevich Polevoi (1839–1902). Another version of this tale, illustrated by Uri Shulevitz, won the Caldecott Medal for distinguished illustration for children in 1969. *The Frog Princess: A Russian Folktale* (Dial, 1994) by Patrick J. Lewis and *The Tale of Tsar Saltan* (Dial, 1995) by Alexander Pushkin are two other Russian folktales.

84   Early, Margaret. *Robin Hood.* Illus. by author. Abrams, 1996. ISBN 0–8019–4428–6. Folk Art. Oils. Legends, England. Middle Ages. Robin Hood (legendary character). Outlaws.

Resplendent paintings depict the honor and dedication of the legendary outlaw Robin Hood, hero to common folk and bane to the unjust ruler of

England in the twelfth century. Robin, formerly Robert Locksley, became an outlaw when he was disinherited. Devoted to his cause, Robin uses the wealth gained from thievery for good purpose and gives his spoils to the poor. Those familiar with the Robin Hood legends will enjoy the richly detailed paintings reminiscent of medieval art. Early's prose is very formal and could be compared with other Robin Hood retellings such as *The Adventures of Robin Hood* (Candlewick Press, 1995) by Marcia Williams, a lighthearted look at the famous outlaw of Sherwood Forest. Hollywood has popularized the legend of Robert of Locksley. Have students research the origins of Robin Hood and his Merrymen with emphasis on Robin Hood as a real figure from history.

85   Eliot, T. S. *Mr. Mistoffelees with Mungojerrie and Rumpelteazer.* Illus. by Errol Le Cain. Harcourt Brace, 1990. ISBN 0–15–256230–3. Watercolors. Expressionism. Poetry, American/English. Eliot, Thomas Stearns (1888–1965). Cats. *Old Possum's Book of Practical Cats* (1939). Illustrated Classics. Poets, American/English.

Errol Le Cain's homage to the fanciful cat poetry by T. S. Eliot, which was published posthumously. Follow the antics of Eliot's feline characters as they stir up mischief in the cobblestone streets and elegant sitting rooms of London. T. S. Eliot's Old Possum tales inspired Andrew Lloyd Webber, composer of numerous hit Broadway musicals, to write *Cats.* Le Cain also illustrated *Growltiger's Last Stand and Other Poems* (Farrar, Straus & Giroux, 1986). Introduce students to Eliot's poetry with *Old Possum's Book of Practical Cats* (Harcourt Brace, 1982), a delightful edition of with illustrations by Edward Gorey, renowned illustrator of PBS series *Mystery!*

86   Frost, Robert. *Birches.* Illus. by Ed Young. Henry Holt, 1988. ISBN 0–8050–0570–6. Impressionism. Watercolors. Poetry, American. Robert Frost (1874–1963). Illustrated Classics. Poets, American.

"Birches" is a reminiscent poem of the endurance and strength of life. Beginning with an image of a boy swinging from the branches of a birch tree, Frost ends his poem by recalling his own days swinging from a tree of the same sort. Insightful and imaginative, "Birches," one of Frost's most quoted poems, first appeared in *Mountain Intervals* (1916). Robert Frost (1874–1963) is one of America's best-loved poets and during his lifetime managed to capture in his poetry the essence of human beings' connection to nature and the land. Ed Young's delicate watercolors evoke the subtle tones of the poem and extend its meaning. As an introduction to the works of Robert Frost, this illustrated version ranks high for the powerful images it evoked for the illustrator. *Robert Frost* (Creative Education, 1994) provides more detailed information in picture book format and is an ideal companion title.

87   Frost, Robert. *Christmas Trees.* Illus. by Ted Rand. Henry Holt, 1990. ISBN 0–8050–1208–7. Impressionism. Watercolors. Poetry, American. Robert Frost (1874–1963). Illustrated Classics. Poets, American.

Robert Frost's poem is about a Christmas tree farmer's deal with an urban businessman and the commercialization of the farmer's trees. When the deal falls through, the farmer comes to realize the importance of his Christmas tree forest and the true value of his friends and farm. The poem first appeared in Frost's collection *Mountain Intervals* (1916). The poem, called a circular letter by Frost, has become a Christmas favorite. Robert Frost (1874–1963) is one of America's favorite poets, and his keen sense of people and their connection to nature and the land is evident in his poetry. *A Restless Spirit: The Story of Robert Frost* (Holt, 1997) by Natalie S. Bober is a biographical sketch of the poet.

88   Frost, Robert. *Stopping By Woods On A Snowy Evening.* Illus. by Susan Jeffers. Dutton, 1978. ISBN 0–525–40115–6. Representational. Pen and Ink/Pencil Overlay. Poetry, American. Frost, Robert (1874–1963). Illustrated Classics. Poets, American.

An illustrated version of Robert Frost's best-loved poem, this book captures the wonderment of a winter day. Each illustration was lovingly drawn to match a line of the poem, bringing an added visual element to Frost's eloquent writing. Each icy scene delicately captures the auspicious offerings of winter. This poem is from Robert Frost's collection *The Poetry of Robert Frost*. Use this book to introduce students to the works of Robert Frost. Jeffers's illustrations are an example of the impact the poem had on one individual. This book will inspire students to view Frost's poetry from an artistic perspective. Follow up with a class discussion of the poem to examine Jeffers's interpretation of the poem through her illustrations. *Robert Frost* (Creative Education, 1994) provides more detailed information in picture book format and is an ideal companion title.

89   Frost, Robert. *Versed in Country Things.* Photographs by B. A. King. Bulfinch Press/Little, Brown, 1996. ISBN 0–8212–2288–0. Representational. Photographs. Poetry, American. Illustrated Classics. Poets, American.

A magnificent series of spare black-and-white photographs captures the simple beauty of twenty of Robert Frost's poems. This collection is strong enough to serve as the sole source for studying the poetry of Frost. Pair with the illustrated texts of other Robert Frost poems—*Birches* (illustrated by Ed Young), *Christmas Trees* (illustrated by Ted Rand), and *Stopping by the Woods on a Snowy Evening* (illustrated by Susan Jeffers)—for an artistic take on the work of Robert Frost. *Road Not Taken: An Introduction to Robert Frost* (Holt, 1985) is an ideal title to help students explore the poetry of Robert Frost.

90   Garland, Sherry. *Why Ducks Sleep on One Leg.* Illus. by Jean and Mousien Tseng. Scholastic, 1993. ISBN 0–590–45697–0. Cartoon Art. Watercolors. Folktales, Vietnam. Ducks—Folklore. Vietnam. Pourquoi Tales.

Long ago three ducks with one leg each lived in Vietnam. Unable to maintain balance, the three ducks fell when chasing worms and were not able to paddle in the water. A means of amusement to the other animals, the trio resolve to remedy their situation by appealing to the Jade Emperor in the Celestial Palace. With the aid of a petition, the three ducks journey to heaven to make their request. This pourquoi tale explains how ducks came have two legs but still sleep on one leg. *Why Ducks Sleep on One Leg* is based on an ancient tale that developed from beliefs in animism—the belief that all life is crated by a force separate from physical matter. Three other picture books about Vietnamese culture are *Lotus Seed* (Harcourt Brace, 1993) by Sherry Garland, *Tuan* (R & S Books, 1988) by Eva Boholm-Olsson, and *Grandfather's Dream* (Greenwillow, 1994) by Holly Keller.

91   Gerson, Mary-Joan. *Why the Sky Is Far Away.* Illus. by Carla Golembe. Little, Brown, 1992. ISBN 0–316–30852–8. Folk Art. Mixed Media. Folktales, Africa. Africa, Nigeria. Sky—Folklore. Pourquoi Tales.

Long ago the sky was the source of food for people, but the people were wasteful and took more than they needed and threw the rest away. This angered the sky, who warned the people, "I will not tolerate this wasteful behavior. Learn to be thrifty or lose my gifts forever!" And for awhile the people did. Eventually the people returned to their wasteful ways, and the sky moved far from their reach. "What will we eat?" they cried. "Learn to plant and harvest. Show nature you are grateful for her gifts," said the sky. To this day the sky is far, far away. The power of nature and the force of the elements had influence over ancient cultures. Examine the power storytelling has within societies by exploring pourquoi tales. Verna Aardema is a noted storyteller who often employs pourquoi form in her books.

92   Glass, Andrew. *Folks Call Me Appleseed John.* Illus. by author. Doubleday, 1995. ISBN 0–385–32045–0. Cartoon Art. Oils. Folklore, America. Chapman, John (1774–1845). Frontier and Pioneer Life. Johnny Appleseed. Tall Tales.

Johnny Appleseed is one of the few tall tale characters who was a real person. Born John Chapman in Pennsylvania in 1774, Johnny Appleseed spent the better part of his adult life planting apple trees across the eastern part of the United States. This version of his adventures is the story of Johnny and his brother, Nathaniel. Johnny loved to tell folks of his brother's reaction to Johnny's burlap clothes and choice of a black cooking pot for headgear. Nathaniel, a gentleman used to comfortable living, had a difficult time adjusting to Johnny's lifestyle and his home: a hollow sycamore tree. Compare this version to other illustrated versions of stories about Johnny Appleseed or any tall tale character. Other books with tall tale characters are *John Henry* (Dial, 1994) by Julius Lester and *Swamp Angel* (Dutton, 1994) by Anne Isaac.

93   Goble, Paul. *Love Flute.* Illus. by author. Bradbury, 1992. ISBN 0–02–736261–2. Folk Art. Watercolors. Legends, Great Plains Indians. Indians of North America. Courting—Folklore. Flutes—Folklore.

A frustrated young man, unable to express his love for a beautiful girl, leaves his village in shame. His lack of courage inspires mystical visitors to give him a special gift that will reveal his deep feelings for the maiden. This Great Plains legend about the sacred flute that was used exclusively for courting is an excellent example of the masterful skill of Paul Goble. This courting tale is based on a version of the Santee Dakota myth recorded by Ella Delorian and Jay Brandon in *The Origin of the Courting Flute* published in 1961. Paul Goble's extensive body of work includes many picture books about Great Plains Indians. Examine the entire design of a Goble title to see an exquisite example of the attributes exhaustive research adds to both text and illustrations in a picture book format.

94   Goble, Paul. *Iktomi and the Boulder.* Illus. by author. Orchard, 1988. ISBN 0–531–05760–7. Folk Art. Watercolors. Legends, Great Plains Indians. Iktomi (trickster figure). Indians of North America. Trickster Tales.

Iktomi [eek-toe-me] is a trickster figure from Native American literature whose escapades are a source of the humorous side of American Indian folklore. Iktomi, foolish and rash, attempts to trick others and in the process tricks only himself. Iktomi is the Lakota name for the trickster figure and means spider. The spider is also a trickster figure in African and Caribbean cultures and is known as Anansi. Paul Goble has written three other Iktomi books that feature the Plains Indian trickster figure: *Iktomi and the Berries* (Orchard, 1989), *Iktomi and the Ducks* (Orchard, 1990), and *Iktomi and the Buffalo Skull* (Orchard, 1991). Paul Goble designed the text to be read the way the tales are told by a storyteller. When the text is grayed out and italicized, the audience is supposed to comment about Iktomi and his actions. Iktomi's thoughts are small text meant not to read aloud but to be enjoyed when sharing the pictures. Have students compare other trickster figures from different cultures.

95   Grahame, Kenneth. *The Open Road from* The Wind in the Willows. Illus. by Beverly Gooding. Scribner's, 1979. ISBN 0-684-16471-X. Cartoon Art. Watercolors. Children's Literature. Grahame, Kenneth (1859-1932). *The Wind in the Willows* (1907). Illustrated Classics.

An illustrated version of the second chapter from Kenneth Grahame's beloved animal fantasy *The Wind in the Willows*. The novel was published in 1907, with hundreds of printings and several illustrated editions since that time. Arthur Rackham, Michael Hague, and Ernest Shepard, illustrator of A. A. Milne's Winnie-the-Pooh books, are among the esteemed illustrators who have honored Grahame's classic novel with their interpretation of Toad, Rat, Mole, and Badger's adventures in the English countryside. *The Jumblies* (Putnam, 1989) illustrations by Ted Rand and *The Owl and the Pussycat* (Putnam, 1991) with illustrations by Jan Brett will allow students to explore the nonsense verse of Edward Lear, a prominent nineteenth-century illustrator, in picture book format.

96   Grahame, Kenneth. *The River Bank from* The Wind in the Willows. Illus. by Adrienne Adams. Scribner's, 1977). ISBN 0-684-15046-8. Cartoon Art. Watercolors. Children's Literature. Grahame, Kenneth (1859-1932). *The Wind in the Willows* (1907). Illustrated Classics.

An illustrated version of the first chapter from Kenneth Grahame's beloved animal fantasy *The Wind in the Willows*. Grahame's tales of Toad, Rat, Mole, and Badger's adventures in the English countryside began as bedtime stories for his son. The novel was published in 1907 and has been through hundreds of printings and several illustrated editions since that time. Arthur Rackham, Michael Hague, and Ernest Shepard, illustrator of A. A. Milne's Winnie-the-Pooh books, are among the esteemed illustrators who have honored Grahame's classic novel with their interpretation of one of children's literature's classic animal fantasies.

97   Granfield, Linda. *In Flander's Field: The Story of the Poem by John McCrae.* Illus. by Janet Wilson. Doubleday, 1995. ISBN 0-385-32228-3. Representational. Mixed Media. Nonfiction. McCrae, John (1872-1918). World War I. Poetry, Canadian. Illustrated Classics.

An illustrated context for John McCrae's war poem "In Flanders Field." McCrae, a Canadian medical officer, cared for hundreds of wounded and dying soldiers each day. This moving tribute to McCrae through this poignant picture book is profound in its scope and purpose. The supplemental information in the form of a map of Europe that graces the endpapers and a reproduction of the poem make this book a visual feast. *In Flanders Field: The Story of the Poem by John McCrae* is an ideal example to illustrate the many creative and exciting ways to gather information and present it in a new format as Granfield did with McCrae's poem.

98   Greene, Ellin. *Billy Beg and His Bull.* Illus. by Kimberly Bulcken Root. Holiday House, 1994. ISBN 0-8234-1100-1. Expressionism. Watercolors. Fairy Tales, Ireland. Cinderella Tales. Gender Roles. Ireland.

Once upon a time in Ireland there lived a boy named Billy. Right before her death, as a parting gift, Billy's mother gives him a bull. Billy prizes his bull over any of his other possessions. When his father remarries a jealous and wicked woman, Billy and his bull must run away from home. Many adventures befall young Billy—including the death of his beloved bull, a magic quest to kill three giants, and the winning of the hand of a lovely princess. This story features a male Cinderella figure. *Billy Beg and His Bull* is based on a tale by Seamus MacManus (1869-1960) that appears in his collection of Irish tales *In Chimney Corners* (1899). Locate other Irish folktales and legends to introduce Irish literature. Billy Beg is a male protagonist who will challenge students to look at the Cinderella tale from a gender perspective. *The Irish Cinderlad* (HarperCollins, 1996) by Shirley Climo is another picture book version with a male Cinderella figure. Both *Billy Beg and His Bull* and *The Irish Cinderlad* come from Irish folklore, have student compare the versions, which are quite distinct despite the common thread of male protagonists.

99   Grifalconi, Ann. *Village of Round and Square Houses.* Illus. by author. Little, Brown, 1986. ISBN 0-316-32862-6. Representational. Pastels. Folktales, Cameroon. Africa, Cameroon. Gender Roles. Volcanoes. Pourquoi Tales.

In the village of Tos the men live in square houses and the women live in round ones. Men and women come together at night to share the evening meal and then return to their respective homes. Osa's Gran'ma Tika tells her about the eruption of a volcano and why men and women live apart to this day because of it. Even today in the village of Tos you will find, if you visit, that the men live inside square houses and the women in round ones. A folktale from Cameroon, this title is sure to spark debate about gender roles. Other folktales from Cameroon include *The King and the Tortoise* (Clarion, 1993) by Mollel Tololwa and *The Elephant's Wrestling Match* (Dutton, 1992) by Judy Sierra.

100 Grimm, Jacob and Wilheim. *Cinderella.* Illus. by Nonny Hogrogian. Greenwillow, 1981. ISBN 0–688–80299–0. Fairy Tales, Germany. Cinderella Tales. Germany.

The Brothers Grimm version of "Cinderella" from Germany. In this version Cinderella's father is alive, but he remains ignorant of the plight of his child. Instead of a Fairy Godmother, there are doves who appear before Cinderella as she weeps beside her mother's grave, where she plants a hazel twig. As with many of the Brothers Grimm's tales, this story is violent; it retains the haunting image of the stepsisters deliberate maiming of their bodies in order to fit the shoe and win the hand of the prince. Compare this version with Charles Perrault's subdued French variant. The Brothers Grimm version originally appeared in *Grimm's Fairy Tales* (1814) as "Ashenputtel." Nonny Hogrogian used the Brothers Grimm's text, which accounts for the violent details and may be offensive to some people. Other picture book versions of the Brothers Grimm fairy tales include *The Twelve Dancing Princesses* (Dutton, 1996) with illustrations by Jane Ray, *The Goose Girl* (Holiday House, 1995) with illustrations by Robert Sauber, and *Snow White and Rose Red* (Philomel, 1992) with illustrations by Gennady Spirin.

101 Grimm, Jacob and Wilhelm. *Hansel and Gretel.* Illus. by Paul O. Zelinsky. G. P. Putnam's, 1984. ISBN 0–399–21733–9. Representational. Watercolors. Folktales, Germany. Siblings. Brothers and Sisters. Witches.

"Hansel and Gretel" was one of the first tales collected by Wilhelm and Jacob Grimm. Originally called "Little Brother and Little Sister," "Hansel and Gretel" appeared for the first time in *Children's and Household Tales* (1812). The Grimm Brothers traveled through their German countryside collecting tales from the peasants, compiling numerous oral versions into their own written version of such favorites as "Cinderella," "Snow White," and "Hansel and Gretel." There were seventeen editions of the *Grimm's Fairy Tales* alone in their lifetime. Since that time hundreds of people have retold the tales and numerous versions have been illustrated. Because the original tale is considered to be violent by today's standards, some modern versions are toned down to eliminate some of the violence. Discuss the aspects of adaptation and how fairy tales are affected when violence and stereotypes are eliminated. Other illustrated versions of the Brothers Grimm fairy tales include Trina Schart Hyman's *Iron John* (Holiday House, 1994), Alix Berenzy's *Rapunzel* (Holt, 1995), and Paul O. Zelinsky's *Rumpelstiltskin* (Dutton, 1986).

102 Haley, Gail E. *A Story, A Story.* Illus. by author. Atheneum, 1970. ISBN 0–689–20511–2. Expressionism. Woodcuts. Folktales, Africa. Ananse (trickster figure). Stories. Africa—Folklore. Trickster Tales.

Long ago there were no stories on earth. All the stories belong to Nyame the Sky God, who kept them in a box. Ananse the Spider Man spins a web and climbs to the sky to ask Nyame for some stories. Nyame will part with his stories for a price: Osebo, the leopard-of-the-terrible-teeth; Mmboro, the hornet-who-stings-like-fire; and Mmoatia, the fairy-whom-men-never-see. *A Story, A Story* is the tale of how Ananse the Spider Man pays the Sky God's price and brings stories to the world. Ananse the Spider is an prominent trickster figure from African folklore that assumes human or animal form, usually as a spider.

103 Han, Suzanne Crowder. *The Rabbit's Escape.* Illus. by Yumi Heo. Henry Holt, 1995. ISBN 0–8050–2675–4. Expressionism. Watercolors. Folktales, Korea. Turtles—Folklore. Rabbits—Folklore. Bilingual Materials, Korean. Trickster Tales.

When the Dragon King of the East Sea falls ill, it is up to his loyal subject, Turtle, who lives on land and sea, to find the cure for his lord's illness. Beneath the simple story of a king's illness are currents of vanity and loyalty as Turtle strives through trickery to convince Rabbit of his duty. Rabbit manages to escape his fate by using clever tactics. The text is presented in both English and Korean, which adds an interesting design dimension to the bold illustrations. An author's note in the front matter explains the origins of the tale, which has roots in India, and tells how it came to Korea with the introduction of Buddhism into Asian cultures. Also included is an explanation of the Korean alphabet, Han-gul. Suzanne Crowder Han also wrote *The Rabbit's Judgment* (Holt, 1994), which is written in both English and in Korean. Companion folktales include Shirley Climo's *The Korean Cinderella* (HarperCollins, 1993), Holly H. Kwon's *The Moles and the Mireuk: A Korean Folktale* (Houghton Mifflin, 1993), and Nami Rhee's *Magic Spring: A Korean Folktale* (G. P. Putnam's, 1993).

104 Hastings, Selina. *Sir Gawain and the Green Knight.* Illus. by Juan Wijngaard. Lothrop, Lee & Shepard, 1981. ISBN 0–688–00592–6. Folk Art. Watercolors. Legends, Arthurian. Gawain (legendary character). England.

Gawain's deeds make him one of King Arthur's most legendary knights. His heart brims with loyalty, and he never shuns performing deeds of honor. In this Arthurian legend he faces the Green Knight, an adversary with powers beyond human ability. The Green Knight challenges any knight of Arthur to kill him with one blow of an ax. If the knight fails, his price will be a return blow by the Green Knight in one year's time. Gawain's heart is heavy for the next year but he can finally tarry no longer and must ride in search of the Green Chapel, home of the Green Knight. Gawain is a legendary figure from medieval literature. Have students locate other Gawain tales. Assign portions of Malory's *Le Morte d'Arthur* to compare a medieval voice with Hastings's modern retelling. Have students compare this version of the Gawain legend with *Gawain and the Green Knight* (G. P. Putnam's, 1994) by Mark Shannon.

105 Hastings, Selina. *Sir Gawain and the Loathly Lady.* Illus. by Juan Wijngaard. Lothrop, Lee & Shepard, 1985. ISBN 0-688-05823-X. Folk Art. Watercolors. Legends, Arthurian. Gawain (legendary character). England.

King Arthur, celebrating Christmas court at his castle in Carlisle, is challenged by the fierce Black Knight during a hunt. The Black Knight challenges Arthur to a duel, which Arthur will surely lose because the knight is an enchanted being. If Arthur can answer a riddle in three days' time, the Black Knight will admit defeat and spare his life. "What is it women most desire?" The riddle is puzzling because every woman Arthur asks has a different answer. On final the day, Arthur meets a misshapen hag who gives him the answer if he grants her the hand of one of his knights in wedlock. Arthur shudders but promises the loathly lady that he will take her to his court. Gawain, Arthur's youngest but most honorable knight, takes the loathly lady in marriage. What follows is a timeless tale of love and honor. Hastings's retelling of the medieval legend is deftly handled and will inspire serious readers to explore Malory's *Le Morte d'Arthur*.

106 Heins, Ethel. *The Cat and the Cook and Other Fables of Krylov.* Illus. by Anita Lobel. Greenwillow, 1995. ISBN 0-688-12311-2. Expressionism. Watercolors. Fables, Russia. Krylov, Ivan Andreevich (1768–1844). Russia.

Ivan Andreevich Krylov's fables have been favorites of Russian children for generations. Twelve of Krylov's fables have been retold for American readers to enjoy. Each fable is complemented with rich illustrations reminiscent of Russian life, capturing the wit and charm in each fable. This collection is a must for any library. Source notes and introduction by the author provide interesting background information about Ivan Andreevich Krylov and his fables. Compare the Russian fables with Aesop's fables as an examination of this literary form. Picture book versions of Aesop's fables include *The Lion and the Mouse* (Millbrook Press, 1995) illustrated by Ian Andrews, *The Tortoise and the Hare* (Holiday House, 1984) illustrated by Janet Stevens, and *Town Mouse, Country Mouse* (G. P. Putnam's, 1994) illustrated by Jan Brett.

107 Heller, Ruth. *Behind the Mask: A Book about Prepositions.* Illus. by author. Grosset & Dunlap, 1995. ISBN 0-448-41123-7. Expressionism. Watercolors. English Language—Usage. Parts of Speech. Prepositions.

One title in the series of books about the eight parts of speech. In this title, prepositions are the featured part of speech. Bright, engaging illustrations and lyrical prose invite the reader to explore the sometimes confusing world of prepositions. Heller introduces prepositional phrases and phrasal prepositions, and she assures the reader that is okay to end a sentence with a preposition in this modern day. When explored in a rhythmic text, prepositions as a necessary part of speech and as a contribution to the language are not so daunting. Have students try to carry on a conversation without using prepositions to demonstrate the part they play in speech.

108 Heller, Ruth. *Kites Sail High: A Book about Verbs.* Illus. by author. Grosset & Dunlap, 1988. ISBN 0–448–10480–6. Expressionism. Watercolors. English Language—Usage. Parts of Speech. Verbs.

One title in the series of books about the eight parts of speech. In this title, verbs are the featured part of speech. Vibrant watercolor illustrations and lyrical prose invite the reader to explore the sometimes confusing combination of verbs. Heller introduces regular and irregular verbs, auxiliary verbs, and helping verbs. A necessary part of a sentence presented in an enticing fashion, verbs become manageable in this text, which clarifies many of the confusing rules taught in a tighter structure. This title can be used alone or with the other books in this series. Either way, Heller has pulled off an amazing feat with this book.

109 Heller, Ruth. *Many Luscious Lollipops: A Books about Adjectives.* Illus. by author. Grosset & Dunlap, 1989. ISBN 0–448–83151–5. Expressionism. Watercolors. English Language—Usage. Parts of Speech. Adjectives.

One title in the series of books about the eight parts of speech. In this title adjectives are the featured part of speech. Heller's illustrations are vividly unusual, incorporating unusual typefaces to point out significant parts of the text. Heller's approach to language usage is engaging and will invite the reader to explore the sometimes confusing world of adjectives. Language would be very bland without descriptive words. Put Heller's book to the test by asking students to describe a topic or a place without adjectives.

110 Heller, Ruth. *Merry-Go-Round: A Book about Nouns.* Illus. by author. Grosset & Dunlap, 1990. ISBN 0–448–40085–5. Expressionism. Watercolors. English Language—Usage. Parts of Speech. Nouns.

One title in the series of books about the eight parts of speech. In this title, nouns are the featured part of speech. Bright watercolor illustrations of people, places, and things and bouncy, enticing prose invite the reader to explore the nouns. Simple definitions of compound nouns, proper nouns, abstract nouns, and concrete nouns make learning the difference easy and less confusing. Heller includes simple rules for forming plural nouns and possessive nouns and distinguishing the two. The strength of this book is Heller's style, which makes correct usage easy to grasp.

111 Heller, Ruth. *Up, Up and Away: A Books about Adverbs.* Illus. by author. Grosset & Dunlap, 1991. ISBN 0–448–40249–1. Expressionism. Watercolors. English Language—Usage. Parts of Speech. Adverbs.

One title in the series of books about the eight parts of speech. In this title adverbs are the featured part of speech. Bold watercolor illustrations and rhythmic text invite the reader to explore adverbs. Heller's playful text introduces double negatives and superlatives, making the subject of adverbs less confusing. Heller's series is innovative and proves that learning grammar and the rules governing correct usage can be interesting.

112 Henry, O. *The Gift of the Magi.* Illus. by Lisbeth Zwerger. Picture Book Studio, 1982. ISBN 0–907234–17–8. Impressionism. Watercolors. Literature, American. Porter, William Sidney (1862–1910). Illustrated Classics.

The newly wed Dillingham Youngs have come upon hard times. There never seems to be enough money for the necessities, and when Christmas comes there is no money for gifts. The two treasures the Dillingham Youngs have are James's gold watch and Della's floor-length hair. For Christmas James wants to buy combs for Della's hair, and she wants to buy a chain for his watch. O. Henry (William Sidney Porter) led a varied life, and his experiences with people and different locales are evident in his celebrated short stories. *The Gift of the Magi* has become a classic tale of Christmas. This edition is illustrated by Lisbeth Zwerger with delicate watercolors. Zwerger has also illustrated *The Selfish Giant* (Picture Book Studios, 1984) by Oscar Wilde and *The Seven Ravens* (Morrow, 1981) by the Brothers Grimm.

113 Hepworth, Cathi. *Antics! An Alphabetical Anthology.* Illus. by author. G. P. Putnam's, 1992. ISBN 0–399–21862–9. Expressionism. Watercolors. Fiction. Alphabet Books. Ants.

An unusual alphabet book to anticipate. It explores the pleasant, mutant, and deviant but always brilliant little pests underfoot and under anthill. Ants are everywhere! They are flamboyant dressers, gallant guests, and hesitant near water. Ants are jubilant when they win, and will throw a tantrum when they do not get their way. This A to Z book features twenty-six words with the word ant somewhere in the spelling and will inspire students to create their own antics and find other words with ant in them. The strength of this book is the vocabulary: The text requires an understanding of each word in which the word ant is embedded. Challenge students to create an alphabet book after the fashion of Hepworth using another short word like ANT that is present in other longer words. *Two Bad Ants* (Houghton Mifflin, 1988) by Chris Van Allsburg is an artistic perspective two ants on a mischievous rampage in a kitchen, while *One Hundred Angry Ants* (Houghton Mifflin, 1993) by Elinor J. Pinczes follows a colony of ants en route to a picnic. Both titles are amusing companion books to use with *Antics! An Alphabetical Anthology.*

114 Heyer, Marilee. *The Weaving of a Dream.* Illus. by author. Viking, 1986. ISBN 0-670-80555-6. Representational. Watercolors. Folktales, China. Greed—Fiction. Loyalty—Fiction. China.

A widow in China has a special gift: She can weave any pattern or design into brocade cloth so real that the tapestries seemed to be alive. Her crowning achievement is a cloth woven in the same design that graces the palace wall behind the throne. As soon as she completes the cloth, a fierce wind pulls the tapestry from her hands and carries it to faraway Sun Mountain. The widow begs her sons to retrieve the tapestry, and what follows is a touching tale of how family love and loyalty can turn to envy and greed when circumstances tempt humans. Other Chinese folktales include *The Dragon's Pearl* (Clarion, 1993) by Julie Lawson, *The Jade Stone* (Holiday House, 1992) by Caryn Yacowitz, and *Lon Po Po: A Red Riding Hood Story from China* (Philomel, 1989) by Ed Young.

115 Hickox, Rebecca. *Per and the Dala Horse.* Illus. by Yvonne Gilbert. Doubleday, 1995. ISBN 0-385-32075-2. Representational. Colored Pencil. Folktales, Sweden. Horses—Folklore. Dala Horses. Brothers.

Long ago in Sweden a farmer died leaving all his possessions to his three sons; aside from his farm, these possessions amounted to three horses. To his firstborn he left his work horse; to his secondborn he left his riding horse; and to his youngest son, Per, he left a small wooden horse that had been given to the father by a skogsrå, a forest spirit. The elder brothers laugh at Per and his toy, but Per knows that the small horse will one day be useful. What follows is a tale of faith and commitment that will enthrall readers. The author included source notes and a brief history of the Dala Horse—the name of the toy horse given to Per. The soft colored pencil illustrations are reminiscent of Swedish culture. Borders grace the outside edges of *Per and the Dala Horse* and add dimension to the tale.

116 Higginson, William J. *Wind in the Long Grass.* Illus. by Sandra Speidel. Simon & Schuster, 1991. ISBN 0–671–67978–3. Representational. Pastels. Haiku. Haiku, Japanese Poetry. Nature. Seasons.

This collection of haiku poems by poets all around the world, arranged by season, which makes it very adaptable for curriculum use. Soft pastel illustrations gently compliment the beautiful but effective brevity of haiku poetry.

117 Hodges, Margaret. *The Arrow and the Lamp: The Story of Psyche.* Illus. by Donna Diamond. Little, Brown, 1989. ISBN 0–316–36790–7. Representational. Watercolors. Mythology, Greek. Psyche (Greek deity). Eros (Greek deity). Aphrodite (Greek deity).

A retelling of the Greek myth of love and the painful consequences of betrayal. Psyche, a beautiful and intelligent girl, with the grace of a deer and the kind heart of an angel, is a threat to Aphrodite, the Greek goddess of love and beauty. Jealous of Psyche, Aphrodite sends her son Eros to ruin any chance of happiness Psyche may have in life. Aphrodite's plan fails when Eros, struck by Psyche's beauty, fails to carry out his mother's commands and spares Psyche. He takes Psyche to his palace and gives her all she desires, exacting one promise in return: That she not look upon his face or form. He warns her to ignore any temptation to discover his identity. But Psyche, with only unseen hands to wait on her and a mysterious husband for company, becomes lonely and wishes for human companionship. At the malicious insistence of her jealous sisters, Psyche betrays Eros and looks upon his sleeping form. To regain her husband, she must complete three tasks set to her by Aphrodite, that include traveling to Hades. The story "Eros and Psyche" can be found in *Metamorphoses, or the Golden Ass*, written in the second century A.D. by Lucius Apuleius. Compare Hodges's version with *Cupid and Psyche* (Morrow, 1996) by M. Charlotte Craft. Explore the tale of "Eros and Psyche" in conjunction with other famous lovers in literature: Tristan and Isolde from the Celtic legend, Arthur and Guinevere from British legend, and the romantic escapades of Don Juan from Spain.

118 Hodges, Margaret. *Comus.* Illus. by Trina Schart Hyman. Holiday House, 1996. ISBN 0–8234–1146–X. Representational. Acrylics/Pen and Ink. Fairy Tales, England. Milton, John (1608–1674). Magicians.

A retelling of the old English fairy tale *Childe Roland.* Three children, one girl and two boys, lose their way in the forest when they stray too far from the castle grounds. The brothers venture in search of water and berries for their sister when her strength is spent. Comus, an evil magician with malicious intentions, seeks out the lost child and leads her from her resting place to his secret domain. What ensues is a tale with motifs identifiable in many fairy tales.

The dark and gloomy forest the children become lost in is reflected in Trina Schart Hyman's evocative paintings. The final illustration is one of the cast of characters from the story taking a bow as they would on stage after a performance. The poet John Milton liked the tale so much that he adapted it into a play, which he called a masque because of the disguises worn by the players. *Comus* was presented for the first time on Michaelmas Eve, 1634 at Ludlow Castle and is still performed in England today. Use this book to explore the dramatic form, masques, which are medieval plays.

119 Hodges, Margaret. *The Kitchen Knight*. Illus. by Trina Schart Hyman. Clarion, 1989. ISBN 0-8234-0787-X. Expressionism. Acrylics/Pen and Ink. Arthurian Romances. Gareth (legendary character). Knights and Knighthood. England.

Gareth of Orkney was one of King Arthur's most celebrated knights, and his deeds have been the source of many poems and songs. This adaptation, culled from Thomas Malory's *Le Morte d'Arthur*, relates Gareth's battle with the feared Knight of the Red Plain, his knighting by Sir Lancelot, and his reward of the hand of a fair maiden. Discuss the historical aspects of knighthood and the code of chivalry adopted by knights. *Young Lancelot* (Doubleday, 1996) by Robert D. San Souci and *The Knight and the Lion: The Story of Yvain* (Little, Brown, 1996) by John Rowe are two other titles about Arthur's valiant knights. *Knights in Shining Armor* (Little, Brown, 1995) by Gail Gibbons is an excellent companion title.

120 Hodges, Margaret. *Saint George and the Dragon*. Illus. by Trina Schart Hyman. Little, Brown, 1985. ISBN 0-316-36789-3. Expressionism. Acrylics/Pen and Ink. Legends, English. Saint George (legendary character). Knights and Knighthood. England.

A rich retelling of the English legend of Saint George and his clash with a dragon so fierce that his tale "swept the land behind him for almost a mile." Hodges's prose retelling is adapted from Edmund Spenser's *The Faerie Queen*, and Trina Schart Hyman's detailed watercolors bring to life the fearsome dragon who is defeated in battle by the legendary Saint George. The illustrations in this book earned Trina Schart Hyman the coveted Caldecott Medal in 1985. This tale is destined to become a classic for future generations. Use the title to introduce *The Faerie Queen* and have students compare Spenser's writing with Hodges's adaptation.

121 Hooks, William H. *Moss Coat.* Illus. by Donald Carrick. Clarion, 1987. ISBN 0–89919–460–5. Representational. Watercolors. Fairy Tales, United States. Cinderella Tales.

Moss Coat is a Cinderella tale set in North Carolina with elements of *King Lear*. Candace is banished from her home, lost in the woods and helped by a gris-gris woman who offers assistance whenever Candace sings a chant to summon her. Her greedy sisters are none too eager to see Candace found because they will have more of their father's fortune if she remains lost. After her rescue, Candace finds work as a scullery maid in a mansion. The young man who owns the estate plans a grand ball, during which he becomes enchanted by a girl who appears suddenly in gown that shines as sun. The girl is Moss Gown, as she is known in the kitchens, who must part company before the Morning Star fades. Have students read this Cinderella tale after reading *King Lear* to identify the elements that mark the story.

122 Hooks, William H. *The Ballad of Belle Dorcas.* Illus. by Brian Pinkney. Knopf, 1990. ISBN 0–394–84645–1. Expressionism. Scratchboard. Folktales, United States. African Americans. Conjurers. Slavery—United States.

This picture book is based on a conjure tale from the Carolinas in the southern United States. Belle Dorcas is he daughter of a house slave and the master of the plantation. Her birth father gives her papers granting her freedom to come as go and she pleases. Many free-issue men want her hand in marriage, but Belle has eyes only for a slave named Joshua. When her master dies and a new master intends to sell Joshua, Belle turns to a conjure woman, who helps her and Joshua remain together. As explained in an author's note, conjurers were both feared and respected for their spells and the powerful influence they had over people's lives. The power of conjurer's has diminished over the years, but their legacy is a canon of conjure tales still told today.

123 Huck, Charlotte. *Princess Furball.* Illus. by Anita Lobel. Greenwillow, 1989. ISBN 0–688–07837–0. Expressionism. Watercolors/Gouache. Fairy Tales, Germany. Cinderella Tales.

A beautiful princess is betrothed to a hated ogre by her father. The princess refuses to marry the ogre unless she receives three seemingly impossible gifts. When her father grants her requests, the princess has no choice but to flee. She hides her royal identity under a coat made from a thousand furs, thereby fooling a king in a neighboring kingdom who finds her in the forest. He takes her to his palace, where he places her under the charge of the cook as a cinder maid. Meanwhile, the king throws three balls and becomes enchanted by the mysterious girl who wears dresses as golden as the sun, as silvery as the moon, and as glittering as the stars. This tale based on "Many Furs" by the Brothers Grimm. The "hated marriage" motif in Princess Furball is the second most popular theme in Cinderella tales after the "glass slipper" motif in Perrault's Cinderella version. Explore the two motifs using a Cinderella version by Perrault.

124 Irving, Washington. *The Legend of Sleepy Hollow.* Illus. by Gary Kelley. Creative Education, 1990. ISBN 0-88682-328-5. Expressionism. Chalk. Literature, American. Irving, Washington (1783-1859). Illustrated Classics.

The tale of a schoolmaster's infamous meeting on a bridge with an unimagined horror was kept safe for many years in the papers of Diedrich Knickerbocker. Ichabod Crane, a learned man who stands out among the farmers, comes to the peaceful village of Tarry Town and listens with rapt attention to the tales of the Headless Horseman who haunts the valley. When Ichabod leaves a party and is never seen again, the residents of Sleepy Hollow fear they know why. Following Ichabod's path home, the townspeople find a smashed pumpkin and are left to wonder what really happened to Ichabod Crane. Washington Irving was born in New York City but often visited the Hudson River Valley area, which is the setting for the "Legend of Sleepy Hollow" and his other famous story "Rip Van Winkle." Gary Kelley has also illustrated *The Necklace* (Creative Editions, 1993) by Guy de Maupassant and *Tales of Mystery and Imagination by Edgar Allan Poe* (Creative Editions, 1996).

125 Isaac, Anne. *Swamp Angel.* Illus. by Paul O. Zelinsky. Dutton, 1994. ISBN 0-525-45271-0. Expressionism. Oils. Folklore, United States. Frontier and Pioneer Life. Gender Roles. United States—Tennessee. Tall Tales.

An original tall tale with a female protagonist. This tall tale heroine is an unusual child, standing tall as her mother and able to climb trees without assistance at age two, Angelica Longrider is destined for trouble. Other than that Angelica is a perfectly normal child who grows up to become the greatest legend to come out of the Tennessee Smoky Mountains. Swamp Angel, capable of amazing feats, is best remembered for her battle with the huge bear Thundering Tarnation—because that is what people always said when they saw him. Swamp Angel and Thundering Tarnation fight a battle that will end in defeat for one of them. To this day no skirmish has come close to their great battle. Who won? Look up in the sky at Ursa Major and you will know the answer. Paul O. Zelinsky's stunning oil paintings rendered on veneer wood are exquisite! Examine the roles of males versus females in tall tales. Read about other female tall tale heroines such as Old Sally Cato, Sal Fink (daughter of Mike Fink), Annie Christmas, and Pohaha in Robert D. San Souci's *Cut from the Same Cloth: American Women of Myth, Legend, and Tall Tale* (Philomel, 1993).

126 Jacobs, Joseph. *Tattercoats*. Illus. by Margot Tomes. G. P. Putnam's, 1989. ISBN 0-399-21584-0. Representational. Watercolors. Folktales, England. Cinderella Tales. England.

The death of her mother in childbirth leaves Tattercoats without a female figure in her life. Grief-stricken, her grandfather sends her away to be raised by servants, and he never lays eyes on the grandchild who reminds him of his beautiful daughter. Tattercoats's only companion is a gooseherd who plays lovely music with his pipe. Denied a chance to attend the ball at the elbow of her grandfather, she runs to her gooseherd and weeps her sad tale. The gooseherd offers himself as an escort to the ball. On the way they meet a handsome stranger who falls deeply in love with Tattercoats despite her ragged appearance. What follows are the classic motifs of a Cinderella tale as both Tattercoats and the gooseherd reveal their true natures and find love. "Tattercoats" first appeared in a collection of English folktales by famed folklorist and historian Joseph Jacobs (1854–1916). Other picture books version of Joseph Jacob's folktales include *The Fine Round Cake* (Four Winds, 1991) by Arnica Esterl, a book based on his folktale "Johnny Cake" and *The Hobyahs* (Doubleday, 1994) by Robert D. San Souci, a story based on his folktale "The Hobyahs."

127 Keens-Douglas, Richardo. *La Diablesse and the Baby: A Caribbean Folktale*. Illus. by Marie Lafrance. Annick, 1994. ISBN 1-55037-993-3. Expressionism. Acrylics. Folktales, West Indies. La Diablesse (legendary character). Pied Piper Tales. West Indies.

Rich acrylic paintings complement this Caribbean folktale about La Diablesse, a beautiful woman with one human foot and one cow foot, who walks in the night and takes people's babies to her mountain home. Beware of La Diablesse and be cautioned when you meet a stranger who asks the same question three times, for this a clue to her identity. The character La Diablesse is similar to the Pied Piper character found in European folktales. Compare with Robert Browning's "Pied Piper of Hamelin" or the picture book version *The Pied Piper of Hamelin* by Michele Lemieux (Morrow, 1993).

128 Kimmel, Eric A. *Anansi and the Moss-covered Rock*. Illus. by Janet Stevens. Holiday House, 1988. ISBN 0-8234-0689-X. Cartoon Art. Watercolors. Folktales, Caribbean. Ananse (legendary character). Caribbean.

Anansi the spider is up to his old tricks again! After stumbling upon a moss-covered rock in the forest, Anansi quickly learns the power of the rock and tricks all the forest animals out of the delicious fruits they have laid aside for dinner. But unknown to Anansi, Little Bush Deer is watching and turns the table on the tricky spider. *Anansi and the Moss-covered Rock* is a trickster tale from the West Indies. Anansi is also a trickster figure in many African cultures. Compare Kimmel's insect Anansi with other versions such as Gail Haley's *A Story, A Story* (Atheneum, 1970), in which Anansi is a man. *Anansi and the Talking Melons* (Holiday House, 1994) is another title by Kimmel about the trickster, Anansi.

129 Kimmel, Eric A. *Rimonah of the Flashing Sword: A North African Tale.* Illus. by Omar Rayyar. Holiday House, 1995. ISBN 0-8234-1093-5. Impressionism. Watercolors. Fairy Tales, Egypt. Snow White Tales.

Based on a story from Howard Schwartz's collection of Jewish folktales *Miriam's Tambourine.* When a childless queen wishes for a daughter with skin as dark as a pomegranate, eyes as bright as its seed, and a voice as sweet as the juice from its tender pulp, heaven hears her words and grants her a child. The queen, thankful for her gift from heaven, names the child Rimonah, which means "pomegranate." In time the queen dies, but before she does she leaves her with a vial filled with three drops of her blood. "If ever the blood turns red and liquid," she promises, "you will know that danger threatens." After the queen's death the king takes a new wife despite a vow not to remarry. Meanwhile Rimonah becomes a great horse woman and with her mother's gift is able to survive her stepmother's plans to kill her. Have students compare this tale with the European Snow White and discuss the themes and motifs threading each tale. A parody version of the Snow White story is *Snow White in New York* (Oxford University Press, 1986) by Fiona French.

130 Kimmel, Eric A. *The Witch's Face: A Mexican Tale.* Illus. by Fabricio Vanden Broeck. Holiday House, 1993. ISBN 0-8234-1038-2. Expressionism. Watercolors. Folktales, Mexico. Witches—Folklore.

On the way to Mexico City Don Aurelio stops for a rest at the home of three strange women. He is struck by the strong resemblance the women have to each other; what he sees is the face of the same woman in three different stages of life. Too late he realizes that the women are witches who take off their human faces off and don straw wings to fly in the night skies. The youngest witch takes pity on Don Aurelio and warns him of the plan to take his life, thus beginning a love story that will have a tragic ending because humans and immortals may never live together side by side. This folktale is based in part on a story from the Mazahua Indians of Central America. Kimmel's text promotes negative images of witches, and the stereotypes of women in the book may be offensive. However, the book sets up discussion of society's obsession with beauty. Explore the witch archetype in literature with *Rapunzel* (Holiday House, 1982) by the Brothers Grimm with illustrations by Trina Schart Hyman, *The Christmas Witch* (Hyperion, 1991) by Ilse Plume, and *Vasilissa the Beautiful: A Russian Folktale* (HarperCollins, 1991) by Elizabeth Winthrop. Another folktale from Mexico about masks is *Uncle Snake* (Tambourine, 1996) by Matthew Gollub.

131 Kipling, Rudyard. *The Beginning of the Armadillos.* Illus. by Lorinda Bryan Cauley. Harcourt Brace, 1985. ISBN 0-15-206380-3. Children's Literature. Kipling, Rudyard (1865-1936). *Just So Stories* (1902). Illustrated Classics.

An illustrated version of Kipling's *The Beginning of the Armadillos* from his classic collection *Just So Stories*. In this tale Stickly-Prickly Hedgehog and Slow-Solid Tortoise must escape the hungry intentions of Young Painted Jaguar. In a magical transformation, the pair manage to survive and create a new creature: the armadillo. Kipling's *Just So Stories* are imaginary tales of the unusual characteristics some animals have. Explore the masterful storytelling power of Rudyard Kipling by introducing other illustrated versions from his *Just So Stories*. Some include *The Elephant's Child* (Knopf, 1986) with illustrations by Tim Raglin and *How the Camel Got His Hump* (Bedrick, 1985) Quentin Blake. *Rikki-Tikki-Tavi* (Harcourt Brace, 1992) with illustrations by Lambert Davis is another classic short story by Rudyard Kipling.

132 Kurtz, Jane. *Fire on the Mountain.* Illus. by E. B. Lewis. Simon & Schuster, 1994. ISBN 0-671-88268-6. Representational. Watercolors. Folktales, Ethiopia. Siblings. Brothers and Sisters. Ethiopia.

Young Alemayu and his sister live as servants in the house of a ruthless, proud man. To win their freedom, Alemayu accepts his master's challenge to spend a night in the frozen desert, but the master is deceitful and cheats. Alemayu is aware of his master's deception and outwits the haughty old man, earning riches for himself and his sister. Jane Kurtz heard this tale growing up in Ethiopia. Although there was not a female in the versions she heard, the author wanted to explore the Ethiopian storytelling tradition and created a sister for the protagonist. Nancy Raines Day's *The Lion's Whiskers* (Scholastic, 1995) is another folktale from Ethiopia. Examine the strong family theme in the Ethiopian folktales by Jane Kurtz and Nancy Raines Day.

133 Lawson Julie. *The Dragon's Pearl*. Illus. by Paul Morin. Clarion, 1993. ISBN 0–395–63623–X. Representational. Oils. Fairy Tales, China. Dragons— Folklore.

Xiao Sheng and his mother live in a small village ravaged by drought, but he never gives up hope. "Who knows what the gods have in store for us," he says to comfort his mother. He then heads far from home to find grass to sell for fuel, but the small amount of money he earns is not enough to put food on the table. When Xiao Sheng discovers a pearl in a field of magic grass, his worries seem to be over. The pearl holds magic of its own, and the discovery of its true source will alter Xiao Sheng's destiny forever. An author's source note explores the history and importance of the dragon in Chinese culture. The illustrations are a blend of oil painting with collage technique and have a border that complements the endpapers. Paul Morin's technique is interesting and worthy of exploration distinct from the text. Graeme Base's *The Discovery of Dragons* (Abrams, 1996) explores the origins of dragons in popular myth. Dragons are very prominent in Asian cultures, springboard into research with *The Dragon's Pearl*.

134 Lemieux, Michèle. *The Pied Piper of Hamelin*. Illus. by author. Morrow Junior, 1993. ISBN 0–688–09849–5. Expressionism. Oils. Legends, Germany. The Pied Piper (legendary character). Germany. Pied Piper Tales.

The Pied Piper is a legendary figure whose deeds have been honored in ballads and tales. Michèle Lemieux's retelling of his actions is based on actual events that occurred in Hamelin, Germany in the year 1284 when over 100 children disappeared from the small town. Many are familiar with the Piper's enchantment of children, whom he entices from the selfish villagers after the town refuses to pay for his services when he rids the town of thousands of rats. In an author's note Michèle Lemieux explains that historians believe that the children left to join the famous Children's Crusade to reclaim Jerusalem from the Muslims. The origins of the Pied Piper are lost, but his deeds were made popular by poet Robert Browning in 1842. Educators will find it interesting to use this adaptation in conjunction with Browning's poem.

135 Lester, Julius. *John Henry*. Illus. by Jerry Pinkney. Dial, 1994. ISBN 0– 8037–1607–9. Representational. Watercolors. Folklore, United States. John Henry (legendary character). African Americans. Tall Tales. United States.

John Henry is one of America's most legendary folk heroes, and this edition brings new aspects to the story. From his birth John Henry was set apart from other men because of his size and strength. His destiny was to forge new paths for others to walk, and his exploits prove the endurance of humans and inspired storytellers for generations. John Henry's legendary race with the steam engine has been retold many times, but this edition by Caldecott Honor winner Julius Lester, with striking watercolor paintings by Jerry Pinkney, is a powerful retelling of the man and the myth that strikes the reader as surely and steadily as John Henry's hammer smashing mountains to rubble.

136 Lewis, J. Patrick. *Black Swan/White Crow*. Illus. by Chris Manson. Atheneum, 1995. ISBN 0–689–31899–5. Representational. Woodcuts. Haiku. Haiku, Japanese Poetry. Nature.

Haiku is the simplest form of poetry, and this book makes a wonderful introduction for students to the powerful imagery of haiku. This collection of haiku centers around the theme of nature with simple yet bold woodcut illustrations that celebrate the beauty and majesty of the natural world. Use *Black Swan/White Crow* to introduce students to the powerful imagery of nature in literature.

137 Loewen, Nancy. *Walt Whitman*. Illus. by Rob Day. Creative Education, 1994. ISBN 0–88682–608–X. Representational. Mixed Media. Biography. Whitman, Walt (1819–1892). Poets, American.

A remarkable volume about American poet Walt Whitman told in alternating biographic sketches and excerpts from *Leaves of Grass*. Photographs of Whitman and original artwork combine to accompany the text, creating a powerful book that will inspire students to explore Whitman's *Leaves of Grass* in its full context. The careful labeling of the excerpts and photographs along with the arrangement is outstanding and rarely matched in biographies for young people. Pair with Robert Sabuda's illustrated version of Whitman's "I Hear America Singing" (Philomel, 1991) to introduce young people to the luminous writing of Walt Whitman. Other titles in the Voices in Poetry series include *e.e. cummings* (Creative Education, 1994) by Barry Skip, *Emily Dickinson* (Creative Education, 1994) by S. L. Berry, *Langston Hughes* (Creative Education, 1994) by S. L. Berry, *Marianne Moore* (Creative Education, 1994) by Dave Page, *Sylvia Plath* (Creative Education, 1994) by Lynn Chapman, and *Edwin Arlington Robinson* (Creative Education, 1994) by Edward E. Goodman.

138 Longfellow, Henry Wadsworth. *Hiawatha*. Illus. by Susan Jeffers. Dial, 1983. ISBN 0–8037–0013–X. Representational. Pen and Ink/Pencil Overlay. Poetry, American. Longfellow, Henry Wadsworth (1807–1882). Narrative Poetry. Illustrated Classics. Poets, American.

An excerpt from Longfellow's narrative poem "The Song of Hiawatha" is illustrated by Jeffers, who focused on the boyhood of Hiawatha. The delicate pen-and-ink illustrations take the reader to the shores of Gitche Gumee, where Hiawatha was born. Because the text is an excerpt from the epic poem, Jeffers attempted to show other stages in Hiawatha's life by illustrating the endpapers with pictures that overview two other sections of the poem. The poem, written in 1855, is a composite sketch of an American Indian. Longfellow's interest and respect for the Native Americans led to the creation of the epic poem loved by generations of people.

139 Longfellow, Henry Wadsworth. *Paul Revere's Ride.* Illus. by Ted Rand. Dutton, 1990. ISBN 0–525–44610–9. Representational. Watercolors. Poetry, American. Longfellow, Henry Wadsworth (1807–1882). American Revolution. Illustrated Classics. Poets, American.

An illustrated version of *Paul Revere's Ride*, Ted Rand's text captures the passion and intensity of Revere's mission to warn the Colonists of the British soldiers arriving in the colonies. Each illustration perfectly captures Wadsworth's poem and is an achievement of interpretation. The picture book format will entice students to look at the poem from an artistic perspective. Introduce students to Wadsworth's body of work. Pair with Susan Jeffers's illustrated *Hiawatha* (Dial, 1983) and explore Longfellow's contribution to American literature.

140 Louie, Ai-Ling. *Yeh-Shen: A Cinderella Tale From China.* Illus. by Ed Young. Philomel, 1982. ISBN 0–399–20900–X. Impressionism. Watercolors. Folktales, China. Cinderella Tales. China.

Yeh-Shen is mistreated by her stepmother and stepsister and turns to the only friend she has, a fish she feeds with her own meager rations. The stepmother stabs the fish out of spite, but she fails to sever the bond between the fish and Yeh-Shen. Yeh-Shen is a Cinderella tale from China whose roots are 1000 years older than those of the European Cinderella by Charles Perrault, making it the first recorded version. Use this tale to compare with other Cinderella tales, paying attention to the distinct motifs that mark them as Cinderella tales. A version written in Chinese and the source notes are in the front matter.

141 Mahy Margaret. *The Seven Chinese Brothers.* Illus. by Jean and Mou-sien Teng. Scholastic, 1990. ISBN 0–590–42055–0. Expressionism. Watercolors. Folktales, China. Siblings. Brothers. China.

A retelling of the Han tale of seven identical Chinese brothers who are pitted against an angry emperor and sentenced to death. Each brother has a special power that enables him to avoid execution; the brothers exchange places as the ruler invents new ways to put what he thinks is one man to death. The seven brothers are true tall tale characters as each is capable of amazing contortions of the body or has the capacity to withstand elements of fire and water without damage to his body. An editor's note gives background information about Emperor Ch'in Shih Huang (2559–210 B.C.), who planned the construction of the Great Wall in China, which figures prominently in this tale. A 1938 picture book, *The Five Chinese Brothers* (Coward-McCann) by Claire Hutchet Bishop and illustrated by Kurt Wiese, considered a classic by many, is marred by the stereotyped illustrations. Have students compare the two versions for cultural authenticity.

142 Martin, Rafe. *Foolish Rabbit's Big Mistake.* Illus. by Ed Young. G. P. Putnam's, 1985. ISBN 0–399–21178–0. Impressionism. Pastels. Jataka Tales (birth stories). Rabbits—Folklore. Rumors. Cumulative Tales.

Little rabbit is sound asleep under a shady apple tree when one of the ripened fruits drops from the branches and lands on his head. Fearing the worst, foolish rabbit runs to tell everyone that the earth is breaking apart. The powerful influence of rumors leads the whole village to panic. *Foolish Rabbit's Big Mistake* is told in the traditional style of Jataka tales, which have flourished in Asia for the last 2,500 years. Jataka tales, or birth stories, are tales of Buddha's birth and are believed to be the inspiration for Aesop's fables and the Arabian Nights stories. Compare with "Henny Penny" or "Chicken Little," which are modern versions of this tale. Jataka tales relate the origin and teachings of Buddha. Other Jataka tales include *The Golden Goose* (Parvardigar Press, 1995) by Judith Ernst and *The Monkey and the Crocodile* (Clarion, 1969) by Paul Galdone.

143 Martin, Rafe. *The Rough-Face Girl.* Illus. by David Shannon. G. P. Putnam's, 1992. ISBN 0–399–21859–9. Expressionism. Oils. Legends, Algonquin Indians. Indians of North America. Cinderella Tales. Siblings. Sisters.

The Rough-Face Girl, whose face is scarred from the flying embers that escape the campfire she tends because her lazy sisters refuse to do chores and instead preen themselves all day, dreams of a life free of her hard labor. Her naive father cannot see beyond his elder daughters' vanity and refuses to step in on the Rough-Face Girl's behalf. When the vain and selfish sisters strive to gain the love of the Invisible Being, laughing at the Rough-Face Girl for imagining that such a great man could love one as ugly as she, they fail. It is the true and compassionate heart of the Rough-Face Girl who triumphs in this Algonquin

Indian version of the Cinderella tale. *Sootface: An Ojibwa Cinderella Tale* (Doubleday, 1994) by Robert D. San Souci is Cinderella Tale similar to *The Rough-Face Girl. Great Rabbit and the Long-Tailed Wildcat* (Whitman, 1993) by Andy Gregg is another Alogonquin folktale.

144   Merrill, Jean Fairbanks. *The Girl Who Loved Caterpillars.* Illus. by Floyd Cooper. Philomel, 1992. ISBN 0–399–21871–8. Representational. Oils. Fiction. Gender Roles. Insects—Caterpillars. Japan.

Young Izumi is an embarrassment to her family because instead of collecting something beautiful such as butterflies, Izumi collects caterpillars. She refuses to conform to fashion and conduct herself as a proper lady. In addition, she has no interest in rich suitors, preferring to play with the boys who have the same interest in insects as she does. This tale, adapted from a twelfth-century manuscript, depicts the struggle of women from all cultures who have chosen an independent life over one of convention. Pair this title with Katherine Paterson's eighteenth-century folktale *The Tale of the Mandarin Ducks* (Lodestar, 1990) for a glimpse at Japanese folklore.

145   Millay, Edna St. Vincent. *The Ballad of the Harp-Weaver.* Illus. by Beth Peck. Philomel, 1991. ISBN 0–399–21611–1. Impressionism. Oils. Poetry, American. Millay, Edna St. Vincent (1892–1950). Poets, American.

Edna St. Vincent Millay was born in Rockland, Maine, in 1892 and grew up to become one of America's greatest poets. Her mother was a pivotal force in her life, encouraging Vincent, as she is known to her family, to be creative even as a small child. Millay attended Vassar College and began writing full time upon graduation. Millay's best-known poem is "The Ballad of the Harp-Weaver," which was included in the collection *Harp-Weaver and Other Poems.* The collection contained some of Millay's best work and was awarded the Pulitzer Prize in 1923. Millay was the first woman to receive this distinguished award. The poem, which celebrates the bond between mother and child, is a haunting tribute to the emotional ties of family. Edna St. Vincent Millay died in 1950. Introduce students to Millay's body of work with this magical picture book.

146   Mohr, Nicholasa. *The Song of El Coqui.* Illus. by Antonia Martorell. Viking, 1995. ISBN 0–670–85837–4. Watercolors. Folktales, Puerto Rico. Puerto Rico. Animal Stories.

From the Taino, African, and Spanish cultures come three interwoven tales that celebrate the many aspects that comprise the heritage of Puerto Rico. The first tale is about La Guinea's escape from slave traders and her marked difference until the kind Don El reveals her gifts to the world. The second tale is about Huracán: The great god awakes to the noise of a coqui and searches for the source that brings sound to the world. Finally, in the last tale La Mula is worked to exhaustion by Spanish bandits until the slave Otilio befriends her and together they escape for a better life. Together the three tales celebrate the richness of Puerto Rican culture. In the introduction the author discusses the source of the tales and the how the stories were chosen to best depict the rich ancestral aspects of Puerto Rico. Other folktales from Puerto Rican culture include *Juan Bobo and the Pig: A Puerto Rican Folktale* (Lodestar, 1993) by Felix Pitre.

147 Mollel, Tololwa M. *The Orphan Boy*. Illus. by Paul Morin. Clarion, 1990. ISBN 0-89919-985-2. Representational. Oils. Folktales, Africa. Masai (African People). Planets—Folklore.

A childless old man searches the skies each evening for a familiar star, but one night the star disappears from the heavens. That same night a mysterious boy appears from the darkness, and the old man takes him home to be the son he never had. The old man, though happy to have a son at last, is curious about his new charge and wonders constantly about where the boy, Kielken, came from and how he is able to complete chores by the time the old man wakes. Kielken tells the old man, "The day you discover my secret will be the end of your good fortune." The old man's curiosity burns nonetheless, and he foolishly follows Kielken to discover his powers. As warned, Kielken must now leave the old man. *The Orphan Boy* is a Masai tale about loyalty and trust, and why the planet Venus is known as Kielken. Other folktales about astronomy include *How Snowshoe Hare Rescued the Sun: A Tale from the Arctic* (Holiday, 1993) by Emery Bernhard and *How Raven Brought Light to People* (Margaret K. McElderry, 1992) by Ann Dixon.

148 Moore, Clement C. *The Night before Christmas*. Illus. by Ted Rand. North-South Books, 1995. ISBN 1-55858-465-X. Representational. Watercolors. Narrative Poetry. Moore, Clement C. (1779-1863). Christmas. Poets, American.

An illustrated version of Clement C. Moore's famous Christmas poem recited by children during the holiday season for over 100 years. Have students research other cultures for traces of a Santa Claus figure including England's Father Christmas and Russia's Grandfather Frost. Pair with Tom Paxton's *The Story of Santa Claus* (Morrow Junior, 1995). Students could also explore the cartoons of Thomas Nast (1840-1902), who is attributed with creating the modern attire Santa Claus wears. Other companion titles include *Silent Night: A*

Christmas Carol Sampler (Knopf, 1995) with illustrations by Belinda Downs, *This is the Star* (Harcourt Brace, 1996) by Joyce Dunbar, *The Angel and the Donkey* (Clarion, 1996) by Katherine Paterson, and *The Polar Express* (Houghton Mifflin, 1985) by Chris Van Allsburg. *Twas the Night B'fore Christmas* (Scholastic, 1996) by Melodye Rosales is an African-American version set in rural North Carolina at the turn of the century and based on Clement C. Moore's poem.

149 Mosel Arlene. *Tikki Tikki Tembo.* Illus. by Blair Lent. Holt Rinehart & Winston, 1968. ISBN 0-590-41622-7. Cartoon Art. Pen and Ink. Folktales, China. Names—Folklore. Siblings. Brothers.

Long ago in China custom dictated that the firstborn and most honored son be given a long name to celebrate his importance. However, secondborn sons were of less importance and given a short name. When Chang, the secondborn son, must save his elder brother, Tikki tikki tembo-no sa rembo chari-bari ruchi pip pari pembo from drowning, his mother realizes that the tradition of giving long names to honor firstborn sons is impractical. This ancient folktale from China explains how custom was abandoned and why today everyone in China has a name that can be said without taking a breath! A folktale from the West Indies *Turtle Knows Your Name* (Macmillan, 1989) by Ashley Bryan is another story about a boy with a very long name. Have students explore the origin of their names. Do they feel that their name suits their personality? Are there comparable names in other languages? For example John (English), Juan (Spanish), and Jean (French), and Johann (German).

150 Murphy, Jim. *Into the Deep Forest with Henry David Thoreau.* Illus. by Kate Kiesler. Clarion, 1995. ISBN 0-395-60522-9. Representational. Oils. Biography. Thoreau, Henry David (1817–1862).

A handsome biography, based on Thoreau's actual journal, about the wilderness wanderings that inspired the writing of *Walden*, Murphy's narrative is faithful in style to the specific details found in Thoreau's own writing. Rich oil paintings and small pencil vignettes grace each page and combine with the narrative to form an evocative book. *Into the Deep Forest* makes an ideal introduction to the writing of Thoreau. Use with Thoreau's *Walden*, with bold linoleum cut illustrations by Robert Sabuda (Philomel, 1990) and *A Man Named Thoreau* (Atheneum, 1985) by Robert Burleigh to entice students to explore the more lengthy works by Henry David Thoreau. *The Tyger* (Harcourt Brace, 1993) by William Blake, illustrations by Neil Waldman. William Blake (1757–1827) *Catskill Eagle: Chapter 96 from* Moby-Dick (Philomel, 1991) by Herman Melville, paintings by Thomas Locker. Melville, Herman (1819–1891) *The Highwayman* (Harcourt Brace, 1990) by Alfred Noyes, illustrations. by Neil

Waldman. *The Lady of Shalott* (Oxford University Press, 1986) by Alfred Tennyson.

151 O'Brien, Anne Sibley. *The Princess and the Beggar.* Illus. by author. Scholastic, 1993. ISBN 0-590-46092-7. Representational. Pastels. Folktales, Korea. Kings, Queens, Rulers. Beggars. Korea.

In the city of Pyung-yang lives a princess known to her subjects as the Weeping Princess because any and all situations make her cry. Her royal parents wonder who will wed a girl who is constantly wiping tears from her eyes. When they find a suitable match, the Weeping Princess refuses to marry, saying she would rather wed the town beggar, Pabo Ondal, before she would marry a man she does not love. Granting her request, her father banishes her from her home. As fate would have it, the princess meets with Pabo Ondal in the wilderness, and what follows is a tender love story. The tale is based on an old Korean folktale, Pabo Ondal, which dates back to the sixth century. An author's notes contains further background information of the tale and the explanation of the illustrations, which were inspired by the Yi Dynasty (1392-1910). Companion Korean folktales include *The Rabbit's Judgment* (Holt, 1994) and *The Rabbit's Escape* (Holt, 1995), both by Suzanne Crowder Han and *Older Brother, Younger Brother* (Viking, 1995) by Nina Jaffe.

152 Olaleye, Isaac. *The Distant Talking Drum.* Illus. by Frané Lessac. Wordsong/Boyds Mills, 1995. ISBN 1-56397-095-3. Naive. Gouache. Poetry, Nigeria. Africa, Nigeria.

Isaac Olaleye captures the calm, simple life of villagers in Nigeria. Villagers saunter through their day grinding grain for bread and spinning thread for cloth in the manner that has been common in the village for hundreds of years. This collection of poetry about life in a Nigerian village evokes strong images of a way of life that seems far away from the hustling world of cars, computers, and telephones. Bright, colorful illustrations make the distant talking drums, sparkling stream, and steady rhythm of the grinding stone come to life. Include this title with *Why the Sky is Far Away: A Nigerian Folktale* (Little, Brown, 1992) by Mary-Joan Gerson and *The Flying Tortoise: An Igbo Tale* (Clarion, 1994) by Tololwa Mollel, two Nigerian folktales. *Ogbo: Sharing Life in an African Village* (Harcourt Brace, 1996) and *Emeka's Gift: An African Counting Book* by Ifeoma Onyefulu are two touching portraits of day to day life in Nigeria.

153   Paterson, Katherine. *The Tale of the Mandarin Ducks*. Illus. by Leo and Diane Dillon. Lodestar, 1990. ISBN 0–525–67283–4. Expressionism. Watercolors. Folktales, Japan. Folklore—Ducks. Greed—Fiction. Japan.

A greedy lord captures a mandarin duck and cages the bird so that he can take pleasure in its beauty. A kitchen maid and a servant take pity on the duck, who is pining for its mate, and free the bird from its prison. Their act earns their lord's displeasure, and as a result they are sentenced to death. The grateful drake and his mate repay the kindness of the couple and in a glorious ending help them escape the wrath of the lord. An eighteenth-century tale from Japan, *The Tale of the Mandarin Ducks* celebrates kindness and the goodness found in generous hearts. Leo and Diane Dillon surpass themselves with the *ukiyo-e* (woodblock) prints inspired by Japanese art. Ruth Wells's *The Farmer and the Poor God* (Simon & Schuster, 1996) is another folktale from Japan with a message about generosity.

154   Perrault, Charles. *Cinderella*. Illus. by Diane Goode. Knopf, 1988. ISBN 0–394–896603–3. Expressionism. Watercolors. Fairy Tales, France. Perrault, Charles (1628–1703). Cinderella Tales.

An illustrated version of Charles Perrault's "Cinderella," which is the basis for the Walt Disney version. This Cinderella tale has the traditional fairy godmother, pumpkin coach, and glass slipper, which will lead the prince to his true love. Considered by many to be the first recorded Cinderella tale, this French version is actually one of the newer versions; many other cultures have Cinderella tales 500 to 1000 years older. This version is sweet compared to the Brothers Grimm version, in which Cinderella punishes her cruel sisters. Charles Perrault lived in France during the extravagant reign of Louis the XIV, and the pomp and luxury of the times are evident in his telling of Cinderella. Another Perrault version is *Cinderella, or the Little Glass Slipper* illustrated by Marcia Brown (Charles Scribner's Sons, 1954). Nonny Hogrogian's *Cinderella* (Greenwillow, 1981) was based on the Brothers Grimm version from Grimm's Fairy Tales (1814). Compare the Brown's version with the Hogrogian's version using the illustrations as points of comparison. Other fairy tales by Charles Perrault include *Toads and Diamonds* (Greenwillow, 1995) retold by Charlotte Huck with illustrations by Anita Lobel and *Puss in Boots* (Farrar, Straus & Giroux, 1990) retold and illustrated by Fred Marcellino. *Pedro and the Monkey* (Morrow, 1996) by Robert D. San Souci is a Filipino version of Perrault's *Puss in Boots*.

155   Poe, Edgar Allan. *Tales of Mystery and Imagination*. Illus. by Gary Kelley. Creative Editions, 1996. ISBN 0–15–100234–7. Expressionism. Chalk. Literature, American. Poe, Edgar Allan (1809–1849). Illustrated Classics.

Acclaimed artist Gary Kelley selected three of Edgar Allan Poe's most celebrated short stories and illustrated them with frightening accuracy. As explained in artist's note, Kelley chose "The Black Cat," "The Fall of the House of Usher," and "The Cask of the Amontillado" for the dark characters and Gothic images present in each story. Although Poe's horrific tales are very popular with young adults, the collection will appeal to fans and newcomers alike. Other famous literary works illustrated by Gary Kelley include *Legend of Sleepy Hollow* (Creative Education, 1990) and *Rip Van Winkle* (Creative Education, 1987) by Washington Irving. Gary Kelley has also illustrated *The Necklace* (Creative Editions, 1993) by Guy de Maupassant.

156 Pollock, Penny. *The Turkey Girl: A Zuni Cinderella Tale.* Illus. by Ed Young. Little, Brown, 1996. ISBN 0–316–71314–7. Impressionism. Oil Crayon and Pastels. Legends, Native American. Indians of North America. Zuni Indians. Cinderella Tales.

A Cinderella tale from the Zuni Indians of New Mexico. The Turkey Girl, shunned by the villagers and dressed in rags, longs to be part of the community and all the hustle and bustle of village life. An opportunity to attend the Dance of the Sacred Bird is an impossible dream until the intervention of the turkeys she tends. The birds grant her the means to attend. For fine clothes and a chance to mingle with the villagers, the turkeys ask for one thing in exchange: her return before the Sun-Father returns to his sacred place. What follows are the classic motifs of the Cinderella tale, which has a variant in almost every culture. Ed Young's pastel illustrations tempered with the colors prevalent in the southwestern desert complement Pollock's deft retelling based on a version found in a collection of Zuni tales compiled by Frank Hamilton Cushing. Compare with the Algonquin Cinderella tale *The Rough-Face Girl* (G. P. Putnam's, 1992) by Rafe Martin. Other legends from the Zuni Indians include *Coyote: A Trickster Tale from the American Southwest* (Harcourt Brace, 1994) by Gerald McDermott and *Dragonfly's Tale* (Clarion, 1991) by Kristina Rodanas.

157 Rockwell, Anne. *The One-Eyed Giant and Other Monsters from the Greek Myths.* Illus. by author. Greenwillow, 1996. ISBN 0–688–13809–8. Naive. Watercolors/Gold Ink. Mythology, Greek. Monsters.

A collection of tales featuring the monsters from Greek mythology. A menagerie of classical beasts from literature are featured: Cyclops, the one-eyed monster, blinded by Odysseus during his long voyage home; the Minotaur, half man and half bull, who reigns over the deadly labyrinth from which no one, not even the monster, can escape; and Medusa, a creature with a writhing mass of snakes for hair. The brief tales of each monster paired with a series of abstract illustrations make this book a perfect title to introduce study of Greek mythology. Pair with *The Olympians: Great Gods and Goddesses of Ancient Greece* (Holiday House, 1984) by Leonard Everett Fisher. Some other Greek myths in picture book format include *Wings* (Harcourt Brace, 1991) by Jane Yolen, *Persephone and the Pomegranate: A Myth from Greece* by (Dial, 1993) Kris Waldherr, and *Cyclops* (Holiday House, 1991) by Leonard Everett Fisher. Warwick Hutton also created a series of illustrated Greek myths that includes *Persephone* (Margaret K. McElderry, 1994), *Perseus* (Margaret K. McElderry, 1993), *Theseus and the Minotaur* (Margaret K. McElderry, 1989), and *The Trojan Horse* (Margaret K. McElderry, 1992). *The Book of Goddesses* (Beyond Words, 1995) by Kris Waldherr is a glorious book that explores the goddess figure in cultures all around the world.

158 Rodanas, Kristina. *Dance of the Sacred Circle.* Illus. by author. Little, Brown, 1994. ISBN 0–316–75358–0. Representational. Colored Pencil. Legends, Native American. Indians of North America. Horses—Folklore. Shiasapa Indians.

A young boy journeys far from his home to find the Great Chief and ask for help to feed his starving people. Unknown to him, the Great Chief has followed the boy's journey, aware all along that the boy was seeking him. The boy's bravery and perseverance are rewarded with a creature the Great Chief shapes to help the people hunt for food and to travel to new hunting grounds. *Dance of the Sacred Circle* is based on a Shiasapa legend of the creation of an animal that forever changes the way the tribe lives: a horse. *Sky Dogs* (Harcourt Brace, 1990) by Jane Yolen is a Blackfoot Indian variation of the creation of horses. *The Girl Who Loved Wild Horses* (Bradbury, 1978) and *The Gift of Sacred Dog* (Bradbury, 1980), both by Paul Goble, are Plains Indians legends of horses and their importance to Native American culture. Explore folklore about buffaloes, another animal that was vital to Native American culture with *Buffalo Dance: A Blackfoot Legend* (Little, Brown, 1993) by Nancy Van Laan and *Crow Chief: A Plains Indian Story* (Orchard, 1992) by Paul Goble.

159 Sabuda, Robert. *Arthur and the Sword.* Illus. by author. Atheneum, 1995. ISBN 0–689–31987–8. Expressionism. Watercolors. Legends, England. *Morte d'Arthur.* Arthur (legendary character). Arthurian Romances. England.

King Arthur's reign in Camelot has been the subject of film, works of literature, epic poems, and ballads. This version begins with Arthur's claiming of the sword Excalibur, an act that made a beardless boy a king. Arthur's right to the throne was challenged by powerful lords and his life placed in danger until his royal destiny was accepted. Was there a real Arthur? Sources verify the existence of a man called Artos who lived during the sixth century—but real or not, the man has become a legend whose story reaches across centuries. Stunning stained-glass illustrations evoke images of the sixth-century, the period for the Arthurian romances. Based on Sir Thomas Malory's fifteenth-century manuscript *Le Morte d'Arthur*.

160 Sage, James. *Coyote Makes the Man*. Illus. by Britta Teckentrup. Simon & Schuster, 1994. ISBN 0–689–80011–8. Expressionism. Collage. Legends, Native American. Creation Stories. Animal Stories.

A creation myth from Native American culture. Coyote's last task in the creation of the world is man. But what should man look like? Coyote gathers the other animals together to ask what they think man should look like. Owl thinks man needs good eyes and excellent hearing; Otter thinks sharp teeth and swimming ability are essential. But what about wings? says Goose. Coyote gives the animals a lump of clay each and asks them to sculpt their ideas. When the animals sleep that night, Coyote examines each clay figure and discovers that each animal has made man in its own likeness. Knowing this was not good, Coyote takes the clay figures and makes man using the best features from all the animals. The expressionistic collage illustrations contribute to James Sage's examination of the necessity of collaboration in the creative process. Sage's strong storytelling opens discussion of the differences in people, which should be celebrated rather than negatively promoted through racism.

161 San Souci, Robert D. *Sukey and the Mermaid*. Illus. by Brian Pinkney. Four Winds Press, 1992. ISBN 0–02–778141–0. Expressionism. Scratchboard. Folktales, United States. Mermaids. Cinderella Tales.

Sukey's ma is married to a no-good man Sukey refers to as Mister Hard Times. That lazy man lies about all day while Sukey hoes and rakes the garden. One day a brief jaunt to the seashore brings about a meeting with a mermaid who answers to the name Mama Jo. For weeks Sukey visits the mermaid, who gives her a gold coin at the end of each day to prevent Sukey's parents from scolding her. Eventually Sukey's ma and step-pa discover her secret, and the only way to see Mama Jo is to go beneath the sea to live in her watery domain. *Sukey and the Mermaid* is a Cinderella tale from South Carolina with its roots deep in West African folktales. Have students research other West African tales for common threads. *Mermaid Tales from Around the World* (Scholastic, 1993) by Mary Pope Osborne is an exquisitely illustrated collection based on noted sources of mermaid lore. *Nicholas Pipe* (Dial, 1997) by Robert D. San Souci is a companion title featuring a merman.

162 San Souci, Robert D. *The Talking Eggs*. Illus. by Jerry Pinkney. Dial, 1989. ISBN 0–8037–0619–7. Representational. Watercolors. Folktales, United States. Cinderella Tales. Greed—Fiction.

Blanche, a sweet, fair, and generous girl, and her mean, spiteful sister, Rose, are both given tasks by an old woman. The good heart of Blanche and the greedy heart of Rose reveal their true natures, and each is rewarded in due kind by an old woman with mysterious powers. This Creole tale in the Cinderella tradition has its roots in the European tale on which it is based. Compare *The Talking Eggs* with *Moss Coat* (Clarion, 1987) by William H. Hooks, another Cinderella version with roots deep in the southern tradition. The finely wrought details in the facial expressions of Jerry Pinkney's characters are his hallmark. Other picture book variants of this tale include *Chinye: A West African Folktale* (Viking, 1994) by Obi Onyefulu and *Toads and Diamonds* (Greenwillow, 1995) by Charles Perrault (retold by Charlotte Huck).

163 San Souci, Robert D. *The Samurai's Daughter*. Illus. by Stephen T. Johnson. Dial, 1992. ISBN 0–8037–1135–2. Expressionism. Pastels. Folktales, Japan. Gender Roles. Japan. Fathers and Daughters.

Tokoyo was raised by her samurai father and is schooled in the virtues of discipline and honor; she places a warrior's duty to protect above her own safety. When her father decides it is time for her to learn more ladylike skills such as music and art, she is faced with dilemma. After her father is exiled to the Oki Islands, Tokoyo must find the strength to endure his absence; but one day she decides that her place is with her father and sets out to join him on his lonely island. On this journey discovers that her strength comes from not being bound by notions of proper behavior. Set during the Kamakura period (1185–1333), this tale explores the history and culture of the Oki Islands, where women pearl divers still thrill crowds today. San Souci has created a powerful story with an enduring female protagonist. Use this book to explore the restraints placed on women throughout history.

164 San Souci, Robert D. *The Tsar's Promise*. Illus. by Lauren Mills. Philomel, 1992. ISBN 0–399–21581–6. Representational. Watercolors. Folk-tales, Russia. Russia.

Tsar Kojata is returning home from a journey when he encounters a demon. Before the demon will release him, the tsar must promise to grant the demon that which is waiting for him at home. The tsar and his wife had waited long for a son, and the Tsar Kojata, ignorant of his child's birth, must now hand over his son to the demon. As fate has it, Ivan, the tsar's son, meets the demon, who takes his prize to his enchanted castle. Angry because Ivan has eluded him so long, the demon requires three tasks to be completed or he will kill him. If Ivan is successful, he will gain his freedom and the hand of the demon's captive princess, Maria. This Russian tale is inspired by Andrew Lang's "King Kojata," which appears in *The Green Fairy Book* (1893) and is based on other Russian and Slavic versions.

165 San Souci, Robert D. *The White Cat: An Old French Fairy Tale.* Illus. by Gennady Spirin. Orchard, 1990. ISBN 0-531-05809-3. Representational. Water-colors. Folktales, France. Cats—Folklore. France.

A young prince on a quest to prove his worth to his father encounters a mysterious castle filled with cats that walk, talk, and eat as people do. An even more mysterious White Cat assists the prince and upon parting gives him a gift that will help the youth earn his father's respect. On two more occasions the prince turns to the White Cat for help. On their last visit, the price battles the wicked magician who placed the spell on the White Cat. With determination and a desire to repay the White Cat's kindness, the prince destroys the wizard and frees the White Cat from his spell. Sorely missing the White Cat's companionship, the prince is pleasantly surprised when the White Cat reappears in a new form to renew their bonds. Based on "La Chatte Blanche" by Madame d'Aulnoy (1650-1705) from her collection *Les Contes de Fees*. Other folktales about cats include *On Cat Mountain* (G. P. Putnam's, 1994) by Richard Françoise, *Puss in Boots* (Farrar, Straus & Giroux, 1990) by Charles Perrault with illustrations by Fred Marcellino, and *The Boy Who Drew Cats: A Japanese Folktale* (Dial, 1994) by Arthur A. Levine.

166 San Souci, Robert D. *Young Guinevere.* Illus. by Jamichael Henterly. Doubleday, 1993. ISBN 0-385-41623-7. Representational. Watercolors. Legends, England. Guinevere (legendary character). Arthurian Romances.

A retelling of the romance and betrayal of Guinevere, wife of King Arthur and lover of his best find, Lancelot. A prophecy by a seer when Guinevere was a child guided her destiny to rule along side Britain's most legendary king. San Souci places emphasis on the feminine side of the Arthurian tales, focusing on Guinevere's fateful journey in search of military aid to succor her father, whose castle is under siege. San Souci also gives attention to the mystical elements of the story: The journey is Guinevere's first meeting with Arthur, and her fate is sealed the moment they lay eyes on each other. Artist Henterly was inspired by the illuminated manuscripts from *The Book of Kells*, which is evident in the jewel-tone illustrations. Robert D. San Souci's Arthurian series includes *Young Merlin* (Doubleday, 1990), *Young Lancelot* (Doubleday, 1996), and *Young Arthur* (Doubleday, 1997). All of San Souci's Arthurian titles are illustrated by

Jamichael Henterly with the exception of *Young Merlin*, which is illustrated by Daniel Horne.

167 San Souci, Robert D. *Young Merlin.* Illus. by Daniel Horne. Doubleday, 1990. ISBN 0–385–24801–6. Representational. Oils. Legends, England. Arthurian Romances. Merlin (legendary character). England.

From birth Merlin is destined for a life of adventure and magic. As a child he is scorned and belittled by other children for his ability to predict the future. His powers, which cause the villagers to brand him an outcast, bring him to the attention of King Vortigern, who takes the young boy into service as an advisor. But Vortigern is an evil man, and Merlin escapes his service by living in the forest and communing with nature. When another king calls for his assistance, Merlin realizes his true destiny. A tale of the life of Merlin the magician as a young boy before he went into service for Arthur, High King of Britain. Another picture book version of Merlin's life is *Merlin and the Dragons* (Dutton, 1995) by Jane Yolen. Robert D. San Souci's Arthurian series includes *Young Guinevere* (Doubleday, 1993), *Young Lancelot* (Doubleday, 1996), and *Young Arthur* (Doubleday, 1997). All of San Souci's Arthurian titles are illustrated by Jamichael Henterly with the exception of *Young Merlin*.

168 San Souci, Robert D. *Feathertop.* Illus. by Daniel San Souci. Doubleday, 1992. ISBN 0–385–42044–7. Expressionism. Watercolors. Narrative Poetry (Adaptations). Hawthorne, Nathaniel (1804–1864). Colonial New England. Narrative Poems—Adaptations.

Long ago in New England an old witch with mischief on her mind creates a scarecrow from scraps of cloth and gives him a broomstick for a backbone. Pleased with her creation, Mother Rigby blows life into her puppet and christens him Feathertop. When Feathertop falls in love with a pretty maiden from the village, he flees because after all, he is only a product of magic, and no magic is powerful enough to make him fully human so that he may have the heart of Polly Gookin. San Souci's tale is an adaptation of Nathaniel Hawthorne's poem "Feathertop," which was first published in 1852 under the title *Feathertop: A Moralized Tale*. Compare this retelling with Hawthorne's original tale.

169 San Souci. Robert D. *The Little Seven-Colored Horse: A Spanish Amer-ican Folktale.* Illus. by Jan Thompson Dicks. Chronicle Books, 1995. ISBN 0–8118–0412–7. Expressionism. Acrylics. Folktales, Latin America. Horses—Folklore.

A farmer's *maizal*, cornfield, is trampled mysteriously each night by an animal that the farmer and his eldest sons are unable to catch. When his youngest son, Juanito, volunteers to catch the intruder, his brothers scoff at him. But Little Juan catches the thief, which turns out to be a *caballito*, a horse, which promises lifelong friendship if Juan sets it free. When Juan's destiny takes him to the city, the *caballito* keeps its promise and aids Juan when he must complete three tasks set to him by the *alcalde*, the mayor. This story is based on a tale popular in many Spanish-speaking countries. The source notes provide further discussion about the origin of the tale. A glossary with pronunciation is included to assist the reader with the Spanish words interspersed throughout text.

170 Sanderson, Ruth. *Papa Gatto: An Italian Fairy Tale.* Illus. by author. Little, Brown, 1995. ISBN 0–316–77073–6. Representational. Oils. Fairy Tales, Italy. Cats—Folklore. Italy.

Papa Gatto is a trusted advisor to the prince. His duties often take him from home, and he needs someone to care for his eight kittens. Charmed by the grace and beauty of Sophia, Papa Gatto entrusts his children to her care, only to return home to find his house in shambles and his kittens neglected. Fearful of another helper, Papa Gatto soon comes to realize that the plain features but loving heart of Beatrice make her a perfect caretaker of his kittens. Her devotion reaches the ears of the prince, who wishes to make her his wife. But the crafty Sophia is mistaken for Beatrice and attempts to fool the prince to win his hand in marriage. *Papa Gatto* is an Italian fairy tale based on several versions, including Andrew Lang's "The Colony of Cats" from *The Crimson Fairy Book* (1903). Explore other cultures with folktales with cats as main characters, some ideas are *Traveling to Tondo: A Tale of the Nkundo of Zaire* (Knopf, 1991) by Verna Aardema, *Puss in Boots* (Farrar, Straus & Giroux, 1990) by Charles Perrault with illustrations Fred Marcellino, and *The White Cat: An Old French Fairy Tale* (Orchard, 1990) by Robert D. San Souci. Other Italian folktales include *Count Silvernose* (Holiday House, 1996) by Eric Kimmel and *Caterina the Clever Farm Girl: A Tuscan Tale* (Dial, 1996) by Julienne Peterson.

171 Shannon, Mark. *Gawain and the Green Knight.* Illus. by David Shannon. G. P. Putnam's, 1994. ISBN 0–399–22446–7. Expressionism. Oils. Legends, England. Gawain (legendary character). Arthurian Romances.

A retelling of the meeting of Gawain, a young knight in King Arthur's court, with a mysterious stranger from the North Country. Hearing of Arthur's brave and fearless knights, the Green Knight arrives on Yuletide Eve to challenge one among Arthur's brave knights to exchange deadly blows with a razor-sharp ax. Gawain, wanting to prove himself to Arthur and the other knights, accepts the deadly challenge and begins a quest that makes his deeds among the most popular of all of Arthur's knights. Compare this version, which adds a love interest—the fair Caryn—for Gawain, with Sheila Hastings's more traditional telling (see index) of Gawain's rendezvous with the Green Knight. *Young Lancelot* (Doubleday, 1996) by Robert D. San Souci and *The Knight and the Lion: The Story of Yvain* (Little, Brown, 1996) by John Rowe, and *The Kitchen Knight* (Clarion, 1989) by Margaret Hodges are other titles about Arthur's valiant knights.

172   Singer, Marilyn. *The Maiden on the Moor.* Illus. by Troy Howell. Morrow, 1995. ISBN 0–388–08674–8. Representational. Colored Pencils. Folktales, England. Brothers. England.

Two brothers, shepherds returning home after tending their herds, discover a maiden lying still as death on the frozen, barren moor. The eldest brother runs from the maiden, fearing she is bewitched because she is breathing although barefooted and dressed in a flimsy gown. The youngest brother takes the maiden home and attempts to warm her by the fire. Despite days of careful nurturing, the maiden remains asleep. The brother, who has fallen in love with the sleeping girl, pleads to her to awaken and be his true love and ease his loneliness. Finally exhausted by his constant vigil, he falls asleep. He awakens to a glorious surprise. *The Maiden on the Moor* is based on an medieval English ballad by an anonymous poet. Compare the sleep motif with *Princess Florecita and the Iron Shoes*. Other English folktales include *The Old Woman Who Lived in a Vinegar Bottle* (August House, 1995) by Margaret Read MacDonald, *The Magpie's Nest* (Clarion, 1995) by Joanna Foster, and *Comus* (Holiday House, 1996) by Margaret Hodges, which is an adaptation of the English fairy tale *Childe Roland*.

173   Singer, Marilyn. *The Painted Fan.* Illus. by Wenhai Ma. Morrow, 1994. ISBN 0–688–117429. Representational. Watercolors. Fairy Tales (literary). China. Fans.

When two royal families, Chen and Li, are unable to settle a feud between them, a greedy warlord named Shang intervenes. He gains control of the land and prospers as the people suffer. After his conquest, he consults a seerer to find out what other great things are in store for a man so great as himself. He is surprised when the seer predicts his death and warns him to beware of fans. Ha! Shang laughs at such foolishness but nonetheless has every fan in the land burned. Years pass and Shang becomes more cruel. One day he spies a lovely girl and wishes to make her his wife. The girl has no choice but to marry him and takes the one memento she has to remind her of her mother—the very thing that will be the undoing of Shang. Marilyn Singer's tale is a fine example of a literary fairy tale.

174 Stanley, Diane, and Peter Vennema. *Bard of Avon: The Story of William Shakespeare.* Illus. by Diane Stanley. Morrow, 1992. ISBN 0-688-09108-3. Expressionism. Gouache. Biography. Dramatists, English. Shakespeare, William (1564-1616).

An exciting biography of one the of the greatest writers in the English-speaking language. Teachers will find this book very adaptable when exposing students to Shakespeare's sonnets and plays for the first time. Share this title to incite interest in the person so students will have an understanding of the man responsible for one of the largest bodies of work by an individual. The life of the man responsible for *Romeo and Juliet* and *King Lear* is often obscured by his literary achievements, but in this biography the authors managed to bring the man to the forefront. Diane Stanley's gouache illustrations are very detailed and transport the reader back to the sixteenth century. Today there are hundreds of published editions of Shakespeare's plays and sonnets, and teachers should include this biography when assigning titles in the study of Shakespeare. A great writer in his day, Shakespeare remains as popular today as he was 400 years ago. Keep him alive for your student with *Bard of Avon*.

175 Stanley, Diane, and Peter Vennema. *Charles Dickens: The Man Who Had Great Expectations.* Illus. by Diane Stanley. Morrow Junior, 1993. ISBN 0-688-09111-3. Representational. Gouache. Biography. Dickens, Charles (1812-1870). Novelists, English. England.

Charles Dickens's life was an example of art imitating life. In Diane Stanley and Peter Vennema's stunning biography, students will get to glimpse the man responsible for *Great Expectations* and *The Pickwick Papers*. Thoroughly researched information about Dickens's boyhood in nineteenth-century England will open a door for students to explore the literature by learning about Dickens's life. This book takes the reader through time to walk the crowded, polluted streets of London with Dickens as a boy and as a man. Revealing information about his marriage and shows the creative process. Dickens's novels are full of the most lively characters in literature; particularly evocative are his child characters: Little Nell, Tiny Tim, and Oliver Twist, who are imaginative sketches of people Dickens met in his life. The illustrations evoke images of Dickens's world transported into his books. The hilarious and heartrending portrayals of Victorian life and the plot twists and turns reveal the world in which he lived. This illustrated biography is a perfect introduction to Dickens's imaginative world.

176 Steptoe, John. *Mufaro's Beautiful Daughters: An African Tale.* Illus. by author. Lothrop Lee & Shepard, 1987. ISBN 0–688–04045–4. Representational. Watercolors. Folktales, Africa. Siblings. Sisters. Cinderella Tales. Africa.

In Africa, Mufaro lives with his two beautiful daughters. Manyara and Nyasha are as different in temperament as night is different from day. A proclamation is sent by messenger to the village with the news of the king's intention to marry the most worthy and beautiful daughter in the land. During their trip to the city both Manyara and Nyasha must prove who between them is worthy to wed the king and rule by his side. This African Cinderella tale was inspired by a folktale collected and published by G. M. Theal in 1895 in *Kaffir Folktales*. The names of the principal characters are from the Shona language: *Nyasha* [nee-AH-sha], the Cinderella figure in this *Mufaro's Beautiful Daughters*, means "mercy."

177 Stewig, John Warren. *Princess Florecita and the Iron Shoes.* Illus. by K. Wendy Pope. Knopf, 1995. ISBN 0–679–84775–8. Representational. Watercolors. Fairy Tales, Spain. Gender Roles. Sleeping Beauty Tales. Spain.

One day as Princess Florecita is sewing by her window, a bird flies near and sings of a sleeping prince trapped in a evil spell placed on him by a magician envious of the prince's charm and handsome face. Determined to find this prince and free him from his magical bonds, Florecita beseeches the bird to tell her how to find the prince. Although the bird does not know of the prince's whereabouts, he tells Florecita to don a pair of iron shoes she must wear out in her search for the prince; but there is one condition: The prince wakes once a year on Midsummer's Eve, when his brow must be stroked with a black feather. So saying, the bird vanishes and leaves Florecita to her task. The tale of Florecita is based on the fairy tale "The Sleeping Prince" collected by Alison Lurie in *Clever Gretchen and Other Forgotten Folktales* (1980). The gender reversal makes a strong statement. Compare this version with other Sleeping Beauty tales and examine the traditional fairy tale's passive females. Picture book versions include *Sleeping Beauty* (Abrams, 1993) by Margaret Early and *Sleeping Beauty: The Story of the Ballet (*Atheneum, 1994) by Marian Horosko.

178 Talbott, Hudson. *King Arthur and the Round Table.* Illus. by author. Books of Wonder, 1995. ISBN 0–688–11340–0. Representational. Watercolors. Watercolors. Legends, England. Arthurian Romances. Knights and Knighthood. Arthur (legendary character). England.

Arthur has been High King of Britain for only a short time when twelve of his lesser lords declare war, refusing to be ruled by a boy of a mere sixteen years of age. In a battle to defend his right to the throne, the idea of the Round Table to unite factions of Britain is born. It is also during this period that Arthur meets Guinevere, who will become his queen and rule by his side. This story is a retelling of the legend of Arthur, High King of all Ancient Britain. This title is second in a trilogy that traces Arthur from the moment he pulled the sword from the stone, setting his destiny in motion. The trilogy is based on the work *Le Morte d'Arthur* by Sir Thomas Malory. The other two titles in the series are *King Arthur: The Sword in the Stone* (Books of Wonder, 1991) and *Excalibur* (Books of Wonder, 1996).

179 Talbott, Hudson. *King Arthur: The Sword in the Stone.* Illus. by author. Books of Wonder, 1991. ISBN 0-688-09403-1. Representational. Watercolors. Legends, England. Arthurian Romances. Knights and Knighthood. Arthur (legendary character). England.

Young Arthur, squire to his brother Kay, travels to London, where Sir Kay will try to pull the sword Excalibur from the stone so that he may become the next king of Britain. Kay will attempt to earn a chance to free the sword by defeating all the other knights in a contest to prove his strength. It is said the blade can be removed only by the next king of Britain. Arthur, forgetting Kay's sword at home, sees Excalibur and frees the sword from the stone intending to give it to Kay, who will use it in battle in place of the forgotten sword. *King Arthur: The Sword in the Stone* is a retelling of the legend of Arthur, High King of all Ancient Britain. This title is first in a trilogy that traces Arthur from the moment he pulled the sword from the stone, setting his destiny in motion. The trilogy is based on the work *Le Morte d'Arthur* by Sir Thomas Malory. The other two titles in the series are *King Arthur and the Round Table* (Books of Wonder, 1995) and *Excalibur* (Books of Wonder, 1996).

180 Thayer, Ernest Lawrence. *Casey at the Bat.* Illus. by Barry Moser. Atheneum, 1988. ISBN 0-87923-772-8. Representational. Watercolors. Poetry, American. Thayer, Ernest Lawrence (1863-1940). Baseball.

When "Casey at the Bat" appeared in the *San Francisco Examiner* on June 3, 1888, its creator never expected the simple poem to gain the attention it did. In fact, Ernest Thayer Lawrence did not even sign his name nor did he write another poem after "Casey at the Bat." This centennial edition of "Casey at the Bat" is illustrated by Barry Moser, whose watercolor paintings were inspired by historical photographs from the National Baseball Library in Copperstown, New York. Many children grow up with a partial knowledge of the poem. "Casey at the Bat" is not of high literary merit, but this has never hampered the success of the poem. Generate discussion about what makes a piece of writing literature and why this poem has endured.

181   Thoreau, Henry David (Text selections by Steve Lowe). *Walden.* Illus. by Robert Sabuda. Philomel, 1990. ISBN 0-399-22153-0. Expressionism. Linoleum Cuts. Literature (Adaptations). Thoreau, Henry David (1817-1862). Nature. Writers, American.

For two years, two months, and two days Henry David Thoreau lived in small wood cabin he built with his own hands. The retreat was the suggestion of his good friend Ralph Waldo Emerson, who was the recipient of the cabin after Thoreau returned to civilization. Robert Sabuda's bold woodblock illustrations perfectly suit Thoreau's study of nature. Sabuda captures the majestic beauty that inspired Thoreau to write *Walden.* After he returned to Concord, Thoreau wrote this, his most favorite book, which was an account of his time in the woods. Introduce *Walden* to your class with this picture book. Discuss the selections chosen by the author. The brevity of the text makes this book an ideal example of nature writing.

182   Uchida, Yoshiko. *The Magic Purse.* Illus. by Keiko Narahashi. Macmillan, 1993. ISBN 0-6889-50559-0. Expressionism. Watercolors. Folktales, Japan. Wealth. Good Deeds.

A young farmer saves every spare penny so that he may take a journey with his friends to a sacred shrine. As hard as he tries, he is unable to save the money he needs to make the trip. After his friends leave for the shrine, the farmer hears a voice cry out, "Go with them! Hurry!" And so he does. Unfortunately, he is unable to catch up with his friends and wanders into the Black Swamp. Here he happens upon a beautiful maiden who is the prisoner of a demon. She asks him to carry a letter to her parents so that they may know she is well. For his kindness, he is rewarded with a magic purse that never runs out of gold coins. The farmer, once poor, prospers for all his days. *The Magic Purse* is based on an ancient Japanese folktale. Other Japanese folktales include *Screen of Frogs: An Old Tale* (Orchard, 1993) by Sheila Hamanaka, *On Cat Mountain* (G. P. Putnam's 1994) by Richard Françoise, *The Bee and the Dream* (Dutton, 1996) by Jan Freeman Long, and *The Terrible Eek* (Simon & Schuster, 1991) by Patricia Compton.

183   Uchida, Yoshiko. *The Wise Old Woman.* Illus. by Martin Springett. Margaret K. McElderry, 1994. ISBN 0-689-50582-5. Expressionism. Airbrush. Folktales, Japan. Old Age. Wisdom—Fiction. Japan.

In ancient Japan a young and cruel lord decrees that all people over the age of seventy are useless and must be carried into the mountains to die. A farmer does the lord's bidding as much as it breaks his heart to abandon his mother. At the last moment he changes his mind and returns with his mother to the village under the cover of darkness. He digs a secret room under his home, and there she lives in secret. When a powerful overlord of the region intends to destroy the village unless three seemingly impossible tasks are performed, it is the old woman's wisdom gleaned from years of living that saves the village from certain destruction. Wisdom coming with age is a difficult concept to explain to young people. Other books that explore wisdom are: *Seven Blind Mice* (Philomel, 1992) by Ed Young and *Zomo the Rabbit: A Trickster Tale from West Africa* (Harcourt Brace, 1992) by Gerald McDermott.

184 Whitman, Walt. *I Hear America Singing*. Illus. by Robert Sabuda. Philomel, 1991. ISBN 0-399-21808-4. Impressionism. Linoleum-Cut. Poetry, American. Walt Whitman (1819–1892). Illustrated Classics. Poets, American.

This illustrated version of Walt Whitman's "I Hear America Singing" with bold linoleum cuts is a perfect introduction to his body of work. The opportunity to examine a work of literature in a picture book format will encourage students to apply visual attributes to discussion of the poetic form. Use with Whitman's collection *Leaves of Grass* (1855) and discuss the text layout in conjunction with the illustration. The muted tones chosen by Sabuda suit the somber tribute to the working-class Americans, who inspired the poem. As Whitman said in the opening of *Leaves of Grass*: "I celebrate myself. For every atom belonging to me as good belongs to you."

185 Wilde, Oscar. *The Selfish Giant*. Illus. by S. Saelig Gallagher. G. P. Putnam's, 1995. ISBN 0-399-22448-3. Surrealism. Oils. Fairy Tales (literary). Wilde, Oscar (1854–1900). Dramatists, Irish. Giants. Illustrated Classics.

An illustrated version of Oscar Wilde's famous literary fairy tale about a selfish giant who will not allow children to play in his garden. The power of the garden draws the children, who seek to slip through the cracks in wall every chance they get. After the giant spies a lonely child separate from the others, he begins to sense the loneliness in his own life. The expressionistic paintings by Gallagher are stunning. Wilde's timeless tale of selfishness paired with the illustrations revives an old classic and breathes new life into the story. There are several illustrated versions of *The Selfish Giant*, including one by Lisbeth Zwerger (Picture Book Studio, 1984. Lisbeth Zwerger also illustrated Wilde's *The Canterville Ghost* (Picture Book Studio, 1986). *The Happy Prince* (Simon & Schuster, 1989) by Oscar Wilde with illustrations by Ed Young is another picture book of Oscar Wilde's literary tales.

186 Williams, Marcia. *The Adventures of Robin Hood*. Illus. by author. Candlewick Press, 1995. ISBN 1-56402-535-7. Cartoon Art. Watercolor and

Ink. Legends, England. Robin Hood (legendary character). Middle Ages. Outlaws. England.

Robin Hood, legendary outlaw of Sherwood Forest, reputed savior of the
poor and hungry, is presented with his Merrymen and Maid Marian in an
engaging comic-strip picture book. Fans of Robin's adventures and those new to
the legends will enjoy the fresh approach to his outrageous exploits as he baffles
the greedy and foolish King John. Comic touches with asides from characters
make this version of the Robin Hood's adventures entertaining and exciting to
compare with more legitimate versions.

187 Williams, Marcia. *King Arthur and the Knights of the Round Table.* Illus.
by author. Candlewick Press, 1996. ISBN 1–56402–802–X. Cartoon Art.
Watercolor and Ink. Legends, England. Knights and Knighthood. England.
Arthur (legendary character).

A comic retelling of King Arthur and his noble knights. King Arthur and
the Knights of the Round Table is a collection of standard Arthurian tales,
including the origin the round table, Arthur and Guinevere's romance, and
Galahad's quest for the Holy Grail. Marcia Williams has taken some of history's
legendary figures and parodied their glory and achievements in a playful,
lighthearted manner. The cartoon-style caricatures will delight younger as well
as older readers. The design in the book is similar to a comic strip and will
inspire students to create their own parodies of other historical figures. Use
Marcia Williams's title with more serious picture books about the gallant deeds
of Arthur and his noble followers.

188 Winthrop, Elizabeth. *Vasilissa the Beautiful.* Illus. by Alexander Koshkin.
HarperCollins, 1991. ISBN 0–06–021662–X. Expressionism. Gouache. Fairy
Tales, Russia. Baba Yaga (legendary character). Cinderella Tales. Russia.

As a token of remembrance, Vasilissa's mother gives her a doll as a gift
before she dies. She tells Vasilissa, "feed the doll a morsel of food and give it
drink whenever you need someone to talk to." Eventually Vasilissa's father
remarries; his new wife is a cruel woman with two petty, selfish daughters who
are jealous of Vasilissa's kind heart and beauty. When Vasilissa's father leaves
on a long journey, her stepmother sells all his possessions and moves the family
to a barren forest near the witch Baba Yaga. A vile plan by her stepmother and
sisters places Vasilissa in the home of Baba Yaga. Vasilissa's escape and return
to her home brings about the deaths of her wicked stepsisters.

189 Wisniewski, David. *Elfwyn's Saga.* Illus. by author. Lothrop. Lee & Shepard, 1990. ISBN 0-688-09589-5. Expressionism. Cut Paper. Fairy Tales, Iceland. Vikings—Folklore. Physical Handicaps. Iceland.

Angered that the greenest valleys were granted to Anlaf Haraldson and his descendants by the Hidden Folk, Gorm the Grim lays a curse on all of Anlaf's line. Anlaf's daughter, Elfwyn, is born blind because of the curse. Although she cannot see, Elfwyn is graced with a second sight that aids her kin when Gorm returns with a gift that blinds the rest of her people to his true nature. The author drew upon Icelandic history and legend to create this original tale. An author's note briefly outlines Viking history and the elements that are interwoven into *Elfwyn's Saga.* David Wisniewski, famous for his original cut paper illustrations, used over 1000 blades and an X-Acto knife to create the bold illustrations. His book *Golem* (Clarion, 1996), set in sixteenth century Prague, won the coveted Caldecott Medal for most distinguished contribution to the field of children's literature in 1997.

190 Wisniewski, David. *Golem.* Illus. by author. Clarion, 1995. ISBN 0-395-72618-2. Expressionism. Cut Paper. Legends, Jewish. Judah Loew ben Bezalel (1525-1609). Golem (legendary character). Czechoslovakia.

In this cautionary tale a good-intentioned rabbi creates a clay giant to help him protect the Jewish people in sixteenth-century Prague. The word Golem [GO-lem] is the Hebrew for "shapeless mass." As with all of his books, Wisniewski skill as both an illustrator and a writer shine through, and won him won the 1997 Caldecott Medal for this Jewish legend. The author's note is methodically researched and serves to answer any question a person may have while reading this book. *Golem: A Giant Made of Mud* (Greenwillow, 1995) by Mark Podwal is another version of the Golem legend. Have students compare the two books for similarities. Other folktales from Czechoslovakia include *Marushka and the Month Brothers* (North-South, 1996) by Anna Vojtech and *Tall, Wide, and Sharp-Eyed* (Holt, 1994) by Mirko Gabler.

191 Wisniewski, David. *The Warrior and the Wise Man.* Illus. by author. Lothrop, Lee & Shepard, 1989. ISBN 0-688-07890-7. Expressionism. Cut Paper. Folktales, Japan. Siblings. Brothers. Japan.

Two brothers, Tozaemon and Toemon, must face the demons who control the elements of earth, fire, water, wind, and cloud to prove to their father which is worthy of the throne. Using different approaches, each son manages to gain the elements and prove his worth. Tozaemon takes up his sword and heads into the fray using his strength to reach his goal. Toemon's nonviolent and gentle approach to the tasks set to him by his father prove that might and strength are not always the way to rule. *The Warrior and the Wise Man* is based on twelfth-century Japanese history, revealing a culture that reveres strength of the warrior as well as the patience of the wise man. The author's source notes outline the origins of the tale and also provides interesting facts that enrich the story. Other folktales about brothers include *The Woman Who Fell from the Sky: An Iroquois Story of Creation* (Morrow, 1993) by John Bierhorst, *The Magic Tapestry* (Holt, 1994) by Demi, *Boots and His Brothers: A Norwegian Tale* (Holiday House, 1992) and *Three Sacks of Truth: A Story from France* (Holiday House, 1993), both by Eric Kimmel.

192 Yep, Laurence. *The Boy Who Swallowed Snakes.* Illus. by Jean and Mou-sien Tseng. Scholastic, 1994. ISBN 0–590–46168–0. Expressionism. Watercolors. Folktales, China. Greed—Fiction. China.

A greedy rich man, whose fortune is ill gained, dumps his source of magic—a ku snake that rewards its owner by cheating and stealing other people's treasure. When honest Chou finds the snake, he attempts to return it—only to have the rich man claim the snake is not his. Chou tries to stamp, burn, and bury the snake to no avail. He finally swallows the snake to prevent harm from coming to others. What follows is a tale with unexpected results in which a young boy with a courageous and kind heart overcomes an evil and greedy man whose intentions are anything but honest.

193 Yep, Laurence. *The City of Dragons.* Illus. by Jean and Mou-sien Tseng. Scholastic, 1995. ISBN 0–590–47765–6. Expressionism. Watercolors. Fairy Tales (literary). Prejudice—Fiction. Dragons—Folklore. China.

A young boy, born with a face so sad that no one can bear to look at him, leaves his family because he cannot bear to bring them more sorrow. His travels take him to the City of Dragons, where his unusual face is finally appreciated. As a child Laurence Yep knew a boy with a deformed face and he used this association and Chinese folktales to create his fictional story. This tale provides powerful messages about aspects of beauty and how society shuns people deemed ugly or unattractive. Laurence Yep has also written *Tiger Woman* (Bridgewater, 1995), *The Khan's Daughter* (Scholastic, 1996), and *The Man Who Tricked a Ghost* (Bridgewater, 1993), all three are folktales from Chinese culture.

194 Yep, Laurence. *The Shell Woman and the King.* Illus. by Yang Ming-Yi. Dial, 1993. ISBN 0–8037–1395–9. Representational. Ink and Watercolors. Folktales, China. China.

A beautiful woman who is able to change from a human into a seashell falls in love with a fisherman and weds him. Her proud husband brags of her magic, and when the cruel emperor hears of her powers, he abducts her husband in order to force Shell to become his queen. She refuses but agrees to perform three difficult tasks so that her husband can be released from prison. This tale was discovered by the author in an eighteenth-century collection of Chinese folktales and adapted to create this version set in the kingdom of Han (917–971). Yang Ming-Yi's soft, luminous illustrations set against the sea are stunning. *The Rainbow People* (HarperCollins, 1989) and *Tongues of Jade* (HarperCollins, 1992) compiled by Laurence Yep are collections of folktales brought to the U. S. by Chinese immigrants in the 1930s that are reflections of their homeland.

195 Yolen, Jane. *Good Griselle.* Illus. by David Christiana. Harcourt Brace, 1994. ISBN 0–15–231701–5. Representational. Watercolors. Fairy Tales (literary). Angels.

Griselle, aging and widowed, spends her days tatting lace and helping those less fortunate tan she is. Griselle's goodness is admired by the angels and sneered at by the gargoyles that perch atop the cathedral she passes each day. Believing that her kindness has its limits, the gargoyles wager the angels that Griselle's goodness has a limit; they and test the woman to find the crack in her kind heart. The gargoyles send an ugly baby to the old woman's doorstep on Christmas Eve, sure that even Griselle's heart will turn from the horrible face. *Good Griselle* is a literary fairy tale would be model title for students interested in creating original fairy tales in English classes. The works of Hans Christian Anderson are perhaps the most famous literary fairy tales in the world. This modern tale by Yolen could be compared with Anderson's fairy tales in an comparative literature unit. The title could also serve as a springboard to discussion of the attributes of goodness in a human relations class.

196 Yolen, Jane. *Merlin and the Dragons.* Illus. by Li Ming. Dutton, 1995. ISBN 0–525–65214–0. Representational. Watercolors. Arthurian Romances. Merlin (legendary character). Dragons—Folklore.

An Arthurian tale about the boyhood of Arthur and the influence of the magician, Merlin, on his journey to manhood and his rule as High King of Britain. In this version, Arthur is frightened by the awesome responsibility of sovereignty and wakes from bad dreams seeking comfort. Merlin whispers tales from the childhood of an anonymous boy to comfort Arthur. After listening to the old magician's tales, Arthur is confident with his destiny and slips into sleep where he dreams peacefully with a calm heart. Jane Yolen, renowned for years for her fantasy and science fiction writing, spellbinds with this rousing tale of

Merlin's boyhood. Use with Robert D. San Souci's *Young Merlin* (Doubleday, 1990) and with Hudson Talbott's Arthurian trilogy that includes *King Arthur: The Sword in the Stone* (Books of Wonder, 1991), *King Arthur and the Round Table* (Books of Wonder, 1995), and *Excalibur* (Books of Wonder, 1996).

197   Yolen, Jane. *Tam Lin.* Illus. by Charles Mikolaycak. Harcourt Brace, 1990. ISBN 0-15-284261-6. Expressionism. Watercolors/Colored Pencil. Folktales, Scotland. Ballads, Scotland. Fairies.

In the Scottish countryside there stands a ruined castle with stones strewn about. It was once the ancestral home of the MacKenzie clan, but for many generations faeries have claimed the stones and mortar of the walls. Young Jennet MacKenzie, a lass with spark, intends to take back her home despite the warnings of her parents and the village elders. On her sixteenth birthday, Jennet drapes her clan's tartan across her shoulder and begins her quest to reclaim her family home. When Jennet plucks a rose from a thorn bush and summons Tam Lin, a human held captive by the Faery Queen, her journey across the misty border between the human world the and faery world begins. *Tam Lin* is based on an old ballad from the border country in Scotland. First mention of the Tam Lin or Tamlane can be traced to a ballad book published in 1549.

198   Yolen, Jane. *Wings.* Illus. by Dennis Nolan. Harcourt Brace, 1991. ISBN 0-15-297850-X. Representational. Watercolors. Mythology. Daedalus (Greek character). Greek Mythology.

A retelling of the Greek myth featuring the architect Daedalus, revered for his graceful and beautiful buildings. Jealous of his nephew's talent and fearing the boy's skill will surpass his own, Daedalus kills the boy and loses all favor with the people of Athens. Exiled to Crete, Daedalus builds the famed Labyrinth, where the Minotaur is to be held prisoner. After completing the maze, Daedalus is imprisoned because it is feared he will reveal the secret way out. The attempted escape and death of his son, Icarus, during their famed flight from Crete has been recorded by the Roman poet Ovid and mentioned by Homer in *The Iliad*. The myth of Daedalus and his deeds is retold is evocative prose by Jane Yolen. The oil illustrations by Dennis Nolan capture the foolish choices and the consequences of Daedalus's actions in a series of magnificent paintings. Pair this title with *The One-Eyed Giant and Other Monsters* (Greenwillow, 1996) by Anne Rockwell, which features a story of the Minotaur.

199   Young, Ed. *Lon Po Po: A Red-Riding Hood Story From China.* Illus. by author. Philomel, 1989. ISBN 0-399-21619-7. Impressionism. Pastels. Folktales, China. China. Red Riding Hood.

Long ago in China three children lived with their mother in the countryside. When their mother leaves to visit their granny, their Po Po, she reminds them "to close the door tight at sunset and latch it well." Shang, Tao, and Paotze do as their mother has bid and wait for her return. But a wolf is watching as the mother leaves, and it hears her instructions. Under the guise of an old woman, the wolf approaches the children and tricks them into letting it in. What follows are the identifiable motifs of the European Red Riding Hood story. *Lon Po Po: A Red Riding Hood Tale from China* is an excellent book to use with students when comparing folk and fairy tales from other cultures. Other versions of Little Red Riding Hood include *Goblin Walk* (Putnam, 1991) by Tony Johnston, *Something Called Ruby* (Little, Brown, 1990), and *Little Red Riding Hood: A New Fangled Prairie Tale* (Simon & Schuster, 1995) by Lisa Campbell Ernst.

200 Young, Ed. *Moon Mother: A Native American Creation Story.* Illus. by author. HarperCollins, 1993. ISBN 0-06-021302-7. Impressionism. Pastels. Legends, Native American. Indians of North America. Creation Stories. United States.

Long ago a spirit person came to earth and saw the beauty of the land and stayed. Before long he grew lonely and created beings in his likeness. The spirit and the men lived together for a long while. But then a woman spirit came, and the man spirit longed to be with her because they were as one. When the spirits leave the earth, the men are sad but discover a gift left behind: the woman spirit's baby. Now the woman is the moon and travels with her husband through the night skies playing with the stars. Moon Mother's gift is the gift of life, and from the sky the Moon Mother still watches her earth children. This Native American creation story about the spirit who created animals and people and his love for a woman spirit who becomes the moon is based on a collection of tales published by Charles Erskine Scott Wood in 1901.

Chapter 4

Mathematics

The titles are not intended to replace mathematics textbooks or to teach math concepts. Rather, they are ideal for introducing math concepts or for recreation. Challenge students to use skills already learned and to apply their knowledge when using the titles from this section.

201 Anno, Mitsumasa. *All in a Day*. Illus. by Anno and others. Philomel, 1986. ISBN 0–399–21311–2. Cartoon Art. Watercolors. Fiction. Time Zones. Mathematical Recreation.

Eight international illustrators joined Mitsumasa Anno to create a book that looks at every corner of the world in just a glance. Each illustration is a double-page spread with eight pictures by eight different artists in eight different time zones. The pages are designed to coincide with the time zones according to Greenwich Time—when it is 6:00 A.M. in Russia, it is 3:00 P.M. in Tokyo and so on. By the end of the book one week has passed and each country has been visited in the morning, afternoon, and evening simultaneously. The book has an exceptional afterword with an explanation of world time zones, the prime meridian, the international date line, and hemispheres and other time-related terms that make this an ideal text to introduce or review topics of time.

202 Anno, Mitsumasa. *Anno's Counting Book*. Illus. by author. Harper Collins, 1977. ISBN 0–690–01288–8. Cartoon Art. Watercolors. Fiction. Counting. Mathematical Recreation.

Anno's Counting Book was based on the idea of how counting systems developed. Beginning with one of each detail in the illustrations and then adding two, then three, and so on, each picture in *Anno's Counting Book* will have students scanning the pages looking for additions. The confusion will encourage young people to look for the pattern and develop a system to calculate the answer. In an author's note, Anno gives a brief history of how counting systems might have developed to help keep records of groups of items larger than one. His innovative picture books take everyday math operations and make them exciting by challenging children to figure out the answer for themselves.

203 Anno, Mitsumasa. *Anno's Counting House.* Illus. by author. Philomel, 1982. ISBN 0–399–20896–8. Cartoon Art. Watercolors. Fiction. Counting. Mathematical Recreation.

Illustrator-author Anno believes all children are natural mathematicians and that they naturally look for pattern, hidden pictures, order, and numbers even when they are embedded within the text. *Anno's Counting House* gives children an opportunity to learn counting skills from 1 to 10 by using simple subtraction and addition rules to arouse curiosity and engage children in a game to figure out who has moved in and who has moved out of Anno's Counting House! An author's note to parents and educators explains Anno's philosophy of teaching and background for readers who are interested in the development of *Anno's Counting House.*

204 Anno, Mitsumasa. *Anno's Magic Seeds.* Illus. by author. Philomel, 1995. ISBN 0–399–22538–2. Cartoon Art. Watercolors. Fiction. Arithmetic. Multiplication. Mathematical Recreation.

Jack is given two magic seeds by a wizard and told to eat one and plant the other. If he follows directions, he will have two plants in the spring that will yield two more seeds. Jack does as he is told and is rewarded with two more seeds. Clever Jack soon learns that planting more than he eats will yield an even bigger crop! Anno has cleverly interwoven his story with numbers that will have students poring over the pages trying to figure out the hidden math problems to find exactly how Jack doubles, triples, and quadruples his original seeds. Anno has dedicated his literature for children to making math concepts fun by encouraging participation through reading. While this book may not seem challenging, students will nonetheless find themselves trying to solve the problem as they read. Include a reading of the English folktale Jack and the Beanstalk, which has similar themes.

205 Baum, Arline and Joseph. *Opt: An Illusionary Tale.* Illus. by author. Viking, 1987. ISBN 0–670–80870–0. Cartoon Art. Watercolors. Fiction. Visual Perception. Symmetry. Mathematical Recreation.

Visit the kingdom of Opt, where nothing is as it appears to be. The portraits in the great hall are pictures of the princess or are they the king's mother? Find faces within faces at the Opt Zoo, and fly kites with the king. At a grand party he prince is given a set of blocks. Are their six or seven blocks? It depends on whether you stand on your head as you look at his gift. Arlene and Joseph Baum have hidden optical tricks on every page, and depending on how you look, a person may appear tall or short, and one arrow can easily become two arrows if you learn to master your own optical orbs.

206 Bolton, Linda. *Hidden Pictures.* Reproductions. Dial, 1993. ISBN 0–8037–1378–9. Reproductions. Nonfiction. Art Appreciation. Visual Perception. Mathematical Recreation.

Linda Bolton has collected a series of famous paintings by celebrated artists that have held centuries of people captive by the subtext embedded in their canvas. Each page is full of distorted figures, altered perspectives, and color tricks that demand a closer look. In each painting, from *Paranoiac Figure* by Salvador Dali to *Three Musicians* by Pablo Picasso, the artists challenge viewers to look beyond the obvious—because upon further inspection, nothing is quite what it appears to be.

207 Chwast, Seymour. *The 12 Circus Rings.* Illus. by author. Harcourt Brace, 1993. ISBN 0–15–200627–3. Cartoon Art. Colored Markers. Fiction. Ordinal Numbers. Cardinal Numbers. Mathematical Recreation.

A circus adventure in the tradition of "The Twelve Days of Christmas." Join two children who begin the adventure with one daredevil on one high wire in first ring and end up with twelve animals in the twelfth ring. Use the lively text to compare ordinal numbers and cardinal numbers as the author has done. The bright, engaging illustrations are reminiscent of an old-fashioned circus. The author includes a math challenge at the end of the story that encourages further math exploration.

208 Geisert, Arthur. *Roman Numerals I to MM: Numerabilia Romana Uno Ad Duo Mila.* Illus. by author. Houghton Mifflin, 1996. ISBN 0–395–74519–5. Cartoon Art. Watercolors. Fiction. Roman Numerals. Counting. Mathematical Recreation.

Roman numerals appear everywhere yet can be confusing for, or even misunderstood by people. A series of cartoon-style illustrations featuring pigs (yes, pigs) introduce the seven letters that represent numbers: I, V, X, L, C, D, and M. Pigs feature prominently in the illustrations, challenging readers to use Roman numerals to count the oinkers on each page. The text incorporates explanation for using and placing Roman numerals in a simple, direct manner. Arthur Geisert has developed an engaging book that takes the confusion out of Roman numerals and adds a unique twist. Suitable for all ages, this book is an animated way to introduce the concept of Roman numerals or to refresh the memory of students who have forgotten how to translate cardinal numbers.

209 Hoban, Tana. *Spirals, Curves, Fanshapes, and Lines.* Photographs by author. Greenwillow, 1992. ISBN 0–688–11228–5. Representational. Photographs. Nonfiction. Geometry. Geometric Shapes. Mathematical Recreation.

Have you ever noticed the pattern in the weave in a basket? Or the curve in a piece of ornate furniture? Take an exciting adventure and find amazing patterns and shapes in everyday things. This book of photographs will encourage students to apply geometric solutions to everyday ordinary objects. Tana Hoban has pulled together an extensive collection of everyday objects that have geometric properties and displayed them in an attractive photographic book. Although the book is not challenging, it is suitable to introduce the necessity of geometry in everyday life.

210 Hulme, Joy N. *Sea Squares.* Illus. by Carol Schwartz. Hyperion, 1991. ISBN 1–56282–080–X. Representational. Gouache. Fiction. Square Roots. Multiplication. Mathematical Recreation.

Take a trip to the seashore to find out what numbers and the sea have in common. Joy Hulme has incorporated information about sea creatures and sea fauna to help connect math and the sea. The seaside illustrations and poetic text make the book engaging despite the simplicity. A strength of the book is the wealth of information; *Sea Squares* is full of interesting facts that will capture students interest. A glossary of informative tidbits about the creatures and plants featured in the book that makes this title useful in a science class as well.

211 Maestro, Betsy. *The Story of Money.* Illus. by Giulio Maestro. Clarion, 1993. ISBN 0–395–56242–2. Cartoon Art. Watercolors. Nonfiction. Currency. Money. Mathematical Recreation.

A historical journey of stuff many believe makes the world go around. Beginning with the ancient Sumerians, who invented silver money, and the

Chinese, who were the first to use paper money, this book is an engaging exploration of currency. Today there are 140 different currencies, and calculating the exchange rate is confusing. This text covers international aspects of money, with special emphasis on United States currency. The cartoon-style illustrations are engaging and make this book ideal to introduce topics about currency.

212 Moss, Lloyd. *Zin! Zin! Zin! A Violin.* Illus. by Marjorie Priceman. Simon & Schuster, 1995. ISBN 0–671–88239–2. Expressionism. Gouache. Fiction. Musical Instruments. Counting Books. Mathematical Recreation.

"Soaring high and moving in, with a ZIN! ZIN! ZIN! A VIOLIN, stroking strings that come alive! Now a QUINTET, let's count them: FIVE." The lyrical prose is exciting and tempts the reader to discover the next sentence before turning the page. Ten orchestra instruments enter the stage one by one in this musical counting book, which introduces the connection of numbers with music. Vivid and a perfect accompaniment for the bouncy text, the expressionistic watercolors earned the illustrator a Caldecott Honor in 1995. The strength of this book lies in its connection of math with music, which dispels the myth that math is not necessary in the real world.

213 Parker, Nancy Winslow. *Money, Money, Money.* Illus. by author. HarperCollins, 1995. ISBN 0–06–023412–1. Cartoon Art. Nonfiction. Currency. Money—History. Mathematical Recreation.

United States paper currency is known to most people as simply "money," but it is also known as "dough," "bucks," "clams," "loot," and "moolah." Officially in the United States, money is classified as "Federal Reserve notes." This is only part of the fascinating history behind the green stuff that keeps the American dream alive and kicking. Nancy Parker explains the meaning of the symbols on the paper currency, reveals the three bills that have portraits of men who were not presidents with the reasons they were selected, and discloses techniques used by the Bureau of Engraving and Printing (BEP) to prevent counterfeiters from duplicating United States currency. The illustrations complement the information but do not make a bold artistic statement.

214 Sandburg, Carl. *Arithmetic.* Illus. by Ted Rand. Harcourt Brace, 1993. ISBN 0–15–203865–5. Anamorphic Images. Mixed Media. Poetry, American. Arithmetic. Anamorphic Images. Poets, American. Illustrated Classics. Mathematical Recreation.

Carl Sandburg's most celebrated poem for children, "Arithmetic," has been illustrated by Ted Rand, who used anamorphic images—images that have been distorted to create an optical illusion—to make the experience of math fun and exciting. The last pages in the book include information about anamorphic images and instruct how to create them. Students will enjoy applying the directions to explore the ordinary from an altered angle. Further exploration of the details of Ted Rand's illustrations will reveal the dedication he applied to this project. The drawings are small masterpieces worthy of Carl Sandburg's poem. Encourage students to apply math and art in the fashion of Rand's book.

215 Schwartz, David M. *How Much is a Million*. Illus. by Steven Kellogg. Lothrop, Lee & Shepard, 1985. ISBN 0–688–09933–5. Cartoon Art. Watercolors. Fiction. Large Numbers. Multiplication. Mathematical Recreation.

Have you ever wondered how big of a fish bowl you would need to hold a million fish? Picturing a million of anything is a daunting task, unless you have the help of Steven Kellogg and David Schwartz, who joined forces to assist readers in the adventure. The cartoon-style illustrations are delightful, full of mind-boggling accuracy. If one million children stood on each others shoulders, they would be taller than the tallest building and higher than airplanes can fly. It would take a fishbowl large enough to hold a whale to hold one million fish! Mathematician David M. Schwartz has written a delightful story that challenges children to explore large numbers. He has included the calculations he used to figure out how much a million really is. But how about a billion? A trillion? Steven Kellogg's cartoon paintings are fun and perfectly complement the playful question, "How much is a million?"

216 Scieszka, Jon. *Math Curse*. Illus. by Lane Smith. Viking, 1995. ISBN 0–670–86194–4. Expressionism. Acrylics. Fiction. Math Problems. School. Mathematical Recreation.

Why does everything have to be a problem? You look in your closet and find three shirts, and two pairs of pants—is this enough to make one outfit? To make matters worse, when you get to school, your teacher tells you "You know, you can think of almost everything as a math problem." The next day our unhappy heroine begins to have problems all over the place. So she can set her alarm correctly, she scrambles through the day subtracting the time it takes her to get ready plus the time it takes her to get to school. But she needs to consider the time it takes her to eat breakfast. To further confuse her she wonders how many teeth she has and how long will it take to brush them all. This makes her wonder about how many quarts are in a gallon, how many pints in a quart, how many inches in a foot, how many feet in yard, how many yards in a neighborhood. Arrghhh!! Obviously her teacher has put a math curse on our hapless heroine. Math problems are embedded throughout the entire text. Students will enjoy finding a solution to the math curse.

217 Westray, Kathleen. *Picture Puzzlers*. Illus. by author. Ticknor & Fields, 1994. ISBN 0–395–70130–9. Folk Art. Gouache. Nonfiction. Visual Perception. Afterimages. Mathematical Recreation.

A picture is worth a thousand words or at least second look in the case of *Picture Puzzlers* by Kathleen Westray. The bright folk art illustrations will entice young people to explore the pictures to discover that not everything is as simple as it at first seems. This book will challenge students to look at a picture with different eyes. Compare with *Opt* (Viking, 1987) by Arline and Joseph Baum. Each book uses afterimages to illustrate properties of geometry, but each has a different theme. Challenge students to create their own book with a theme that unites a story, illustrations, and afterimages.

218 Wiesner, David. *June 29, 1999*. Illus. by author. Clarion, 1992. ISBN 0–395–59762–5. Representational. Watercolors. Fiction. Vegetables. Size Relations. Mathematical Recreation.

Young Holly Evans launches her vegetable seedlings into the ionosphere for a school science experiment, with unexpected results. Within weeks turnips the size of boats land in Billings, Montana, and heads of lettuce as big as houses grow in Iowa. What has Holly done? The playful text and rich details will engage students. The book is full of opportunities to explore calendar concepts, size relations, and proportions. Challenge your students to estimate the size and weight of the vegetables in relation to the other objects in Wiesner's illustrations.

Chapter 5

Science and Nature

The titles in the science and nature section can be used individually but will be most effective if used conjointly with other books on a similar topic (e.g., group together books about environmental protection and books about rainforests). Consider looking in the literature section for folktales concerned with environmental and science issues. I encourage teachers to explore the published body of work by Seymour Simon, Barbara Bash, Carol Lerner, and Gail Gibbons. All these authors have published extensively in the field of science for children and young adults.

219   Appelbaum, Diana. *Giants in the Land.* Illus. by Michael McCurdy. Houghton Mifflin, 1993. ISBN 0-395-64720-7. Expressionism. Scratchboard. Fiction. Logging. Shipbuilding. Human Influence on Nature. Botany. Earth Sciences.

A visually enticing history of the logging business in America prior to the American Revolution. Giant white pines, 250 feet tall and 4 feet wide, were chopped down and transported from the forests of the area now called New England by oxen to the sea, where they were taken to England and fashioned into ship masts. The incredible tale of this lesser known slice of American history comes alive in Diane Appelbaum's lively retelling of shipbuilding during the eighteenth century. Read this title aloud to your class to introduce units about the Revolutionary War or as an example of the effects commerce had on the environment before people understood how their actions would affect future generations.

220   Arnosky, Jim. *A Kettle of Hawks and Other Wildlife Groups.* Illus. by author. Lothrop, Lee & Shepard, 1990. ISBN 0–688–09280–2. Representational. Watercolors. Nonfiction. Animal Societies. Animal Behavior. Biology. Life Sciences.

Biologists use specific terms to describe how distinct animal societies herd: bees, for example, swarm. People are familiar with many grouping names, but some, such as a kettle of hawks, are unfamiliar. Jim Arnosky has chosen six animal societies to explore. The group names used for the animal societies derive from a characteristic or behavior displayed by the animals. Each animal society is introduced with a short poem that is followed by a page of facts about each animal group. The approach is unique, combining creative writing with nonfiction writing. As with his other books, Arnosky's strength is his keen eye for the natural world, evident in the watercolor illustrations.

221   Arnosky, Jim. *I See Animals Hiding.* Illus. by author. Scholastic, 1995. ISBN 0–590–48143–6. Representational. Watercolors. Nonfiction. Animals— Vertebrates. Animal Camouflage. Biology. Life Sciences.

A simple, straightforward book introducing animal camouflage. Animals live in very dangerous environments and are always potential targets for predators and hunters. Nature has given animals the ability to blend into their surroundings. Shedding or growing fur coats and feathers is just one of the ways animals blend with the changing seasons and defend against predators. Animals will also altar their body shapes and seem to melt into the trees and bushes surrounding them. Jim Arnosky's watercolors are designed with care so that each animal appears to blend into the illustrations just as it would in its natural surroundings. A respected illustrator of thirty environmentally conscious books for children, Jim Arnosky has hosted a PBS series based on one of his ALA award-winning books, *Drawing from Nature.* The text is concise and effective. Step beyond the simple text to use the illustrations—the strength of this book— to springboard into a wildlife unit.

222   Baker, Jeannie. *The Story of Rosy Dock.* Illus. by author. Greenwillow, 1995. ISBN 0–688–11493–8. Representational. Collage. Nonfiction. Plants— Rosy Dock (*rumex vesicarius*). Human Influence on Nature. Plant Introduction. Botany. Life Sciences.

Throughout history immigrants have introduced aspects of their culture to their adopted countries. In many cases the additions can enrich and enhance the new culture, but often the introduction of alien plants and animals to a new environment has adverse effects. Jeannie Baker's exquisite collage illustrations show how an unintentional act can have adverse effects on the environment.

Rosy dock (*rumex vesicarius*), a European plant introduced to Australia by immigrants, spread across the landscape affecting the plants and animals indigenous to the continent. The text falls short of the powerful illustrations because although Baker centers her text on the theme of the destruction of a natural environment, she fails to reveal which animals and plant life in Australia were affected by the introduction of rosy dock. However, the illustrations are powerful and teachers can use them to explore the consequences of plant and animal introduction.

223   Bang, Molly. *Chattanooga Sludge*. Illus. by author. Harcourt Brace, 1996. ISBN 0-15-216345-X. Expressionism. Collage. Nonfiction. Rivers—Chattanooga. United States—Appalachian Mountain Region. Human Influence on Nature. Environmental Sciences. Earth Sciences.

A fictionalized account of the history of the Chattanooga River in the Tennessee River Valley, nestled in the Appalachian Mountains. The bulk of the text follows the efforts of John Todd, a biologist from Massachusetts, who developed a system to clean up the river. The layout of the book is unusual because the book does not have a cover. Bang's brief history of the formation of the Appalachian Mountains and concise overview of the events that led to the pollution of the river's water is succinct and energetic. Her collage illustrations, although exciting to explore, are very busy and might distract many readers from finishing the book. The small cartoon frogs border the illustrations, offering commentary on the story, hinder the overall effect of the book. The book contains almost too much information to be absorbed in one sitting. Science teachers will find that this book will encourage students to explore aspects of living machines or bioassay tanks—tanks of the kind John Todd used to clean the thirty-three poisons from the waters of the Chattanooga River.

224   Bash, Barbara. *Ancient Ones: The World of the Old Growth Douglas Fir*. Illus. by author. Sierra Club, 1994. ISBN 0-87156-561-7. Representational. Watercolors. Nonfiction. Trees—Douglas Firs. Forest Ecology. Botany. Life Sciences.

In the silent forest the air is moist and the forest floor is covered with fallen needles, which decompose and feed the soil. It is here that a tree grows to majestic heights. Upon closer inspection, one might hear the skittering of tiny feet and see a flash of life as a small bird flies to nest in the protective branches of the ancient one—the old-growth Douglas fir tree. Barbara Bash has created an enticing tribute to the noble trees that support an amazing amount of animal life. Capturing the tiny life forms that depend on the Douglas fir for life, Bash's watercolor illustrations vividly depict the tree's lasting endurance and inspire respect for the ancient one growing silently in the forest. This is a title from

Bash's Tree Tales series published by Sierra Club. Use the title as part of a life cycle study or to explore the wondrous contributions trees make to the environment.

225   Bash, Barbara. *Desert Giant: The World of the Saguaro Cactus.* Illus. by author. Sierra Club, 1989. ISBN 0-316-08301-1. Representational. Watercolors. Nonfiction. Habitats—Deserts. Cacti. Plant Groups. Botany. Life Sciences.

Author and illustrator Barbara Bash's Tree Tales series is sure to enhance any library or classroom collection. This tree tale features the magnificent saguaro cactus, native to desert environments in the southwestern United States and Mexico. The cactus grows to be over fifty feet tall and supports many animals in the desert. The saguaro cactus begins life as a small seedling. Most seedlings die, but the few that survive take over 150 years to mature and to grow the arms for which the saguaro cactus is so famous. During its lifetime the cactus is home to many animals who build nests inside its trunk. The white blossoms that in May appear and are treats for birds, bats, and people. After the birds have fertilized the blossoms, the blooms wither and dry; fruit forms at the base of the flower. At harvest time each year the Tohono O'odham Indians pick the fruit and make jams, syrups, and wine. The text and illustrations are thoroughly researched, making this title a reliable source for study purposes. Use this title with Bash's other Tree Tales or as a selection for a desert habitat unit. Pair with Diane Siebert's *Mojave* (Crowell, 1989), an affecting poem inspired by the beautiful Mojave desert in California and Richard E. Albert's *Alejandro's Gift* (Chronicle, 1994), a story about an elderly man and his desert animal friends.

226   Bash, Barbara. *In the Heart of the Village: The World of the Indian Banyan.* Illus. by author. Sierra Club, 1996. ISBN 0-87156-575-7. Representational. Watercolors. Nonfiction. Trees—Banyan Tree. India. Plant Groups. Botany. Life Sciences.

From Barbara Bash, a tree tale about the banyan tree in India. In the heart of the village stands a tree with so many trunks, it seems to be a forest. Stretching for acres, the banyan tree serves as a gathering place for the villagers to meet for social and economic reasons. The leaves form a canopy under which villagers meet to take refuge from the heat of the sun. From a single trunk in the center, branches extend out and hang toward the earth. Eventually the branches take root and form other trunks. New branches, using the new trunks, follow suit and this is how the banyan tree becomes a forest. The banyan tree has several names, among them Grandfather Tree because of the many generations of trunks that spread outward from the main trunk; it is also known as Many-

Footed One because of the numerous trunks that make up the tree. Bash opens the book with a legend from Indian culture about the ancient beliefs surrounding the tree. Encourage students to explore other aspects of Indian culture or other trees that play pivotal roles in communal life. Pair with folktales from India, some ideas are *The Gifts of Wali Dad: A Tae from India* (Macmillan, 1995) by Aaron Shepard and *One Grain of Rice: A Mathematical Folktale* (Scholastic, 1997) by Demi.

227   Bash, Barbara. *Shadows of the Night: The Hidden World of the Little Brown Bat.* Illus. by author. Sierra Club, 1993. ISBN 0–971–56–562–5. Representational. Watercolors. Nonfiction. Bats. Nocturnal Animals. Mammals, Flying. Zoology. Life Sciences.

The little brown bat is one the most misunderstood mammals in the world. Subject to myth, the little brown bat is often taken for granted, or worse, harmed because humans fail to recognize the contribution the bats make to nature and society. Follow a brown bat through one year of its life and learn about its nesting, sleeping, and eating patterns. Barbara Bash's exploration of this complex and often misunderstood creature is thoroughly researched and presented in a lively and entertaining fashion. The detailed watercolor illustrations take the reader directly to the hidden world of the little brown bat and allow for a close-up examination of the bat's nocturnal world. Bash's tight prose conveys a plethora of information within the small format of a picture book. The text ends with additional information about other bat species and with tips for people who have limited experience with the gracious and useful creatures of the night. *Stellaluna* (Harcourt Brace, 1993) by Janelle Cannon is an anthropomorphic tale of a lost bat. Read this title to your students and generate discussion about bats in literature. *The Elephant's Wrestling Match* (Dutton, 1992) by Judy Sierra) and *A Promise to the Sun: An African Story* (Little, Brown, 1992) by Tololwa Mollel are two folktales about bats.

228   Bash, Barbara. *Tree of Life: The World of the African Baobab.* Illus. by author. Sierra Club, 1989. ISBN. Representational. Watercolors. Nonfiction. Trees—Baobab Tree. Habitats—Savannas. Plant Groups. Botany. Life Sciences.

Barbara Bash's Tree Tales series invites readers to enter the exciting world of trees famous for the pivotal part they play in many cultures. This Tree Tale features the baobab tree, which is scattered across the savannas of Africa. Baobab trees have gnarled branches that resemble roots. According to the !Kung Bushmen, a great spirit once gave each animal who inhabited earth a tree to plant. Lazy hyena arrived last and was given the baobab to plant. Careless as well as slow, hyena planted the tree upside down, and this is why the baobab branches look like roots. Baobabs live to be over 1000 years old and are forty feet wide and sixty feet tall! These impressive trees are leafless for most of the year, but they sprout leaves and delicate flowers that attract birds and bees. Like many other trees, the baobab is home to countless life forms that use the massive trunk and twisted branches to build nests. Bash's watercolor illustrations are finely detailed, making the most use of her talent.

229   Bash, Barbara. *Urban Roosts: Where Birds Nest in the City.* Illus. by author. Sierra Club, 1990. ISBN 0–316–08306–2. Representational. Watercolors. Nonfiction. Birds. Ornithology. Zoology. Life Sciences.

This picture book is a result of Barbara Bash's fascination with the resilient birds that manage to peck out an existence in the glass and cement buildings of an urban setting. Inspired by the adaptable birds that survive in urban environments, Bash spent one year examining the many places birds roost in cities. Her adventures took her to bridges, window ledges, statues, and churches, where she found birds nesting in the most unusual nooks and crannies. Each illustration includes an enlarged inset with details of the nests birds build. Very dependable, this title is an excellent choice for students interested in an unusual aspect of birds. As with her other titles for Sierra Club, Bash's tight prose conveys a wealth of information. *Urban Roosts* will inspire students to step outside to see if they can discover their own bird dwellings.

230   Bernhard, Emery. *Dragonfly.* Illus. by Durga Bernhard. Holiday House, 1993. ISBN 0–8234–1033–1. Expressionism. Gouache. Nonfiction. Insects—Dragonflies. Entomology. Zoology. Life Sciences.

An in-depth look at one of the most beautiful insects: the dragonfly. Dragonflies were present on the earth 100 million years ago. The oddly beautiful insects were flying around before dinosaurs, making them one of the earliest life forms. Despite their fierce name, dragonflies are very beneficial to humans because they control the insect population by killing stinging insects. The text is rounded and ranges from historical aspects of the insect to physical traits to feeding habits to folklore about the dragonfly. Bright gouache illustrations of the several types of dragonflies with an inset of magnified sections of the insect, make this title suitable for an introduction to a unit on insects.

231   Brandenburg, Jim. *An American Safari: Adventures on the North American Prairie.* Photographs by author. Walker & Company, 1995. ISBN 0–8027–8320–1. Representational. Photographs. Nonfiction. Prairie Animals. Habitats—Prairies. Ecology. Life Sciences.

Jim Brandenburg, renowned for his incredible wildlife photography, returns to the prairie of his youth. In a series of full-color photographs, the fauna and wildlife of the vast prairie ecosystem unfold. Unfortunately, personal memories of his career in photography bog down the narrative, taking some of the effectiveness away from the text. Despite the impediment of his personal experiences, the information about prairie ecology is fascinating. Brandenburg's photography is stunning even if his writing lacks punch. It is evident that Brandenburg studies his subject thoroughly before taking his camera from his case. Any faults in the text are rectified by the live action shots of the prairie ecosystem.

232   Brandenburg, Jim. *To the Top of the World: Adventures with Arctic Wolves.* Photographs by author. Walker and Company, 1993. ISBN 0–8027–8219–1. Representational. Photographs. Nonfiction. Wolves. Arctic Region. Zoology. Life Sciences.

Wildlife photographer Jim Brandenburg spent one exciting summer with a pack of wolves on the remote Ellesmere Island, located near the Arctic Circle. Because of lack of contact with humans, the wolves were not afraid of Brandenburg, and this afforded him many opportunities: The birth of a litter of pups and a stampede of musk oxen are just a few of the glimpses of wolf behavior never before photographed. This book is a photographic diary of Brandenburg's time spent among the legendary white wolves. This photojournal, although weighted with text, is worth perusing for the stunning full-color photographs. Each photograph has a caption explaining what Brandenburg intended to capture with his lens. A fine example of a photo essay.

233   Cherry, Lynne. *A River Ran Wild: An Environmental History.* Illus. by author. Harcourt Brace, 1992. ISBN 0–15–200542–0. Impressionism. Water-colors. Nonfiction. Rivers—Nashua. Environmental Protection. Pollution. Earth Sciences. Clean Water Act. Pollution. Water.

Lynne Cherry's moving tribute to Marion Stoddart's and the Nashua Indians' fight to clean up the Nashua River in Massachusetts. Cherry's illustrations are complex and warrant thorough exploration. Detailed borders with objects and scenes of passing years mark the history of the polluting as well as the revitalizing of the Nashua River. Although Cherry's text flows smoothly, it is the rich illustrations that convey the historical aspects of the story. Known for her research, Cherry shines in a stunning tale of humankind's influence on nature—both destruction and repair. This book has many possibilities: Springboard into other environmental issues with this book or use the illustrations as part of a history unit on Native Americans or as an outline of United States history. Lynne Cherry is also the author of *The Dragon and the*

Unicorn (Harcourt Brace, 1995), a literary fairy tale about conserving natural resources.

234   Cherry, Lynne. *The Great Kapok Tree.* Illus. by author. Harcourt Brace, 1990. ISBN 0-15-200520-X. Representational. Mixed Media. Fiction. Habitats—Rain Forests. Environmental Protection. Human Influence on Nature. Ecology. Earth Sciences.

In a lush, dense rainforest a man is chopping down a great Kapok tree. The tree is tough, and the man grows tired in the heat of the day. While lying at rest in the moist darkness of the rainforest, he dreams that the animals that call the Kapok tree home are telling him to spare the tree. When he wakes, he looks upon the trees, animals, and insects of the forest with new eyes. Lynne Cherry's story, though fiction, conveys a timely message about the effects of tree desecration in the important ecosystems of the world's rainforests. "What happens tomorrow depends on what you do today." The evocative illustrations, as lush and vibrant as rainforests, enhance the story; maps identifying existing rainforests grace the endpapers and provide additional information about rainforest habitats. When used with other rainforest titles, this book makes an interesting contribution to the study of ecology for its unique approach.

235   Cutchins, Judy, and Ginny Johnston. *Are Those Animals Real: How Museums Prepare Wildlife Exhibits.* Photographs. Morrow, 1995. ISBN 0-688-12854-8. Representational. Photographs. Nonfiction. Museums. Wildlife Exhibits. Zoology. Life Sciences.

Have you ever visited a museum and wondered, "Are those animals real?" This book takes you behind the scenes to watch the process used by museum staff to prepare a wildlife exhibit. Full-color photographs of each stage of the process—from the initial design through production, creation, and completed display—are included. Shot from unique angles, the photographs reveal the details involved in the process. The book is a worthwhile read for anyone interested in museum exhibits. Use it with students preparing to visit a museum; they will then be able to answer the question most asked by visitors to museums, "Are those animals real?"

236   Dunphy, Madeline. *Here is the Southwestern Desert.* Illus. by Anne Coe. Hyperion, 1995. ISBN 0-7868-0049-6. Representational. Acrylics. Poetry. Habitats—Deserts. Natural History. Ecology. Earth Sciences.

A cumulative poem about the Sonoran Desert in the American Southwest. As the poem builds, Dunphy adds the animals and sights found in a desert environment to create an introduction to desert ecology. Despite the poetry format, Dunphy introduces the coyote and the roadrunner as well as many other animals that live in a desert habitat. Coe's vivid three-quarter-page illustrations are finely detailed and enhance the text, giving substance to the light verse. The book cannot stand alone because it lacks additional information about the animals and desert featured in the book, but it will make a nice addition to other books about desert ecology. Madeline Dunphy has written two other books in this series *Here is the Arctic Winter* (Hyperion, 1993) and *Here is the Tropical Rainforest.* (Hyperion, 1994).

237   Esbensen, Barbara Juster. *Great Northern Diver: The Loon.* Illus. by Mary Barrett Brown. Little, Brown, 1990. ISBN 0-316-24954-8. Representational. Watercolors. Nonfiction. Birds—Loons. Ornithology. Zoology. Life Sciences.

The loon, marked with unique white dots, checks, and strips on a black body, is the most primitive bird species known to exist in the United States. After winters in warmer climates along the coast, loons return to the same northern lake to mate. Loons have four distinguishing calls that echo across water, pleasing all who hear the majestic cry. Brown's enticing watercolor paintings capture the loon in many of its most elusive activities: mating and laying eggs. Together Esbensen and Brown create a book that extends beyond mere fact but never relies on sentiment to introduce one of America's most intriguing birds. This book would fit nicely in a unit about migrating birds or in a study of northern territories in the United States.

238   Esbensen, Barbara Juster. *Tiger with Wings: The Great Horned Owl.* Illus. by Mary Barrett Brown. Orchard, 1991. ISBN 0-531-05940-5. Representational. Watercolors. Nonfiction. Birds—Great Horned Owl. Ornithology. Zoology. Life Sciences.

Resembling a tiger with wings, the great horned owl glides through the night air seeking prey. With razor-sharp talons, the great horned owl swoops down from the air and strikes. With grace and dignity, she lifts into the night skies to return to feed her babies. Esbensen's text is thoroughly researched, covering the bird's behavior, habits, and habitat. Although the text is long for a picture book format, Esbensen's crisp writing is strong, particularly for one topic. The arrangement of the text in conjunction with the realistic pencil drawings is inviting and will encourage the reader to explore further about one of nature's most majestic creatures. This book is strong and can stand alone or be used along with other titles to explore owls, birds or other nocturnal animals.

239   Fisher, Leonard Everett. *Marie Curie.* Illus. by author. Macmillan, 1994. ISBN 0–02–735375–3. Expressionism. Acrylics. Biography. Curie, Marie (1867–1934). Women—Biography. Scientists.

A biography of Marie Curie, the first woman professor at the Sorbonne, replacing her husband, after his tragic death. Marie Curie devoted her life to science, winning the Noble prize in both chemistry and physics. Curie discovered polonium and radium, isolating pure radium for the first time in 1902. Perhaps her most notable achievement is her exploration of uranium rays and coining the term radioactivity. Curie was from a family that placed education first, which spurred her in her studies. At age twenty-four, Marie Curie was accepted to the University of Paris, the first woman to be accepted at the prestigious school. In his signature style, Fisher again offers up a picture book worthy of its subject. His stark black-and-white paintings are a haunting tribute to the brilliant Marie Curie.

240   George, Jean Craighead. *Everglades.* Illus. by Wendell Minor. Harper-Collins, 1995. ISBN 0–06–021229–2. Representational. Watercolors. Fiction. Everglades (Florida). Environmental Protection. Human Influence on Nature. Earth Sciences.

In the southeastern United States in the state of Florida lies an ecosystem unlike any other in the world: the Everglades. Jean Craighead George's storyteller travels through the river that is the Everglades and answers the questions of his young passengers. The device imparts abundant information in a lyrical voice that makes the subject exciting. The story of the beginnings and the slow deterioration of the Everglades will fascinate readers if the book is read aloud because of the powerful voice of Craighead George. The lush, detailed paintings by Wendell Minor capture the multitude of life forms that depend on the Everglades for their existence. Generate discussion with your students about America's deteriorating landscape and develop actions to contribute to the conservation of our land. Use this book with *Chattanooga Sludge* (Harcourt Brace, 1996) by Molly Bang and *A River Ran Wild: An Environmental History* (Harcourt Brace, 1992) by Lynne Cherry, two other books about polluted rivers in America.

241   Gibbons, Gail. *Frogs.* Illus. by author. Holiday House, 1993. ISBN 0–8234–1052–8. Cartoon Art. Watercolors. Nonfiction. Amphibians—Frogs. Herpetology. Zoology. Life Sciences.

From egg to tadpole to mature frog, the life of one of 3,800 types of frogs known to exist is outlined by Gibbons. The information is thorough and includes little tidbits about frogs not commonly known. At the end of the text,

Gibbons includes a double-page spread that outlines the differences between frogs and toads—two amphibians frequently mistaken for each other. Gibbons's strong writing enhances her cartoon-style illustrations, which might easily be dismissed because of their simplicity. The illustrations, though simple, are detailed, and Gibbons uses labels to point out significant areas of interest on the pages. Some readers might find the labels distracting, but others will find that the labels enhance the illustrations. Use this title as part of a unit on amphibians or to coincide with studies of life cycles.

242   Gibbons, Gail. *Nature's Green Umbrella: Tropical Rain Forests.* Illus. by author. Morrow, 1994. ISBN 0–688–12353–8. Cartoon Art. Watercolors. Nonfiction. Habitats—Rainforests. Human Influence on Nature. Ecology. Earth Sciences.

Rainforests cover approximately seven percent of the land mass in the world today. Greedy people concerned with so-called progress and profit are destroying rainforests at an alarming rate. Over half the species in the world, from animals to plants to insects, make rainforests their home. Gail Gibbons's book introduces just a few of these creatures. The simple cartoon-style illustrations are jammed with information and open the door to an understanding of the extensive life forms found in the wet, green environment of the rainforest. The pages are graced with borders of flowers indigenous to rainforest ecosystems. Gibbons has written and illustrated many titles for younger children. Like many of her other titles, this book has a tone for younger children, but the text is full of vital information about the rainforest ecosystems. If used as a springboard into other environmental topics, this book is challenging.

243   Gibbons, Gail. *Wolves.* Illus. by author. Holiday House, 1994. ISBN 0–8234–1127–3. Cartoon Art. Watercolors. Nonfiction. Wolves. Zoology. Life Sciences.

An informative book that dispels myths about the hauntingly beautiful gray wolves that live in the territories of North America. Gray wolves, also called timber wolves, run in packs, hunt in packs, and protect each other. Gail Gibbons has arranged a plethora of information about wolves within the tight confines of a picture book format. She includes a list of curious and unusual facts and legends about wolves. Her cartoon-style art might have some people closing the book and dismissing it as a title for elementary children. The curious person will explore this title or any of Gail Gibbons's carefully researched books and come to appreciate the dedication and accuracy to be found in each one. Pair with *To the Top of the World: Adventures with Arctic Wolves* (Walker & Company, 1993) by Jim Brandenburg and *The Wolves* (Dial, 1996) by Brian J. Heinz. Generate discussion about the wolves as they appear in legends using the stories of *The Three Little Pigs* and *Little Red Riding Hood.* John Scieszka is responsible for *The True Story of the Three Little Pigs* (Viking, 1989), which relates the wolf's side the story, offering an opportunity for lively debate with your students.

244   Goodman, Susan E. *Unseen Rainbows, Silent Songs: The World Beyond Human Senses.* Illus. by Beverly Duncan. Atheneum, 1995. ISBN 0–689–31892–8. Representational. Watercolors. Nonfiction. Sense and Sensation. Animal Physiology. Zoology. Life Sciences.

Beyond human senses is a world of sounds, sights, and smells that make up the communication of animals and insects. It is a world with extrasensory perceptions that warn of danger, hint at food sources, and reveal a thousand odors that remain meaningless to humans. Written in second-person narration, this text actively involves the reader by making comparisons between humans and animals. Goodman's strong writing inspires experimentation; readers will pause to try many of Goodman's examples. Second-person narration, though elsewhere rarely used, is highly effective in this book. The watercolor illustrations are pleasing but do not extend or draw attention from the text.

245   Henderson, Douglas. *Dinosaur Tree.* Illus. by author. Bradbury Press, 1994. ISBN 0–02–743547–4. Representational. Gouache. Nonfiction. Trees, Fossils. Dinosaurs, Fossils. Paleontology. Geology. Earth Sciences.

Enticing story of the life cycle of a conifer tree in the Triassic era. A small seed from a parent conifer tree drifts to the earth and is nurtured by the soil. For 500 years, the conifer survives in the continent known as Pangaea. When a windstorm pulls the fragile roots from the soil, the tree's real story begins to unfold. The story of the tree is paralleled with the natural history of the dinosaurs. Detailed watercolor illustrations bring the story to startling life. Told in chapters marked by the passage of time, Douglas Henderson has created a visual feast that will appeal to dinosaur fans as well as to students interested in plant fossils. The text is thoroughly researched, and the resolution of the tree's story as a fossil in the Petrified Forest National Park in Arizona will delight students and teachers.

246   Johnson, Sylvia A. *Raptor Rescue: An Eagle Flies Free.* Photographs by Ron Winch. Dutton, 1995. ISBN 0–525–45301–6. Representational. Photographs. Nonfiction. Birds—Birds of Prey—Eagles. Wildlife Rescue. Life Sciences.

A wounded bald eagle is discovered in a ditch by a conservation worker in Minnesota. Unable to fly, the bird is starving and close to death because it cannot capture and kill prey for sustenance. The worker takes the bird to the Gabbert Raptor Center at the University of Minnesota, where conservation workers begin a process to heal the bird. The center is a nonprofit organization that has helped to rehabilitate and return to nature over 600 raptors and birds of prey. A collection of engaging photographs follow the bird's plight from its rescue to surgery to recovery and eventual release to once again fly free. The text is highly readable and full of fascinating facts about wildlife rescue. A glossary includes further information about raptors. Several photographs show detailed aspects of veterinary careers, making this book appropriate for a study of occupations. *The Book of Eagles* (Lothrop, Lee & Shepard) by Helen Roney Sattler is a useful title for exploring eagles. *Eagle Dreams* (Philomel, 1994) by Sheryl McFarlane is a fictional story of one eagle's rescue. *Spotted Eagle and Black Crow* (Holiday House, 1993) by Emery Bernhard is a Lakota legend about eagles.

247   Jordan, Martin and Tanis. *Angel Falls: A South American Journey.* Illus. by Martin Jordan. Kingfisher, 1995. ISBN 1–85697–541–X. Representational. Oils. Nonfiction. Waterfalls. Animals—Jungle. Hydrologic Sciences. Life Sciences.

Personal account of the author's journey to Venezuela to visit Angel Falls, the highest waterfall in the world. Martin Jordan's lush oil paintings recreate the unique sights the Martins experienced during their journey up Auyantepui, the summit from which Angel Falls descends. Full-color illustrations recreate the breathtaking adventure in the heart of the Venezuelan highlands. Detailed paintings of the animals and plants encountered during their journey make this book a treat for any person with a sense of adventure. Elegant prose relates the sights, sounds, and smells of a jungle deep in the heart of South America without leaning toward sentimentality, a factor often fatal to many personal narratives with a science base. The book includes a glossary of animals indigenous to the Angel Falls region. *Niagara Falls: Nature's Wonder* (Holiday House, 1996) by Leonard Everett Fisher is an ideal companion book.

248   Jordan, Martin and Tanis. *Journey of the Red Eyed Tree Frog.* Illus. by Martin Jordan. Green Tiger Press, 1991. ISBN 0–671–76903–0. Representational. Oils. Fiction. Animals—Rainforests. Amazon River Valley. Zoology. Life Sciences.

A fantasy about a red-eyed tree frog who journeys deep into the Amazon River Valley region in search of the wise Oracle Toad. People have arrived in the valley and have begun to burn acres of forest every day. Along the way, the red-eyed tree frog encounters many animals indigenous to the Amazon River Valley. Included are harpy eagles, uakaris, and howler monkeys. The story is anthropomorphic, but this does not take away from the timely message buried in the fantasy storyline. The oil paintings are exquisite; up-close examination makes this book suitable for young adults. If used with other rainforest information, this book offers a unique angle on environmental protection and habitat conservation.

249   Kroll, Virginia. *Sweet Magnolia.* Illus. by Laura Jacques. Charlesbridge, 1995. ISBN 0-88106-415-7. Representational. Acrylics. Fiction. Habitats— Bayous. Wildlife Preservation. Life Sciences.

When Denise goes to visit her grandmother, a wildlife rehabilitator in the Louisiana Bayou, she learns to care for and nurture injured wildlife. Denise's visit is filled with many Cajun traditions common to Louisiana culture, including Zydeco music, sweet magnolia flowers, and spicy jambalaya stew. When Denise finds an injured bunting bird, she nurses it back to health with her grandmother's help. When the time comes to let the bird return to nature, Denise refuses because she has become attached. Her grandmother helps Denise see the value of freedom for the bird over captivity in a cage. The story is light and simple to comprehend. The topic, wildlife preservation, is rare in picture books and makes up in intent what it lacks in depth. The hanging moss, magnolia flowers, croaking frogs, and marshy water of the Louisiana Bayou come to life in Laura Jacques's detailed acrylic paintings. The illustrations alone make this a book worth perusing.

250   Lasky, Kathryn. *The Librarian Who Measured the Earth.* Illus. by Kevin Hawkes. Little, Brown, 1994. ISBN 0-316-51526-4. Expressionism. Acrylics. Biography. Eratosthenes. Greek Geographers. Geography, Ancient. Astronomy.

An engaging illustrated biography about Eratosthenes, the Greek geographer who measured the circumference of the earth 2000 years ago. With tools such as camels and calculations of shadows, Eratosthenes managed to measure the earth's surface with a reading that was within 200 miles as determined by modern methods. Kevin Hawkes's lively paintings trace the life of Eratosthenes from his birth through his years as librarian at Alexandria to his landmark book *Geographica*, the first geography book written. Hawkes incorporates the methods and applications Eratosthenes used when he measured the earth, making the task the geographer tackled even more miraculous. Lasky based her text on the few facts known about Eratosthenes to create a stunning example of how biography in picture book format should be written. Eratosthenes's natural curiosity was the impetus to figure out the size of the earth, and this book will inspire students to employ their own curiosity to explore a few of life's mysteries. Pair with *Starry Messenger* (Farrar, Straus & Giroux, 1996) by Peter Sis, another exquisitely illustrated book about a famous scientist, Galileo.

251   Lauber, Patricia. *Living with Dinosaurs.* Illus. by Douglas Henderson. Bradbury Press, 1991. ISBN 0–02–754521–0. Representational. Gouache. Non-fiction. Dinosaurs. Paleontology. Geology. Earth Sciences.

Picture yourself standing on a beach 75 million years ago. What would you see? hear? smell? Patricia Lauber uses second-person point of view to take readers back 75 million years to the prehistoric era when dinosaurs still walked the earth and Montana had a seashore. The challenging text is full of interesting facts about reptiles, plants, and geographic details of a world startlingly different form the one we know. Lauber's use of language is spirited; the sights and sounds of a time long gone come vividly to life. Douglas Henderson's exquisite watercolor illustrations do justice to the strong text. The concluding pages are designed to incite young readers to apply scientific facts to solve a few prehistoric mysteries on their own. The entire design of the book is strong and includes captions for illustrations, a glossary, and a pronunciation guide. *Living with Dinosaurs* is an ideal title to add to your dinosaur section or a great title to purchase to build a collection.

252   Lerner, Carol. *Backyard Birds of Winter.* Illus. by author. Morrow, 1994. ISBN 0–688–12819–X. Representational. Watercolors. Nonfiction. Birds. Ornithology. Zoology. Life Sciences.

An incredible number of people bird-watch as a hobby, putting bird feeders in their yards to attract birds. This book by naturalist Carol Lerner is a perfect handbook to use while pursuing this hobby. Winter is the best season to bird-watch because the birds are hungry and to survive depend on the feed provided by humans. The leaves of summer have fallen from the trees, giving bird-watchers ample opportunity to examine the feathered creatures. Carol Lerner has compiled information on forty species commonly found in North America and arranged the information in an enticing display. Each bird is represented in a full-color to-scale illustration with facts about each species, including food preferences and distinguishing features. Teachers will find that this book attracts students without encouragement. An interesting companion title is *When Birds Could Talk and Bats Could Sing* (Scholastic, 1996) by Virginia Hamilton, which is a collection of African American folktales about birds and bats. *The Magpie's Nest* (Clarion, 1995) by Joanna Foster is an English folktale, which explains why birds build nests in different ways. Lerner also wrote and illustrated *Backyard Birds of Summer* (Morrow, 1996).

253   Lerner, Carol. *Cactus.* Illus. by author. Morrow, 1992. ISBN 0–688–09637–9. Representational. Watercolors. Nonfiction. Cacti. Plant Groups. Botany. Earth Sciences.

Carol Lerner, respected naturalist, explores the distinctive group of plants known as cacti. With over 1500 species, the common characteristics of cacti set the species apart from all other plants. The book is heavy with text and has fewer illustrations than the standard picture book; however, Lerner's watercolor illustrations are finely detailed and labeled, which makes up for the lack of drawings. The information is concise and presented in an enticing fashion. Warm desert colors draw attention to the cover of the book. Carol Lerner's tribute to the enduring cacti family can serve as a pivotal book in a botany collection.

254   Lesser, Carolyn. *Great Crystal Bear.* Illus. by William Noonan. Harcourt Brace, 1996. ISBN 0–15–200667–2. Impressionism. Watercolors/Water Soluble Dyes. Fiction. Mammals—Polar Bears. Arctic Region. Zoology. Life Sciences.

Journey to the far north and enter the habitat of one of nature's fiercest beasts: The polar bear. Follow a great polar bear across the frozen tundra as he hunts seals for food, frolics with other bears, and looks for a mate. Polar bears are nature's most resilient creatures, and Lesser and Noonan have paid homage to the great beast in a lyrical and visual feast. Lesser's text, though based on scientific fact, wavers to the poetic side. The illustrations are set against the frozen tundra of the Arctic. This title makes a nice introduction to a study of arctic animals or arctic regions, but the absence of author or artist notes makes the title less reliable than other titles about polar bears or the arctic regions. Lesser hints at Inuit legends about polar bears but fails to cite sources, which would make this a stronger book for the classroom.

255   Locker, Thomas. *Sky Tree: Science through Art.* Illus. by author. HarperCollins, 1995. ISBN 0–06–024883–1. Representational. Oils. Nonfiction. Trees. Seasons. Botany. Earth Sciences.

A series of exquisite oil paintings focusing on the effects of seasonal changes on a lone tree standing on a hill. Sprinkled stars on the boughs, scattered falling leaves and mysterious mists play around the tree trunk as the ravages of time and weather transform the tree from summer to autumn to winter to spring. Each illustration is accompanied by lyrical observations of the passage of time and its effects on the tree. A brief question challenges the reader to use scientific information to describe the changes in the tree and the effect each painting has on emotion. This is a truly outstanding book that can be enjoyed simply for its design and beauty or appreciated as a learning tool by readers who apply scientific data to examine the illustrations. Use with Barbara Bash's books from her Tree Tales series.

256   Long, Matthew, and Thomas Long. *Any Bear Can Wear Glasses: The Spectacled Bear and Other Curious Creatures.* Illus. by Sylvia Long. Chronicle Books, 1995. ISBN 0-8118-0809-2. Cartoon Art. Watercolors/Pen and Ink. Nonfiction. Endangered Species. Animal Conservation. Zoology. Life Sciences.

An engaging and informative book about endangered animals from all around the world. The animals explored have unusual names such as the masked duck and the ringtail cat. Each entry introduces the animals by comparing them to other animals of the same species in a play of words. For example: "Any rabbit can wear shoes but there's only one snowshoe hare." Despite the playful approach, the book contains concise information about each animal and why it is registered on the endangered animals list. The humorous caricatures will appeal to students, who will enjoy the playful comparisons. Teachers might be apt to disregard the book, but are encouraged to explore the title thoroughly because the information is well rounded and presented in a format that will encourage students to explore animal preservation and natural history. A glossary and maps of each endangered animal's habitat are an added bonus. *V is for Vanishing: An Alphabet of Endangered Animals* (HarperCollins, 1994) by Patricia Mullins includes information about twenty-five species facing extinction and is an ideal companion title.

257   Lucht, Irmgard. *The Red Poppy.* Illus. by author. Hyperion, 1994. ISBN 0-7868-0055-0. Representational. Acrylics. Nonfiction. Flowers—Poppies. Life Cycles. Botany. Life Sciences.

An exploration of a red poppy growing wild in a field of rye. Poppies bloom for one day, and in this one day a miracle of life occurs. The information about the poppy is presented in a straightforward, enlightening fashion. The bright oil paintings dominated by the red petals of the poppy are exquisite. Stunning panel illustrations create a window on the natural world, bringing an abandoned field to brilliant life. The illustrations were created by studying poppies under a binocular microscope; thus you may want to use this book to illustrate to students the fascinating microscopic world all around us. Lucht included a note that outlines the inspiration that led to this book—a story as incredible as the book itself. Teachers and librarians will eagerly await another effort from Irmgard Lucht.

258   Mason, Cherie. *Wild Fox: A True Story.* Illus. by Jo Ellen McAllister Stammen. Down East, 1993. ISBN 0–89272–319–X. Representational. Pastels. Nonfiction. Foxes. Wildlife Preservation. Zoology. Life Sciences.

This personal account of one woman's experience with a wounded fox and her efforts to heal the wild animal will inspire everyone. Encouraged by the fox's daily visits, the author researches foxes to learn how to approach the wounded animal and help it recover and return to nature. The first-person narrative follows the author's encounter with the fox from initial visit through recovery. The personable account allows for easy discussion with students about their experiences with wildlife. The stunning full-color double-page illustration on the title page will haunt anyone who has come face to face with a wild animal that has wandered from nature into a quiet neighborhood. The author ends on a note about French folklore and introduces the term "Reynard" (French for fox), which encourages exploration of foxes in a literary aspect. The author's style also makes *Wild Fox* a perfect example to use for exploring nature writing. Two companion folktales about foxes are *Moon Rope: Un Lazo a la Luna: A Peruvian Folktale* (Harcourt Brace, 1992) by Lois Ehlert and *Reynard the Fox* (Tambourine, 1991) by Selina Hastings.

259   Micucci, Charles. *The Life and Times of the Apple.* Illus. by author. Orchard, 1992. ISBN 0–531–05939–1. Representational. Watercolors. Nonfiction. Apples. Fruits. Botany. Life Sciences.

An informational book about the most popular fruit tree in the world. Over 30 million apples trees, which produce 200 million bushels of apples, grow in the United States. This might explain why apple pie is as American as baseball. The information is arranged in an enticing format, with many carefully labeled vignette illustrations. The arrangement of the book is very appealing; chapters covering the life cycle, history, growing techniques, varieties, and folklore of the apple are brief but packed with information. Perhaps the most fascinating fact is that the grafting process, not the apple seed, allows apple growers to determine the type of apple that grows on a tree. The complete design of the book makes it highly adaptable for a science classroom. Pair folk literature about apples with *Johnny Appleseed* (Morrow, 1988) by Steven Kellogg and *William Tell* (Abrams, 1991) by Margaret Early.

260   Micucci, Charles. *The Life and Times of the Honeybee.* Illus. by author. Ticknor & Fields, 1995. ISBN 0–395–65968–X. Representational. Watercolors. Nonfiction. Insects—Bees. Entomology. Zoology. Life Sciences.

An informative tribute to honeybees, this book covers the life cycle of the insect, honey production, and other uses of the busy work of honey bees.

Brought to the forefront are many aspects of the honeybee's lifecycle such as the bee dance, which is used among bees to communicate the location of flowers. Charles Miucci's detailed illustrations are not the standard picture book double-page spread. Instead the author incorporates small vignettes with facts about honeybees and integrates them into the illustrations in the fashion of a textbook. This approach does not push against the overall effect but is instead interactive. The soft watercolor illustrations are thoroughly researched, making this book a dependable source for an insect unit. Explore bee folklore with Dalia Hardof Renberg's Jewish folktale *King Solomon and the Bee* (HarperCollins, 1994), Djemma Bider's Armenia folktale *A Drop of Honey* (Simon & Schuster, 1989), and Jan Freeman Long's Japanese folktale *The Bee and the Dream* (Dutton, 1996). Buzzzzzz!

261   Moroney, Lynn. *Moontellers: Myths of the Moon From Around the World.* Illus. by Greg Shed. Northland, 1995. ISBN 0-87358-601-8. Impressionism. Oils/Colored Pencil. Mythology. Moon—Folklore. Astronomy.

A collection of moon myths from around the world. Lynn Moroney's enchanting verses explore the myths of eleven cultures. The author follows with facts about how cultures developed the myth. From Polynesia comes the tale of Hina, a girl who walked along a rainbow and came to rest in the night sky. Early Polynesian navigators used the stars and moon to guide them from island to island. As they traveled, the sailors spun moon tales that have been handed down for generations. Each illustration has a full moon with shadings designed to help readers find the moon picture for each myth. Greg Shed's luminous oil paintings will encourage readers of all ages to explore their own night sky for a moon legend of their own. As unusual as it seems, moon myths will inspire students to look at the moon in an scientific manner to answer questions about how the myths developed. The author included source notes and titles for further reading. Companion moon tales include *Moon Mother* (HarperCollins, 1993) by Ed Young, *Moon Rope: Un Lazo a la Luna: A Peruvian Folktale* (Harcourt Brace, 1992) by Lois Ehlert, and *Thirteen Moons on Turtle's Back* (Philomel, 1992) by Joseph Bruchac.

262   Pallotta, Jerry. *The Spice Alphabet Book: Herbs, Spices, and Other Natural Flavors.* Illus. by Leslie Evans. Charlesbridge, 1994. ISBN 0-881106-898-5. Impressionism. Watercolors. Alphabet Book. Spices. Botany. Earth Sciences.

An alphabetical journey of twenty-six herbs, spices, and flavors, some common like ginger and vanilla; others, like zatar and quinine, will be new to many readers. Each entry includes the origin of the spice and recipes featuring the spice or herb. "A is for Anise. Anise is a spice that comes from a seed and tastes like licorice." The alphabet format is enticing for this type of information. The watercolor illustrations are detailed but not outstanding. The glossary invites readers to search pages for hidden spices located on pages outside of their featured letter. All twenty-six spices and herbs are featured on the cover. *The Spice Alphabet Book: Herbs, Spices, and Other Natural Flavors* is worthy of perusing because its topic is unusual for the picture book format. *Onions and Garlic: An Old Tale* (Holiday House, 1996) by Eric A. Kimmel is a Jewish tale about spices.

263   Powell, Consie. *A Bold Carnivore: An Alphabet of Predators.* Illus. by author. Robert Rinehart, 1995. ISBN 1-57098-023-3. Representational. Watercolors. Alphabet Book. Predators. Animals—North America. Zoology. Life Sciences.

A book about twenty-six North American carnivores in an alphabet book format. Brief captions below the outlines tells how the predator lives and how it hunts. For example: "R is for Ringtail, an animal related to raccoons, preys on cactus wren and kangaroo rats." The illustrations show the predators in their natural habitat and are surrounded by smaller illustrations of the animals they prey on. The information is challenging despite the alphabet book format. A glossary includes further information about each predator and lists the names of the prey. If used with other resources, *A Bold Carnivore* becomes a useful introduction to the food chain.

264   Powzyk, Joyce. *Animal Camouflage: A Closer Look.* Illus. by author. Bradbury Press, 1990. ISBN 0-02-774980-0. Representational. Watercolors. Nonfiction. Animal Camouflage. Biology. Life Sciences.

A fascinating exploration of the various applications animals use to camouflage themselves from predators. This title explores coloration, disguise, mimicry, masking, and concealment of the eye. In a note the author explains the conflicting information she uncovered during her research; this note should be considered when using this book. However, despite the conflicting information, the book serves as a suitable introduction to the subject of animal camouflage. The layout of the book is arranged to make the most of the picture book format. The author opens the book by posing a question: "What is animal camouflage?" Brief definitions follow and lead to a series of in-depth examinations of animals who employ camouflage techniques. Powzyk's watercolor illustrations are designed to show each animal in the act of camouflage. Concise, accessible text makes this title appropriate for a biology class exploring animals in their natural habitats, encouraging students to take a closer look at their surroundings to see if they can see animals "in hiding."

265   Robbins, Ken. *Fire: The Elements*. Photographs by author. Holt, 1996. ISBN 0–8050–2293–7. Representational. Photographs. Nonfiction. Elements. Fire. Weather. Atmospheric Sciences. Earth Sciences.

Fire has been a source of mystery and power in many cultures throughout recorded history. This book serves as an outstanding introduction to the many manifestations fire assumes: heat, energy, light, ritual, and uncontrollable danger. Robbins's lyrical text flows smoothly but manages to challenge young readers by questioning previously held beliefs. His approach is an unusual take on exploring the elements; his series is a memorable contribution to science books for young readers. The book makes an ideal springboard into experiments with fire in a controlled classroom environment. Other titles by Ken Robbins in The Elements series include *Water: The Elements* (Holt, 1996), *Earth: The Elements* (Holt, 1995), and *Air: The Elements* (Holt, 1995). Any one of the titles works well alone, or the series may serve for a unit of study about the elements. Have students gather myths about fire, water, earth, and air and then study scientific data to provide explanations as to why cultures may have developed the fear and awe inspired by the elements. Some folktales appropriate to use with The Elements series include *Why the Sun and Moon Live in the Sky* (Lothrop, Lee & Shepard, 1995) by Niki Daly, *Rainbow Crow: A Lenape Tale* (Knopf, 1989) by Nancy Van Laan, *Earth, Fire, Water, Air* (Dutton, 1995) by Mary Hoffman, and *Coyote and the Fire Stick: A Pacific Northwest Indian Tale* (Harcourt Brace, 1996) by Barbara Diamond Goldin.

266   Roop, Peter and Connie (eds.). *Capturing Nature: The Writings and Art of John James Audubon*. Illus. by Rick Farley. Walker & Company, 1993. ISBN 0–8027–8204–3. Representational. Watercolors. Nonfiction. Audubon, John James (1785–1851). Personal Narratives. Ornithology. Zoology. Life Sciences.

A collection of paintings and writings by respected the nineteenth-century naturalist John James Audubon. Connie and Peter Roop have gathered selected writings of Audubon and arranged them in an enticing fashion that will win Audubon new fans. The competent illustrations of Audubon by Rick Farley are unnecessary because the beauty of Audubon's is paintings are the beacon in this book. Students interested in animal extinction and conservation will be surprised that the ideals of preserving the earth began as early as 1803, when Audubon began recording nature in his writing and in his art. This book will work well as an example of scientific writing, for introducing the works of John James Audubon, or as an example of personal narrative as it pertains to education. Pair with *Backyard Birds of Winter* (Morrow, 1994) by Carol Lerner, an exquisite study of birds by a modern naturalist.

267   Siebert, Diane. *Heartland.* Illus. by Wendell Minor. Crowell, 1989. ISBN 0–690–04730–4. Representational. Acrylics. Poetry. Habitats—Prairies. United States—Midwest Region. Geography. Earth Sciences.

Running across the middle of the United States is a patchwork of cornfields, wheat fields, and vast expanses of prairie grass. The land, while outstanding for its beauty, is also the source of food for a nation of people. Expanses of green, brown, and yellow fields, broken by herds of grazing cattle and an occasional prairie dog, are America's heartland. Here dedicated farmers, strong and proud, devote their lives to working the land. In a powerful verse Diane Siebert, a product of midwestern values, celebrates the subtle harmony of the heartland and the people who call the land home. Wendell Minor's captivating paintings are as beautiful as the land itself. Together the two work magic and create a vividly realized work of art. Use *Heartland* to introduce students to the spacious midwestern states of America.

268   Siebert, Diane. *Mojave.* Illus. by Wendell Minor. Crowell, 1989. ISBN 0–690–05655–4. Representational. Acrylics. Poetry. Habitats—Deserts. United States—California, Mojave Desert. Geography. Earth Sciences.

"I am the desert. I am free." So begins Diane's Siebert's mesmerizing tribute to the seemingly endless Mojave Desert in California. Expanses of sun-baked earth give way to rolling hills, where a multitude of life flourishes in an environment of harsh conditions. Darting lizards and slithering snakes thrive in a place where tumbleweeds blow across the earth. Wendell Minor's spectacular paintings add dimension to Siebert's poem, making this book a wonderful introduction to desert habitats. Read aloud, the poem itself will intrigue students and capture their attention. Follow up by having students compare Minor's striking landscape illustrations with photographs of the Mojave Desert.

269   Siebert, Diane. *Sierra.* Illus. by Wendell Minor. HarperCollins, 1991. ISBN 0–06–021639–5. Representational. Acrylics. Poetry. Habitats—Mountain Ranges. United States—California. Geography. Earth Sciences.

Millions of years ago, when the earth was young, a mountain range rose from the surface of the earth and came to be known as the Sierra Nevada. The mountain range, located in California, stands like a sentinel providing shelter for a multitude of plant and animal life. Between the peaks a continuous cycle of life thrives, dependent on the protection of the mountains. Diane Siebert's lyrical poem reverberates with power and celebrates the majesty of evolution. Wendell Minor's stunning acrylic paintings are vividly realized, adding dimension to Siebert's voice. Alone, this title may seem inadequate to the needs of a science teacher, but if used in conjunction with more solid information, *Sierra* will add a evocative touch to the study of land forms.

270   Simon, Seymour. *Stars*. Photographs. Morrow, 1993. ISBN 0–688–05855–8. Representational. Photographs. Nonfiction. Solar System. Astronomy. Stars.

There are few other offerings from nature that surpass the magnificence of a clear night sky splattered with stars. Seymour Simon's journey through the mythical and scientific history of stars will inspire anyone to explore the night sky. Accurate and dependable, this book covers the formation and the fiery death of stars. *Stars* is an exciting examination of the types of stars: periodic, nebulous, and variable, to name a few. Other titles in the Astronomy series include *Galaxies*, *Mars*, *Mercury*, *Neptune*, *Our Solar System*, *Uranus*, and *Venus*. Simon Seymour is the author of more than 100 science book for young readers. His titles are acclaimed by teachers across the country. Dozens of Simon's books have been cited for their outstanding contribution to the field of science. His informative Astronomy series will inspire students to explore the stars with a telescope or from their own backyard on a clear evening. *Exploring Space: Using Seymour Simon's Astrology Books in the Classroom* (Morrow Junior Books, 1994) by Barbara Bourne and Wendy Saul is an indispensable resource for teachers interested in incorporating Simon's books into the curriculum. Encourage students to research the mythology of constellations and then compare the findings with scientific data.

271   Simon, Seymour. *Storms*. Photographs. Morrow, 1993. ISBN 0–688–10546–7. Representational. Photographs. Nonfiction. Weather. Storms. Meteorology. Atmospheric Sciences. Earth Sciences.

A breathtaking study of the atmospheric conditions that lead to thunderstorms, hailstones, tornadoes, and hurricanes. The unpredictability of the weather can often have adverse effects on the environment. The human race is basically at the mercy of the forces of weather, and an understanding of atmospheric processes is beneficial to everyone. The full-color photographs were carefully chosen for their contribution to the text. Other titles in the Earth Science series include *Deserts*, *Earthquakes*, *Icebergs and Glaciers*, *Oceans*, *Weather*, and *Volcanoes*. Simon Seymour is the author of more than 100 science books for younger readers. His titles are acclaimed by teachers across the country. Several titles in the Earth Science series have been cited for their outstanding contribution to the field of science. Together or alone, the titles in this series will add depth to students interested in physical geography.

272   Simon, Seymour. *The Sun.* Photographs. Morrow, 1986. ISBN 0–688–05857–4. Representational. Photographs. Nonfiction. Solar System. The Sun. Astronomy.

The sun, closest star to the earth, furnishes light, heat, and energy to our solar system. The brilliant splendor of the sun is explored in this stunning effort by Seymour Simon. A brief overview of the information packed into this evocative book includes solar energy, solar eclipses, sun spots, and sun mythology. Independently or with other titles from the "Astronomy" series, this book is a must for a unit about the sun, the solar system or the universe. The Astronomy series has garnered awards from American Library Association and the Children's Book Council. Other titles in the series include *Galaxies*, *Mars*, *Mercury*, *Neptune*, *Our Solar System*, *Uranus*, and *Venus*. This book offers endless opportunities for the classroom. *Exploring Space: Using Seymour Simon's Astrology Books in the Classroom* (Morrow Junior Books, 1994) by Barbara Bourne and Wendy Saul is an indispensable resource for teachers interested in incorporating Simon's books into the curriculum. For maximum effect, time the exploration this book with a solar eclipse. Students could also create a sundial to explore how the sun developed as a source of time keeping in ancient cultures. Picture book folktales about the sun are *Raven: A Trickster Tale from the Pacific Northwest* (Harcourt Brace, 1993) by Gerald McDermott and *How Snowshoe Hare Rescued the Sun: A Tale from the Arctic* (Holiday House, 1993) by Emery Bernhard.

273   Simon, Seymour. *Weather.* Photographs. Morrow, 1993. ISBN 0–688–10546–7. Representational. Photographs. Nonfiction. Weather. Climates. Meteorology. Atmospheric Sciences. Earth Sciences.

An exciting exploration of weather and the impact it has have on our lives. How often do you think of the cause of a thunderstorm or the particular formation of clouds? Seymour Simon's engaging and informative prose is accompanied by full-color photographs that capture each aspect of weather as it occurs. You cannot get closer without actually being there. *Weather* includes an examination of wind, jet streams, and the formation of storms and warm fronts. Other titles in the Earth Science series include *Deserts*, *Earthquakes*, *Icebergs and Glaciers*, *Oceans*, *Storms*, and *Volcanoes*. The author of more than 100 science book for younger readers. Seymour Simon is a scientist who pays close attention to the accuracy of his books, which is why they are acclaimed by teachers and librarians across the country. All the Earth Science titles were chosen as ALA notable books. Science teachers honor Simon's books, which have been cited for their outstanding contribution to the field of science. Companion titles include *The Junior Thunder Lord* (BridgeWater Books, 1994) by Laurence Yep and *Rain Player* (Houghton Mifflin, 1991) by David

Wisniewski, which are two folktales about the consequences of altering weather patterns. *The Story of Lightning and Thunder* (Atheneum, 1993) by Ashley Bryan is a West African tale about the origins of thunder and lightning.

274   Simon, Seymour. *Whales.* Photographs. HarperCollins, 1989. ISBN 0–690–04756–8. Representational. Photographs. Nonfiction. Mammals—Whales. Zoology. Life Sciences.

An amazing look at the mammal often mistaken for a fish. Unlike fish, which are cold-blooded, whales are warm-blooded mammals. Whales, like humans, deliver their babies in live birth, and they inhale and exhale air just as people do. The physical characteristics and habits of humpback, blue, sperm, and narwhal whales are a few species explored in the book. Stunning live action shots of various whales in their natural habitats make this book worthy of any unit on whales. The text is well written and simple to comprehend. Simon uses comparisons with everyday objects to make the awesome size of whales easy to understand. Simon Seymour is the author of more than 100 science book for younger readers. His titles are acclaimed by teachers across the country. Dozens of Simon's books have been cited for their outstanding contribution to the field of science. Explore whales in a fictional capacity with Arnica Esterl's literary fairy tale *Okino and the Whales* (Harcourt Brace, 1995) and Peter Sis's wordless picture book *An Ocean World* (Greenwillow, 1992), which follows one whale's migratory journey. *Jonah and the Whale* (Lothrop, Lee & Shepard) by Geoffrey Patterson is an illustrated biblical story about whales.

275   Sis, Peter. *Starry Messenger.* Illus. by author. Farrar, Straus & Giroux, 1996. ISBN 0–374–37191–1. Expressionism. Mixed Media. Biography. Galilei, Galileo (1564–1642). Astronomers. Scientists.

"One man looked at the sky and wondered." So begins the stunning biography of the man who helped the world see the universe from a revolutionary angle. For hundreds of years people believed the earth was the center of the galaxy, until Galileo turned their eyes to the heavens to see the universe from a different perspective. Galileo Galilei challenged tradition when he turned his telescope to the heavens in an effort to create a map of the stars, and instead discovered that earth was not the fixed center of the universe. His findings were exciting for many and disturbing for others. Based on Galileo's own words, *Starry Messenger* is a tightly drawn sketch with exquisite paintings that won Peter Sis a Caldecott Honor in 1997. Compare with Leonard Everett Fisher's *Galileo* (Macmillan, 1992), another title about man who shook up the harmonious balance of the universe.

276   Thornhill, Jan. *The Tree in a Forest.* Illus. by author. Simon & Schuster, 1992. ISBN 0–671–75901–9. Cartoon Art. Watercolors. Nonfiction. Trees— Maple. Habitats—Forests. Botany. Life Sciences.

Chronicles the life cycle of a maple tree that has grown undisturbed for 200 years. Jan Thornhill traces the life the maple tree through the seasons; she details the tree's maturation and eventual death and shows these events as life affirming. Her lively narrative is as exciting as the illustrations. Some people may be put off by the playful, cartoon-style paintings that enhance rather than pull from the information. Each watercolor illustration is bustling with the life forms that depend on the stability of the maple tree. The maple tree, standing on the edge of a suburban area, bursts with a variety of life forms: Owls, raccoons, and squirrels use the sturdy tree as a nesting place. At the base of the tree flourishes a plethora of forest fauna, drawing nourishment from the roots of the tree. In an unusual touch, Thornhill replaces page numbers with the age of the tree as she intended it to be in the illustrations.

277   Whayne, Susanne Santoro. *Night Creatures.* Illus. by Steven Schindler. Simon & Schuster, 1993. ISBN 0–671–73395–8. Representational. Gouache. Nonfiction. Nocturnal Animals. Zoology. Life Sciences.

An enticing introduction to the nocturnal world inhabited by a slew of animals that creep to life as humans lie down for the night. In this book some nocturnal or night-active animals are introduced. Among them are well-known inhabitants of darkness such as owls and bats. Whayne also included animals that many might not realize are nocturnal—lemurs, wombats, and leopards. Whayne's thoroughly researched prose never ventures toward dull or boring. *Night Creatures* covers each animal's preference of darkness, how the animal adapted to the dark, and how and what each animal hunts. The meticulous illustrations are dark and somber; shadows of night play across the pages, giving an eerie quality to the reading experience. Teachers will find that this book is strong and able to carry itself without additional sources.

278   Yolen, Jane. *Welcome to the Green House.* Illus. by Laura Regan. G. P. Putnam's, 1993. ISBN 0–399–22335–5. Representational. Gouache. Nonfiction. Habitats—Rainforests. Human Influence on Nature. Environmental Protection. Environmental Sciences. Earth Sciences.

Jane Yolen, author of more than 100 picture books and novels for young people, has taken a timely subject and made an important topic enticing. Yolen invites readers into the mysterious world of the rainforest: "Welcome to the Green House with a canopy of leaves for a roof and forest trees forming the walls." This is Laura Regan's first picture book. *In Welcome to the Greenhouse* she uses gouache, a new medium for her, to illustrate the lush and wondrous rainforests of South America. In an afterword Yolen informs readers that only six percent of the earth consists of rainforests, yet this six percent is home to two-thirds of the species of plants and animals found in the world. In the last 100 years over half the rainforest has been chopped down in the name of progress. Even today, fifty acres are destroyed every minute.

Chapter 6

Social Sciences and History

The titles in this section cover a broad range of topics from current social issues to historical events. Subjects ranging from the Civil War to immigration to Kwanzaa to Santa Claus to slavery to Saint Francis of Assisi are represented in this section. Use the titles as springboards to introduce sensitive topics, such as the American government's policy during World War II that allowed Japanese American citizens to be forcibly removed from their homes and relocated to internment camps. The rich illustrations in picture books are guaranteed to generate discussion. Grouping titles together will enhance the experience. Begin with this guide and then dive into the rich trove of picture books waiting for you at your library and school media center.

279 Adler, David A. *A Picture Book of Davy Crockett.* Illus. by John and Alexandra Wallner. Holiday House, 1996. ISBN 0-8234-1212-1. Naive. Watercolors. Biography. Crockett, Davy (1786-1836). United States— Tennessee. Pioneers.

A historical overview of Davy Crockett, whose achievements often get lost in the legends surrounding his life. Born in 1786, Davy Crockett would led an extraordinary life that would include three terms in the U. S. House of Representatives. *A Picture Book of Davy Crockett* is one title from a series of picture book biographies that provide adequate background information and timelines of significant events about prominent Americans. The text is simple and direct with accurate and viable information about an array of prominent people. John and Alexandra Wallner's naive watercolors are delightful and thoroughly detailed, capturing the essence and strength of the brave frontiersman who dared to defy President Andrew Jackson. The books in this series, though intended for younger children, are suitable for young adults because they provide an ideal introduction to the achievements of an unusual man chosen by the people to represent them in Congress. Explore the developments of legends with the life of Davy Crockett, John Chapman (Johnny Appleseed), and John Henry, three men whose feats became legendary.

280   Adler, David A. *A Picture Book of Paul Revere.* Illus. by John and Alexandra Wallner. Holiday House, 1995. ISBN 0-8234-1144-3. Naive. Watercolors. Biography. Revere, Paul (1735-1818). American Revolution.

An enticing, attractive sketch of Paul Revere. Born in 1735, Paul Revere would become famous for a midnight ride across the colonies to warn people of the approach of British soldiers. David A. Adler has created a series of picture book biographies that provide adequate background information and timelines of significant events from American history. John and Alexandra Wallner's naive watercolors capture the essence and strength of the brave colonist who dared to fight against the tyranny of the British. Intended for younger children, the picture book biographies by David A. Adler are suitable for young adults because they provide an ideal introduction to American history. Companion books by Adler include *A Picture Book of George Washington* and *A Picture Book of Thomas Jefferson*, both published by Holiday House. Other companion books include Ted Rand's illustrated picture book of Henry Wadsworth Longfellow's *Paul Revere's Ride* (Dutton, 1990).

281   Adler, David A. *A Picture Book of Rosa Parks.* Illus. by Robert Casilla. Holiday House, 1993. ISBN 0-8234-1041-2. Representational. Watercolors. Biography. Parks, Rosa (1913-). Segregation. Race Relations.

A brief overview of the life of Rosa Parks. Born in 1913, Rosa McCauley Parks would astound the nation by the simple act of refusing to sit in a segregated section for colored people. Rosa Parks is just one of the fascinating historical figures David A. Adler has captured in his picture book biographies. Robert Casilla's stark watercolors capture Rosa Parks in several stages in her life, matching the effective simplicity of the text. The books in this series, though intended for younger children, are suitable for young adults if used as springboards for discussion. The brief, accurate text is ideal for introducing topics. Companion books by Adler include *A Picture Book of Martin Luther King, Jr.* and *A Picture Book of Harriet Tubman*, both published by Holiday House.

282   Adler, David A. *A Picture Book of Sitting Bull.* Illus. by Robert Byrd. Holiday House, 1993. ISBN 0-8234-1044-7. Representational. Watercolors. Biography. Sitting Bull (1843?-1890). Indians of North America. Lakota Indians.

A brief overview of the life of Sitting Bull, great chief of the Dakota Indians. Born around 1834, Sitting Bull would grow up to lead his people in the Battle of Little Bighorn. David A. Adler's picture book biographies of historical events and prominent figures from American history are ideal to introduce sensitive topics in history classes. The text is simple and direct with accurate and viable information. Robert Byrd's haunting illustrations capture the proud strength of a great medicine man and compassionate leader. Other companion books include *A Boy Called Slow* (Philomel, 1995) by Joseph Bruchac, which explores the childhood of Sitting Bull.

283   Adler, David A. *Child of the Warsaw Ghetto.* Illus. by Karen Ritz. Holiday House, 1995. ISBN 0-8234-1160-5. Representational. Pastels. Biography. Jews. World War II—Poland. Holocaust. Children and War.

Chilling recount of the formation of the Warsaw Ghetto, a section of the city blocked off for Polish Jews by the Nazis during their occupation of Poland in World War II. The details of the daily existence in the filthy, crime-ridden streets are drawn from the memories of Froim Baum, a boy born and raised in the Warsaw Ghetto. Baum's memories are vivid, making this account a bleak reminder of the inhumane treatment of the Jewish people. The dismal chalk illustrations by Karen Ritz recapture the suffering and injustice of the persecution of the Jewish people during Hitler's domination. Used alone or as part of a study about the Holocaust, this book is a grim tribute to the millions of Jewish people who died at the hands of the Nazis. David A. Adler and Karen Ritz also collaborated on *Hilde and Eli: Children of the Holocaust* (Holiday House, 1991), another harrowing tale of the innocent child victims of the Holocaust. Additional titles to use with this book include *Tell Them We Remember: The Story of the Holocaust* (Little, Brown, 1994) by Susan D. Bachrach and *I Never Saw Another Butterfly: Children's Drawings and Poems from Terezin Concentration Camp, 1942-1944* (Schocken Books, 1993) edited by Hana Volavková.

284   Agard, John. *The Calypso Alphabet.* Illus. by Jennifer Bent. Henry Holt, 1989. ISBN 0-8050-1177-3. Naive. Scratchboard. Fiction. Alphabet Books. Caribbean. Island Cultures.

"A is for Anancy. Spiderman of tricky-tricky fame." So starts this alphabet of twenty-six words indigenous to the Caribbean area. The rhythmic, sing-song verse and bright illustrations inspired by island culture introduce words like "okra," "ugli fruit," and "kaiso." This unique alphabet book of Caribbean words is an ideal way to introduce students to aspects of island cultures. Included is a glossary that explains unfamiliar terms. Use with *A Caribbean Dozen: Poems from Caribbean Poets* (Candlewick Press, 1994) edited by John Agard and Grace Nichols, *La Diablesse and the Baby: A Caribbean Folktale* (Annick, 1994) by Richardo Keens-Douglas, *Hue Boy* (Dial, 1993) by Rita Phillips Mitchell, *One White Sail: A Caribbean Counting Book* (Green Tiger Press, 1992) by S. T. Garne to explore the unique expression of Caribbean artists and writers. *Caribbean Canvas* (Lippincott, 1987) by Frané Lessac combines original paintings of island life with West Indian proverbs and poems to create a pictorial journey through the Caribbean islands. *Caribbean Alphabet* (Tambourine, 1989), also by Frané Lessac, is an alphabet book featuring fruits, flowers, and animals native to the Caribbean Islands.

285 Aliki. *A Medieval Feast.* Illus. by author. HarperCollins, 1983. ISBN 0-690-042450. Cartoon Art. Watercolors. Nonfiction. Medieval Feasts.

In her signature style Aliki has created another engaging picture book. This time the subject is medieval feasts. The text and the captions beneath the illustrations offer a wealth of information. The grandiose event was a time of celebration for the royal and titled people, but it was plain hard work for peasants and servants. This book places perspective on the event and all the preparations required for each feast. Each new feast brought challenges for the cooks, who rivaled to create the most pretentious cakes and breads. The excitement of the feast is captured by Aliki in detailed paintings based upon actual medieval art. The minute details in the borders reveal the fowl, fruits, and breads that were spread across the table—a magnificent array of food. Scrumptious! John Goodall's *The Story of a Castle* (Atheneum, 1986) and David Macualey's *Castle* (Houghton Mifflin, 1997) are excellent companion titles.

286 Aliki. *Mummies Made in Egypt.* Illus. by author. Crowell, 1979. ISBN 0-690-03858-5. Cartoon Art. Watercolors. Nonfiction. Mummies. Egypt. Archaeology.

An interesting but sometimes gruesome exploration of the process used by ancient Egyptians to prepare their people for burial. Aliki's thorough exploration of the mummification process—beginning with the embalmer's slab, where the body was prepared, to the sealing of the sarcophagus over two months later, with the corpses personal effects—is engaging. The mystery surrounding the Egyptians' intent has mystified people for centuries, and Aliki unravels some of the secrets in this picture book. The detailed watercolor illustrations were inspired by actual paintings from ancient Egyptian tombs. Small vignettes with captions provide further information in addition to the narrative. Aliki, noted for her meticulous research, surpasses herself with this attempt. The subject, though grisly, is presented in an entertaining fashion and covers all aspects of the burial preparation. Burial ceremonies are prevalent in all areas of the world, and this book can be used to springboard into discussion of burial practices in other cultures.

287 Aliki. *The King's Day: Louis XIV of France.* Illus. by author. Crowell, 1989. ISBN 0-690-04588-3. Representational (Cartoon Art). Watercolors. Nonfiction. Louis XIV, King of France (1638-1715). France. Kings, Queens, Rulers.

Enticing biography of King Louis XIV of France, who was known for the elaborate ceremonies that centered around every aspect of his daily routine— from dressing in the morning, to multiple-course meals, to retiring each night. The pomp that surrounded Louis XIV has earned him the label the Sun King, a symbol that became his personal insignia. Louis spared no expense when it came to his pleasure, and despite his extravagant nature, he was one of France's most celebrated rulers. Aliki's panel illustrations take the reader frame by frame through glimpses of the ruler's splendid but predictable day, which afforded no digression from the routine. This thoroughly researched book with a focus on routine gives students an example of how to approach a biographical sketch by illustrating the possible topics surrounding a famous person.

288 Armstrong, Carole. *Lives and Legends of the Saints.* Illus. by Reproductions. Simon & Schuster, 1995. ISBN 0-689-80277-3. Reproductions. Nonfiction. Christian Saints. Christianity. Christian Art and Symbolism. Religion.

A treasury of paintings combined with narrative of famous Christian saints. The text includes a brief history of each saint as well as the miracle or legend surrounding the death. The famous paintings include *Saint Francis Preaching to the Birds* by Giotto, *Saint George Slaying the Dragon* by Raphael, and *Saint John the Baptist in Mediation* by Hieronymous Bosch. An index of paintings and a calendar of principal feasts of saints are included. Use with *Patrick: Patron Saint of Ireland* (Holiday House, 1992) and *Francis: The Man of the Poor* (Holiday House, 1982), both by Tomie dePaola. Other books about saints include *Saint Patrick and the Peddler* (Orchard, 1993) and *St. Jerome and the Lion* (Orchard, 1991), both by Margaret Hodges.

289 Aylesworth, Jim. *The Folks in the Valley: A Pennsylvania Dutch ABC.*
Illus. by Stefano Vitale. HarperCollins, 1992. ISBN 0–06–021929–7. Naive.
Oils. Fiction. Alphabet Books. Pennsylvania Dutch. United States.

An alphabet book about the customs and activities of Pennsylvania Dutch
people. Details of scenes common in the Pennsylvania area—such as setting
preserves, stitching quilts, and harvesting crops—come vividly to life in this
unique alphabet book. The text is simple and direct, but the subject makes this
book outstanding. Stefano Vitale's rich folk art paintings capture the charm and
innocence that survive in many parts of America today. The Amish and the
Mennonites are some of the other people who have opted for the simple
lifestyle. Use this book to study aspects of people who have chosen to live
"outside" the pressures and bustle of an urban lifestyle.

290 Bates, Artie Ann. *Ragsale.* Illus. by Jeff Chapman-Crane. Houghton
Mifflin, 1995. ISBN 0–395–70030–2. Representational. Watercolors. Fiction.
Appalachian Region—Social Life and Customs. Shopping.

In a touching portrait of a bygone era, Appalachian author Artie Ann Bates
draws upon childhood memories to create a moving story about a group of
people often misrepresented in literature and movies. Together with
Appalachian artist Jeff Chapman-Crane, Bates successfully creates an authentic
and profound book about a simple way of life left behind in a world concerned
with technology and money. The realistic paintings capture the excitement and
anticipation of a day of ragsalin' with family and friends. Use this book with
Cynthia Rylant's *Appalachia: Voices of Sleeping Birds* (Harcourt Brace, 1991)
and *When I Was Young in the Mountains* (Dutton, 1982). Rylant, like Bates, was
born and raised in the Appalachian region and is evident in the strong voices of
both writers. *Smoky Mountain Rose: An Appalachian Cinderella* (Dial, 1997) by
Alan Schroeder and *Soap! Soap! Don't Forget the Soap!* (Holiday House, 1993)
by Tom Birdseye are folktales from the Appalachian region.

291 Blos, Joan W. *The Heroine of the* Titanic. Illus. by Tennessee Dixon.
Morrow Junior, 1991. ISBN. Cartoon Art. Watercolors. Biography. Brown,
Margaret Tobin. United States. The *Titanic*.

A fictional account of the life of Margaret Tobin Brown, a daring woman
who stormed the mines of Colorado in the 1800s. Margaret, otherwise known as
"The Unsinkable Molly Brown," was most famous for her survival of the
greatest sea tragedies—the sinking of the *Titanic*, which earned her the
nickname. Not much has been written about Molly's life, but live she did—and
how! Tennessee Dixon's authentic watercolor paintings of 1890s Colorado are
inspiring. Molly's notorious life, though based mostly on legend, would make

an interesting glimpse at women who dared to live full lives despite the restrictions imposed by men and society. Joan Blos's striking narrative is thoroughly researched and will inspire students to explore the *Titanic*'s sinking. *Exploring the Titanic* (Scholastic, 1988) by Robert Ballard is a photo essay, a title from the Time Quest series, about the events leading up to and following the destruction of the "unsinkable" ship. Joan W. Blos is also the author of *Nellie Bly's Monkey* (Morrow, 1996), a book in the same playful spirit as *The Heroine of the* Titanic.

292 Bodker, Cecil. *Mary of Nazareth.* Illus. by Bengt Arne Runnerström. R & S Books, 1989. ISBN 91-29-59178-3. Representational. Watercolors. Fiction. Mary, Blessed Virgin, Saint. Biblical Women. Christian Saints.

A picture book about Mary, mother of Jesus and symbol of faith to Christians all around the world. Her story is as astounding as the one of her son, but it is often shrouded in time and myth. This unique book brings forth the human side of Mary through her perspective. The narrative has a vaguely modern feel that allows doubt of Mary's honor when it is discovered she is with child. There is plenty of dialogue, which makes the story very accessible in the third-person format. The emphasis is placed on Mary's maturation from a child to a young woman with an incredible destiny. Use this book when studying significant women in history. Pair with *Eve and Her Sisters* (Greenwillow, 1994) by Yona Zeldis McDonough, *Mary and Martha* (Eerdmans, 1995), *Esther's Story* (Morrow, 1996) by Diane Wolkstein, and *Mary: The Mother of Jesus* (Holiday House, 1995) by Tomie dePaola, four other titles about biblical women.

293 Bowen, Gary. *Stranded at Plimoth Plantation 1626.* Illus. by author. HarperCollins, 1994. ISBN 0-06-022541-6. Expressionism. Woodcuts. Personal Narratives. Pilgrims. New Plymouth Colony.

First-person account of a young boy stranded for many months at Plimoth Plantation. Christopher Sears sails from England six years after the Mayflower lands with a destination of Jamestown. An unfortunate accident at sea blows the ship off course and near Plimoth Plantation. With fortune against him, orphaned Christopher must rely on the kindness of a Puritan family until he can secure passage to Jamestown. Gary Bowen carefully researched documents from 1626 and 1627 to reconstruct with painstaking detail the life of Pilgrims in Colonial America. Woodcut illustrations with extravagant detail reveal a way of life that led to the creation of the United States of America. The combined strength of the illustrations and the first-person narration of a child will bolster young minds to research Pilgrims and Colonial America with new fire.

294 Bray, Rosemary L. *Martin Luther King.* Illus. by Malcah Zeldis. Greenwillow, 1995. ISBN 0-688-13131-X. Naive. Gouache. Biography. King, Martin Luther, Jr. (1929-1968). African Americans—Biography. Civil Rights. Segregation.

A biography as personal and powerful as the man himself. Rosemary L. Bray's vividly detailed portrait seizes the reader from the first page in an engaging tale of one man's triumphant life and ultimate sacrifice for his beliefs. Martin Luther King, Jr., who will always be known as the father of the civil rights movement, grew up in a world divided by the invisible line of segregation that prevented him from going to certain places or doing certain things. The brilliant folk art illustrations by Malcah Zeldis and the taut storyline by Bray make this book an ideal source for a unit about inspiring African Americans who were fundamental in changing the way black people were treated in the United States. Use with *Dear Benjamin Banneker* (Harcourt Brace, 1994) by Andrea Pinkney, *A Picture Book of Rosa Parks* (Holiday House, 1993) by David A. Adler, and *Frederick Douglass: The Last Day of Slavery* (Lee & Low, 1995) by William Miller, three other titles about courageous people whose struggles contributed to African Americans' struggle for freedom.

295 Bruchac, Joseph. *A Boy Called Slow.* Illus. by Rocoo Baviera. Philomel, 1995. ISBN 0-399-22692-3. Impressionism. Acrylics. Biography. Sitting Bull (1843?-1890). Indians of North America. Lakota Indians.

Dark, brooding illustrations gracefully accompany Joseph Bruchac's flowing tale of the childhood of Sitting Bull, one of the Lakota nation's greatest heroes. In the Lakota nation, children are named for outstanding personality traits. As a child, Sitting Bull approached every task in a deliberate and unhurried fashion, earning him the name Slow. Lakota children had to perform a brave task or show maturity before they would be granted an adult name. Bruchac chose to intersperse his text with Lakota words, which strongly flavors the text. With its powerful narrative, this book makes a great read-aloud to ignite interest in the study of Great Plains Indians.

296 Bruchac, Joseph. *Between Earth and Sky: Legends of Native American Sacred Places.* Illus. by Thomas Locker. Harcourt Brace, 1996. ISBN 0-15-200042-9. Representational. Oils. Fiction. Indians of North America.

In Native American folklore all things are sacred and have a place and a purpose. The narrative is composed of ten legends combined with wisdom of an uncle instructing his nephew about the ways of the world. The journey opens the eyes of a young boy as he learns to view all things with respect. All things, whether living or inanimate, have a place in the scheme of things. Joseph

Bruchac and Thomas Locker combine forces to create a stunning picture book of quiet intensity that reminds readers of the majesty of the land we call America. This title is ideal to open discussion about the power of sacred places in different cultures around the world.

297 Bunting, Eve. *Fly away Home.* Illus. by Ronald Himler. Clarion, 1991. ISBN 0-395-55962-6. Representational. Watercolors. Fiction. Homeless Persons. Airports.

Eve Bunting, author of more than one picture books and novels for children and young adults, takes a timely topic, homelessness, and creates a heartrending story sure to shake up the most hardened listener. Bunting's story is plausible and strikes at the seriousness of homelessness in America. Her protagonists are an unlikely middle-class father and son who attempt to fade into the busy atmosphere of a metropolitan airport. Ronald Himler's harshly realistic watercolor paintings are stronger than Bunting's text, which tends to be romantic when the little boy compares himself to a bird, waiting to "fly away home." In a current events class, this title is sure to generate discussion about homelessness, but it would also be ideal to read aloud when exploring issues concerning modern America. Other titles that explore the desperation of homeless persons include *Uncle Willie and the Soup Kitchen* (Morrow, 1991) by DyAnne DiSalva-Ryan and *Mr. Bow Tie* (Harcourt Brace, 1991) by Karen Barbour.

298 Bunting, Eve. *How Many Days to America: A Thanksgiving Story.* Illus. by Beth Peck. Clarion, 1988. ISBN 0-89919-521-0. Impressionism. Pastels. Fiction. Refugees. Thanksgiving Day.

A poignant story of a modern Caribbean family's frantic flight from their war torn home to the promise of freedom in America. After soldiers ransack their home, a young boy and his family flee the harsh rule in their country. Taking only a change of clothing each and what little money they have, the family steals into the night and buys passage on a boat headed for America. What follows is a story of courage and family devotion in the pursuit of personal and religious freedom. Soft, warm watercolors nab the reader in a compassionate tale that will inspire discussion about what it really means to live in a country where freedom is often taken for granted.

299 Bunting, Eve. *The Wall.* Illus. by Ronald Himler. Clarion, 1990. ISBN. Representational. Watercolors. Fiction. Vietnam Veterans. Washington D. C. Vietnam Veterans Memorial.

A touching story about a father and son's excursion to Washington, D.C., to visit the Vietnam Veterans Memorial. The young boy's grandfather, whom the boy never met, died in the war. Told from the point of view of an innocent child, the story makes the horror of war vivid for people familiar with the statistics and realities of the Vietnam War. Ronald Himler's realistic watercolor illustrations are heartrending portrayals of people visiting the memorial to pay respects to the men and women who died serving their country. Read the book out loud to a class to introduce discussion about the Vietnam War. The story is suitable to generate honest discourse about a very volatile subject: war.

300 Burleigh, Robert. *Flight The Journey of Charles Lindbergh.* Illus. by Mike Wimmer. Philomel, 1991. ISBN 0–399–22272–3. Representational. Acrylics. Biography. Lindbergh, Charles Augustus (1902–1974). Aviation. Pilots.

An account of Charles Lindbergh's flight across the Atlantic Ocean. On May 20, 1927, Lindbergh left Long Island to begin a thirty-three-hour flight with a destination of Paris, France. When Lindbergh made the historic journey, airplanes were not common and people, though intrigued, thought he was crazy to attempt the solo flight. Michael Wimmer's energetic illustrations transport the reader from the ground right into the cockpit to make the historic flight along with Charles Lindbergh. Based on Lindbergh's own account *The Spirit of St. Louis* (1953), the text remains historically faithful. This book will inspire anyone who has ever dreamed of accomplishing a feat never before tackled. Companion titles about Charles Lindbergh include *Lindbergh* (Crown, 1993) by Chris Demarest and *View from the Air: Charles Lindbergh's Earth and Sky* (Viking, 1992) by Reeve Lindbergh. Other picture book biographies about pilots include *The Glorious Flight: Across the Channel With Louis Bleriot, July 25, 1908* (Viking, 1984) by Alice and Martin Provensen and *Ruth Law Thrills a Nation* (Ticknor & Fields, 1993) by Don Brown.

301 Cha, Dia. *Dia's Story Cloth: The Hmong People's Journey of Freedom.* Stitched by Chue and Nhia Thao Cha. Lee & Low, 1996. ISBN 1–880000–34–2. Embroidery. Nonfiction. Hmong (Asian People). Hmong Americans.

A personal account of one woman's struggle for freedom. Dia Cha's journey is told through a story cloth stitched by her aunts, who along with Dia emigrated from Thailand to the United States. The story cloths are an important part of Hmong culture and have become vessels for Hmong history. Dia Cha includes an impressive afterword that details the history of the Hmong people and their customs, clothing, and beliefs. There is also a bibliography for readers interested in more information about the Hmong culture. Use this book with *The Whispering Cloth: A Refugee's Story* (Boyds Mills, 1995) by Pegi Deitz Shea, another book about the Hmong people and story cloths. *Jouanah: A Hmong*

Cinderella (Shen's Books, 1996) by Jewell R. Coburn and Tzexa C. Lee is a companion folktale.

302 Cogancherry, Helen. *The Floating House*. Illus. by Scott Russell Sanders. Macmillan, 1995. ISBN 0-02-778137-2. Representational. Watercolors. Historical Fiction. Families. United States—Indiana. Frontier and Pioneer Life.

A family from Pennsylvania journey down the Ohio River on a flatboat in 1815 to build a new life in Indiana. The story, though fictional, is strong and inviting. The watercolor illustrations depict the hardships and joy of settlers who uprooted themselves to find a new life in unknown territories. The endpapers have an adaptation of a map from the 1815 identifying land prior to Indiana's becoming a state. Used with other titles, this book is an ideal introduction to the period of American history when there was still frontier to be claimed. This topic is rarely written about for young people, and would have been stronger had the author included titles for further reading and source notes identifying the inspiration for this book.

303 Cole, Joanna. *A Gift from Saint Francis: The First Crèche*. Illus. by Michèle Lemieux. Morrow, 1989. ISBN 0-688-06502-3. Expressionism. Oils. Fiction. Francis of Assisi, Saint (1182-1226). Crèches (Nativity Scenes). Christian Saints.

An account of the inspiration and creation of the first nativity scene. In the twelfth-century people did not celebrate Christmas with trees or presents; little or no ceremony surrounded the celebration of Jesus Christ's birth. Saint Francis of Assisi, though he had himself cast off personal belongings and the trappings of wealth, wanted to mark the birth with a special commemorative. Michèle Lemieux's soft oil paintings capture the haunting quality of the nativity scene, which still marks the celebration of Christ's birth during the Christmas season. Observance of special days in every culture are celebrated with special ceremonies or rituals; use *A Gift from Saint Francis* to explore the historical or significant aspects of celebrations. Tomie dePoala's *Francis: The Man of the Poor* (Holiday House, 1982) is an excellent companion title.

304 Coles, Robert. *The Story of Ruby Bridges*. Illus. by George Ford. Scholastic, 1995. ISBN 0-590-43967-7. Representational. Watercolors/Acrylic Inks. Biography. Ruby Bridges. Race Relations. School Integration.

In 1960 a judge ordered that segregation of schools based on race was unconstitutional. Ruby Bridges was one of the girls allowed into all-white schools. Each day for months Ruby had to pass through crowds of angry white people who opposed the court's decision. The crowd raised their fists and shouted ugly things at Ruby. The president of the United States ordered federal marshals armed with weapons to escort Ruby into the building each day. The white people retaliated by pulling their children out of school. Twice a day, as she walked to school and on the way home, Ruby said a prayer: "Please, God, try to forgive these people. Because even if they say those bad things, they do not know what they are doing. So You could forgive them, just like You did those folks a long time ago when they said terrible things about You." Use this book to introduce the powerful events surrounding the landmark Supreme Court decision *Brown vs. The Board of Education* (1954).

305 Cooney, Barbara. *Eleanor.* Illus. by author. Viking, 1996. ISBN 0–670–86159–6. Naive. Watercolors. Biography. Roosevelt, Eleanor (1884–1962). First Ladies. Women—Biography.

An astounding illustrated biography of the early years of Eleanor Roosevelt, beloved wife of Franklin Delano Roosevelt, thirty-second president of the United States. Cooney traces Eleanor's early years in a world of wealth and advantage. Despite her privileged birth, Eleanor knows sadness and despair from an early age. The death of her parents, her mother when she is eight and her father when she is nine, leaves her in the care of her Grandma Hall. Little Nell, always a shy child, withdraws even farther. Years later in Europe under the tutelage of a woman, who sees the intelligence and spirit hidden deep within the eyes of lonely child, Little Nell blossoms into the vibrant and compassionate woman known to the world as Eleanor Roosevelt. Barbara Cooney's books should challenge other authors to create such a breathtaking book as *Eleanor*, which captures the spirit and essence of a extraordinary woman.

306 Cooper, Floyd. *Mandela: From the Life of the South African Statesman.* Illus. by author. Philomel, 1996. ISBN 0–399–22942–6. Impressionism. Oils. Biography. Mandela, Nelson (1918–). Presidents—South Africa.

Outstanding biography of South Africa's first black president. Born the son of a tribal chief, Nelson Mandela was raised to be a fair and just ruler of his people. His lessons would help him build the character and the stamina required to endure the hard life ahead of him. Mandela's rebellion against the injustice of oppression and the brutality of racism eventually landed him in prison for twenty-seven years. His mission to help free his people from the bonds of apartheid was undertaken with courage and determination. South Africa's first black president, Mandela represents freedom and courage to people around he world. Persistence and his belief in equality helped Mandela free his people and earn him the Nobel Peace Prize in 1993 for writing the South African constitution. Pair with Elinor Batezat Sisulu's *The Day Gogo Went to Vote:*

South Africa, April 1994 (Little, Brown, 1996). Included is a pronunciation key, bibliography, and author's note.

307 Crum, Robert. *Eagle Drum: On the Powwow Trail with a Young Eagle Dancer.* Photographs by author. Four Winds Press, 1994. ISBN 0–02–725515–8. Representational. Photographs. Nonfiction. Indians of North America. Powwows.

A photo essay about a young boy's first experience participating in a sacred ceremony marking his passage into manhood. A series of full-color photographs capture Pierre Louis's excitement and diligence as he practices moves and creates his costume for the first grass dance. As explained in the introduction by D. Chief Eagle, Rosebud Sioux Hoopdancer, powwows are ancient Indian ceremonies that connect people with the earth. Robert's Crum's book is a worthy tribute to the sacred aspects of such a monumental event. The dedication and commitment to this project is evident in the grand design of the title. Included is a list of significant powwows that take place annually across the United States. *Eagle Drum* is an ideal title to use when exploring the unique traditions of Native American cultures.

308 DePaola, Tomie. *Mary: The Mother of Jesus.* Illus. by author. Holiday House, 1995. ISBN 0–8234–1018–8. Cartoon Art. Watercolors. Fiction. Mary, Blessed Virgin, Saint. Biblical Women. Christian Saints.

The figure of Mary, Blessed Virgin and saint has captured the imagination and hearts of Christians since the birth of Jesus Christ. Over 80,000 visions of Mary have been claimed by people all over the world since the third century A.D. Tomie dePaola has drawn upon the Scriptures, legend, and popular myth to create fifteen segments spanning Mary's life from her childhood to her assumption into Heaven. As usual with his picture books, dePaola has invested thorough research evident in the design of the book. Pair with *Eve and Her Sisters* (Greenwillow, 1994) by Yona Zeldis McDonough and *Lives and Legends of the Saints* (Simon & Schuster, 1995) by Carole Armstrong, which features stories of other holy women who sacrificed their lives in the name of God.

309 DePaola, Tomie. *Francis: The Man of the Poor.* Illus. by author. Holiday House, 1982. ISBN 0–8234–0435–8. Cartoon Art. Watercolors. Biography. Francis, of Assisi, Saint (1182–1226). Christian Saints. Italy.

A man born to a wealthy family in the small Italian village of Assisi in 1182 lived a privileged life afforded those with fortune. After fighting in a bloody war and seeing the suffering of common folk, Francis renounced his family and cast aside his money to live a simple life free of material possessions. His extraordinary change of lifestyle drew followers who accompanied him through the streets to beg for the food and clothing they needed to survive. Francis formed an order of "brothers," an order that thrives today as the Franciscan monks. Tomie dePaola created this picture book to celebrate the 800th birthday of a saint known around the world as Saint Francis of Assisi. The entire design of the book is outstanding, from the detailed illustrations to the source notes and the thoroughly researched text. Use this book with *A Gift From Saint Francis: The First Crèche* (Morrow, 1989) by Joanna Cole and *Brother Francis and the Friendly Beasts* (Charles Scribner's Sons, 1991) by Margaret Hodges to explore another aspects of one man's extraordinary legacy.

310 DePaola, Tomie. *Patrick: Patron Saint of Ireland.* Illus. by author. Holiday House, 1992. ISBN 0-8234-0924-4. Expressionism. Watercolors. Biography. Patrick, Saint (373?–463?). Christian Saints. Ireland.

Lively rendering of the life and times of Patrick, patron saint of Ireland. DePaola combines the historical facts with timeless legends surrounding Patrick to create a pleasing tale accompanied by brilliant watercolor illustrations. Patrick is captured by bandits and enslaved in the strange land of Ireland for six years. He then returns to his home but eventually his travels lead him back to the Emerald Isle to convert thousands of Irish people to the Christian faith. Patrick's accomplishments are shrouded by time, but the effect the man had on the religious history of Ireland is unmistakable. Explore the commercialized celebration of Saint Patrick's Day by comparing modern practices with legends of Saint Patrick's lessons and achievements.

311 Demi. *Buddha.* Illus. by author. Holt, 1996. ISBN 0-8050-4203-2. Naive. Watercolors. Biography. Gautama Buddha (B.C. 563?–483?). Buddhism. Religion.

Demi has crafted an exciting illustrated biography in her distinctive style using traditional Chinese paints and watercolors. Her spirited version of the man who left behind trappings of wealth to discover truth is especially significant because the author herself is a Buddhist. Buddha's famous Deer Park sermon includes his Noble Eightfold Path and the Doctrine of Four Truths, which became the cornerstone of Buddhist teachings. Demi's carefully researched text is accentuated by the loving brush strokes inspired by Asian art through the centuries. The text is historic in presentation and should not offend anyone sensitive to religions with ideas distinct from European teachings. Introduce historical aspects of Buddhism with this title and *Buddha* (Doubleday, 1994) by Susan L. Roth. Continue exploration of this major world religion with three

Jataka tales (birth stories) told by the Buddha to his followers circa the fourth-century B.C. *The Golden Goose* (Parvardigar Press, 1995) by Judith Ernst, *The Monkey and the Crocodile* (Clarion, 1969) by Paul Galdone, and *Foolish Rabbit's Big Mistake* (G. P. Putnam's, 1985) by Rafe Martin.

312 Demi. *Chingis Khan.* Illus. by author. Henry Holt, 1991. ISBN 0–8050–1708–9. Naive. Watercolors. Biography. Genghis Khan (1162–1227). Mongols. Kings, Queens, Rulers.

An account of the legendary rule of Chingis Khan. A small boy, born in the year of the Snow Leopard, 1160, would rise in power to become a great warrior and ruler. The text is simple but loaded with vital information about one of history's most brilliant leaders. Demi based the narrative on legends and historical record and combined the two for this lively account of Chingis Khan's life. The delicate jewel-tone illustrations are vivacious and exciting. Use this book to explore famous rulers who have reached legendary status for their shrewd and cunning leadership. Some suggested titles are *The King's Day: Louis XIV of France* (Crowell, 1989) by Aliki and *Cleopatra* (Morrow, 1994) and *Shaka: King of the Zulus* (Morrow, 1988) by Diane Stanley and Peter Vennema.

313 Demi. *The Dragon's Tale and Other Fables of the Chinese Zodiac.* Illus. by author. Holt, 1996. ISBN 0–8050–3446–3. Folk Art. Traditional Paints. Fables, China. Chinese Zodiac.

A collection of fables about the twelve animals that form the Chinese zodiac. The tales relate characteristics of the each animal, revealing universal truths through the moral threads woven within. Snake's tale warns of judging by appearance when circumstance arouses suspicion until all information is gathered and evaluated. Like Demi's luminous illustrations, each fable is a gem of truth, sparkling with wisdom and humor. Pair with *Cat and Rat: The Legend of the Chinese Zodiac* (Holt, 1995) by Ed Young, another book about the tales surrounding the twelve animals of the Chinese Zodiac. Birth signs in the China are not determined by months, but rather years. Have students explore their Chinese sign and see if the characteristics of the animal is apparent in their personalities.

314 Ehrlich, Amy. *The Story of Hanukkah.* Illus. by Ori Sherman. Dial, 1989. ISBN 0–8037–0718–5. Expressionism. Gouache. Nonfiction. Hanukkah. Religion. Holidays—Jewish.

The powerful and gripping story of the origins of a holiday that represents faith and hope to an entire race of people. In the land of Judea a flame burns brightly to signify the hope and faith of the Jewish people. When the evil King Antiochus storms with a legion of soldiers, bringing destruction and bloody death, the faith of the Jewish people is put to the test. The relighting of the flame begins a tradition that will remind the Jews of their struggles for all time. The fight for religious freedom is a battle people have been fighting since recorded history. Use with *Rose Blanche* (Creative Education, 1985) by Roberto Innocenti, *Let the Celebrations Begin!* (Orchard, 1991) by Margaret Wild, *The Lily Cupboard* by Shulamith Levey Oppenheim (HarperCollins, 1992), and *Child of the Warsaw Ghetto* (Holiday House, 1995) by David Adler, all titles about the persecution of Jews over 2000 years later. Other titles about Jewish holidays include Barbara Goldin's *Cakes and Miracles: A Purim Tale* (Viking, 1991) and David S. Alder's *One Yellow Daffodil: A Hanukkah Story* (Harcourt, 1995).

315   Ernst, Judith. *The Golden Goose King: A Tale Told by the Buddha.* Illus. by author. Parvardigar Press, 1995. ISBN 0-9644362-0-5. Expressionism. Gouache. Fiction. Jataka Tales (birth stories). Gautama Buddha (B.C. 563?–483?). Buddhism.

One from over 500 Jataka tales (birth stories) told by the Buddha to his disciples. In this tale the queen of Benares dreams of a golden goose and longs to see the bird in its feathered glory. A series of events follow, with classic motifs of love and loyalty, that culminate in a glorious ending. The author provides an outstanding introduction about the evolution of Jataka tales from oral transmission to written form. Introduce the figure of the historical Gautama Buddha with *Buddha* (Doubleday, 1994) by Susan L. Roth and *Buddha* (Holt, 1996) by Demi. Follow up with another Jataka tale with Rafe Martin's *Foolish Rabbit's Big Mistake* (G. P. Putnam's, 1985).

316   Everett, Gwen. *John Brown: One Man against Slavery.* Illus. by Jacob Lawrence. Rizzoli, 1993. ISBN 0-8478-1702-4. Naive. Acrylics. John Brown. Slavery. Abolitionists.

John Brown's raid on Harper's Ferry in 1859 is considered to be a pivotal point in the separation of the United States into northern and southern factions over the issue of slavery. John Brown rallied a group of black men from the free northern states to aid him in raiding an arsenal and using the weapons to fight against the white man's oppression of black people. John Brown failed in his attempts, but his determination to right a wrong had permanent effects on the issues of freedom and slavery in a country founded on this principals. Famed artist Jacob Lawrence created a series of paintings celebrating John Brown's attempt to abolish slavery in the United States. These are the illustrations used in *John Brown: One Man Against Slavery.* Author Gwen Brown chose to tell of this historical event through the eyes of John Brown's daughter, Annie. Open a unit about the Civil War with John Brown's achievements fighting against slavery. Companion titles include *A Picture Book of Sojourner Truth* (Holiday House, 1994) by David Adler and *Harriet and the Promised Land* (Simon & Schuster, 1993) by Jacob Lawrence.

317 Feelings, Muriel. *Jambo Means Hello.* Illus. by Tom Feelings. Dial, 1974. ISBN 0–8037–4350–5. Representational. Charcoal. Fiction. Alphabet Books. Swahili Language. Africa.

Introduces the reader to the Swahili language, which is still spoken by 45 million people in eastern Africa. Swahili is one of over 800 languages spoken in Africa. This alphabet book features twenty-four Swahili words representing the letters of the alphabet, with the exception of Q and X because these sounds are not part of the Swahili language. Each letter is accompanied by illustrations depicting aspects of African cultures that still speak Swahili. The author includes a map showing countries that speak Swahili and gives an introduction of intent.

318 Feelings, Muriel. *Moja Means One.* Illus. by Tom Feelings. Dial, 1971. ISBN 0–8037–5776–X. Representational. Charcoal. Nonfiction. Counting Books. Africa. Swahili Language.

Introduces the reader to the Swahili language, which is still spoken by 45 million people in eastern Africa. Swahili is one of over 800 languages spoken in Africa. This counting book features the Swahili words for the numbers one to ten. Each number is accompanied by aspects of African cultures that still speak the Swahili language. The author includes a map showing countries that speak Swahili and gives an introduction of intent.

319 Feelings, Tom. *Soul Looks Back in Wonder.* Illus. by author. Dial, 1993. ISBN 0–8037–1001–1. Expressionism. Colored Pencils. Poetry. African Americans. Poetry Collections.

Tom Feelings has long been praised for his stunning illustrations, which celebrate the tumultuous and proud African American heritage in the United States. The paintings in *Soul Looks Back in Wonder* reflect the struggle and spirit of African Americans though the generations from the middle passage to the civil rights movement of the 1960s. In this collection, Mr. Feelings asked thirteen respected poets and writers to create selections to accompany his paintings. The work of Maya Angelou, Langston Hughes, Lucille Clifton, Walter Dean Myers, and Margaret Walker is represented in this stunning book.

320 Fisher, Leonard Everett. *Gandhi.* Illus. by author. Holiday House, 1995. ISBN 0–689–80337–0. Expressionism. Acrylics. Biography. Gandhi, Mohandas K. (1869–1948). India.

A pictorial biography of one of the world's greatest civil rights leaders— Mohandas Karamchand Gandhi (1869–1948). Leonard Everett Fisher has taken the extraordinary life of Gandhi and developed it into an equally exceptional book. Gandhi and his achievements in civil rights have rarely been given such devoted tribute as Fisher has paid him in this illustrated text. The variations of black and white Fisher used to render his illustrations are stunning and capture Gandhi from his boyhood through his fight to free India from the colonial rule of Britain and end with his assassination. This unprecedented biography will challenge other writers and illustrators to capture a slice of history and bring it to life as Fisher has done repeatedly with historical figures. Other books by Leonard Everett Fisher in this series include *Galileo (*Macmillan, 1992), *Marie Curie (*Macmillan, 1994), and *Gutenburg (*Macmillan, 1992).

321 Fisher, Leonard Everett. *Moses.* Illus. by author. Holiday House, 1995. ISBN 0–8234–1149–4. Expressionism. Acrylics. Biography. Moses (biblical figure). Biblical Figures.

A dramatic account of the life of Moses, who was chosen by God to lead the Israelites out of Egypt. Leonard Everett Fisher's sensational acrylic paintings of the pivotal events in the life of Moses seize the reader. Teachers cautious of introducing Christian philosophy in the classroom may nonetheless find this accurate retelling of the life of Moses suitable for discussion of world religions. Fisher includes a bibliography for further reading and provides maps tracing the Exodus to the Promised Land. Fisher's adaptations of Bible stories include *David and Goliath* (Holiday House, 1993).

322 Fisher, Leonard Everett. *Prince Henry the Navigator.* Illus. by author. Macmillan, 1990. ISBN 0–02–735231–5. Expressionism. Acrylics. Biography. Henry, Infante of Portugal (1394–1460). Explorers.

A lively biography of Prince Henry, visionary and creator of the first school of navigation. Henry, who never participated in sea adventures, made outstanding contributions to the field of navigation that enabled explorers— Christopher Columbus among them—to travel uncharted waters safely. Leonard Everett Fisher takes a section of history and breaths life into the vision of a man who receives little attention in most history books. Fisher's stark black-and-white illustrations are spare but enlightening. The design of the book is ideal for the classroom because Fisher includes maps, timelines, and sources for further reading.

323 Fisher, Leonard Everett. *Pyramid of the Sun, Pyramid of the Moon.* Illus. by author. Macmillan, 1988. ISBN 0-02-735300-1. Expressionism. Acrylics. Nonfiction. Aztecs. Indians of Mexico. Toltec Indians.

A title from the acclaimed architectural series by Leonard Everett Fisher. Thirty miles from the capital of Mexico in the ancient city of Teotihuacán are two monuments representing the proud history of the Mexican people: the Pyramid of the Sun and the Pyramid of the Moon. For over 2000 years these massive structures have stood high above earth, a bleak reminder of the lost Toltec civilization. Fisher combines evocative illustrations and perfectly paced text to invite readers to explore the distant past and enduring presence of the mystical pyramids. Standard features in Leonard Everett Fisher's exquisitely designed books are the maps and timelines, which enhance the carefully researched text and illustrations.

324 Fisher, Leonard Everett. *Stars and Strips: Our National Flag.* Illus. by author. Holiday House, 1993. ISBN 0-8234-1053-6. Representational. Acrylics. Nonfiction. American Flag. Pledge of Allegiance.

A brief historical overview of the transformation of the American flag from its first pattern of thirteen stars and stripes to today's flag with fifty stars and thirteen stripes. Leonard Everett Fisher combines the words from the Pledge of Allegiance with brief passages detailing the names and official dates of fifteen of the flags that have flown proudly to represent America and freedom. Because of the subject, the illustrations are dominated by red, white, and blue; but the use of the entire page for each flag offers details that may be missed in a smaller pictures of the American flag. The trim size of the book is small; an oversized book would have been notable and had more significant visual impact. Other companion titles include Stephen Kroll's *By the Dawn's Early Light: The Story of the Star-Spangled Banner* (Scholastic 1994), Peter Spier's illustrated *The Star-Spangled Banner* (Doubleday, 1983), and Alexandra Wallner's *Betsy Ross* (Holiday House, 1994).

325 Fisher, Leonard Everett. *The Great Wall of China.* Illus. by author. Macmillan, 1986. ISBN 0-02-735220-X. Expressionism. Acrylics. Nonfiction. Great Wall of China. China. Architecture.

A brief overview of the building of the Great Wall of China. Over 2000 years ago King Cheng of Ch'in conquered a dozen surrounding kingdoms and became Ch'in Shih Huang Ti, First Supreme Emperor of China. After developing a uniform system of weights and measures, currency and writing that would be used consistently in the unified kingdom, Ch'in Shih Huang Ti set himself the task of keeping the invading Mongols at bay. His idea was the Great

Wall of China. Over a million people labored to create one of history's greatest architectural achievements. Use this book to introduce exploration of modern China by looking to the distant past to set the stage for discussion. Fisher combines evocative illustrations and perfectly paced text to invite readers to explore the distant past and enduring strength of the people of China. The captions for each illustration are in Chinese characters, a detail that adds an exciting touch to the paintings.

326 Fisher, Leonard Everett. *The Wailing Wall.* Illus. by author. Macmillan, 1989. ISBN 0–02–735310–9. Expressionism. Acrylics. Nonfiction. Western Wall (Jerusalem). Jews. Architecture.

This text takes the reader on a magnificent journey through time beginning 4000 years ago and along the way relates several critical events that surround the creation and history of the Western or "Wailing" Wall. The Wailing Wall, the only remaining stones from the First and Second Temples destroyed during struggles of different nations wanting to curtail the Jewish faith, remains standing as a testament to the power and endurance of faith. As is standard in Leonard Everett Fisher's exquisitely designed books, this title includes maps and timelines to enhance the carefully researched text and illustrations. Fisher chose a unique angle from which to view Jewish history, making this book an exciting addition to other titles chronicling Jewish struggle to worship as they believe. Other titles in this series of architectural achievements include *The Tower of London* (Macmillan, 1987), *The Great Wall of China* (Macmillan, 1986), and *Pyramid of the Sun, Pyramid of the Moon* (Macmillan, 1988).

327 Flournoy, Vanessa and Valerie. *Celie and the Harvest Fiddler.* Illus. by James Ransome. Tambourine, 1995. ISBN 0–688–11457–1. Representational. Oils. Fiction. Halloween. African Americans.

Celie wants to win the contest for best costume at the All Hallows Eve party, but all of her preparations go awry when her costume falls apart. She runs from the celebration with tears in her eyes and meets the mysterious fiddler who gives her a mask that is guaranteed to win the contest. When Celie returns to the gathering, chaos ensues as two wolves chase the winner of the contest from the party. Celie may not get the prize for best costume, but she will sure have a great story to tell at next year's celebration. The strength of this book is its setting: an African American celebration following the emancipation of the slaves. James Ransome's energetic oil illustrations are a visual feast. The text, though well written, lacks details about daily life.

328 Gallaz, Christophe. *Rose Blanche.* Illus. by Roberto Innocenti. Creative Education, 1985. ISBN 0-87191-944-X. Watercolors. Historical Fiction. Jews. Germany. Concentration Camps.

Rose Blanche lives in a small village in Germany that overnight is invaded by German soldiers. As fear engulfs her village and more soldiers begin to arrive, she begins to seek answers on her own. Big trucks with guns bring loads of people through the town and take them into the forest. One day she follows a truck filled with people to the outskirts of town. In the forest are rough wooden buildings surrounded by barbed wire. Inside the fence are scantily dressed people with yellow stars pinned to their clothing. They are thin and cold, including children younger than herself. Rose Blanche begins to sneak food to the hungry children, but there is never enough. Adolph Hitler's reign of terror that led to World War II is vividly portrayed. The persecution of Jewish people and the horrible death camps they were thrown into are depicted as the hell they were. Christophe Gallaz's text has made a difficult subject approachable. Roberto Innocenti's chilling illustrations depict the horror of war through the eyes of a child.

329 Garland, Sherry. *The Lotus Seed.* Illus. by Tatsuro Kiuchi. Harcourt Brace, 1993. ISBN 0-15-249465-0. Impressionism. Oils. Fiction. Vietnamese Americans. Vietnam. Immigration.

A compassionate story of a girl's immigration to the United States from her homeland of Vietnam. The story opens with a young girl witnessing the last days of the rule of her emperor. The girl sneaks down to the royal gardens and plucks a lotus pod to help remind her of the brave emperor and the homeland she has to leave behind. Although the brief text seems to lack challenge, it will spark lively discussion about Vietnamese history and the Vietnam War. The story, from a child's point of view, is powerful because of its intimate associations with the bloody upheaval that resulted in the flight of a million Vietnamese seeking refuge in other countries. The back cover of the book has a poem about the lotus flower, a metaphor for endurance, written in Vietnamese. Tatsuro Kiuchi's impressionistic oil paintings capture the immutable spirit of the brave Vietnamese people. *Why Ducks Sleep on One Leg* (Scholastic, 1993) by Sherry Garland, *Tuan* (R & S Books, 1988) by Eva Boholm-Olsson, and *Grandfather's Dream* (Greenwillow, 1994) by Holly Keller are companion titles about Vietnam culture.

330 Giblin, James Cross. *George Washington: A Picture Book Biography.* Illus. by Michael Dooling. Scholastic, 1994. ISBN 0-590-42550-1. Impressionism. Oils. Biography. Washington, George (1732-1799). Presidents—United States.

Exceptional biography of the life of George Washington, first president of the United States. Giblin's organization is outstanding. His accurate fictional narration pulls the reader into the book. Michael Dooling's luxuriant oil paintings transport the reader back through time to an era that shaped America's future. An interesting afterword dispels the myth of George Washington and the cherry tree. Giblin cites the source of the rumor, a novel for children published in 1800, which will make an exciting springboard for discussion about the accuracy of historical records. Companion titles to use for an illustrated introduction to the American Revolution are *Betsy Ross* (Holiday House, 1994) by Alexandra Wallner, *The Joke's on George* (Tambourine, 1993) by Michael O. Tunnell, *Stars and Stripes: Our National Flag* (Holiday House, 1993) by Leonard Everett Fisher, *Paul Revere's Ride* by Henry Wadsworth Longfellow with illustrations by Ted Rand (Dutton, 1990), *We the People: The Constitution of the United States of America* (Doubleday, 1987) by Peter Spier, and *In 1776* (Scholastic, 1994) by Jean Marzolla.

331   Giblin, James Cross. *Thomas Jefferson: A Picture Book Biography.* Illus. by Michael Dooling. Scholastic, 1994. ISBN 0–590–44838–2. Impressionism. Oils. Biography. Jefferson, Thomas (1743–1826). Presidents—United States.

An exquisite portrayal of the life of Thomas Jefferson, third president of the United States. James Cross Gilbin does a magnificent job of combining fact with prose to create a biography that will entice any student, covering details of Jefferson's boyhood, his education, and his rise to power in the government. Writing the Declaration of Independence was one of Jefferson's many achievements; it also proved to be his most controversial because as a slave owner, Jefferson violated many of the beliefs that he tried to establish with the document. Thorough and engaging, this book will establish itself as an introduction to American presidents. Evocative oil paintings with floral borders inspired by eighteenth-century French wallpaper make the illustrations worthy of several examinations. Teachers will appreciate the excerpts from Jefferson's most famous speeches, essays, and government documents. The author also includes a history of Monticello, Jefferson's Virginia home, and gives a list of significant dates of Thomas Jefferson's life.

332   Goble, Paul. *Beyond the Ridge.* Illus. by author. Bradbury, 1989. ISBN 0–02–736581–6. Folk Art. Watercolors. Legends, Indians of North America. Great Plains Indians. Death.

Another exquisite offering from Paul Goble, who is renowned for his accurate portrayal of Plains Indians. This title explores the death ceremony of the Plains Indians as an old woman prepares to go "beyond the ridge" to the spirit world, where she will continue her journey by shedding her earthly body.

Goble's delicately melds his folk art illustrations with selected prayers that enhance the moving passage of the woman from the earthly world to the spirit world. As with all his titles, Paul Goble thoroughly researched his topic and includes source notes and a bibliography for further reading. The overall design of the *Beyond the Ridge* exemplifies the possibilities of the picture book format as a tool for educators.

333 Goble, Paul. *Death of the Iron Horse.* Illus. by author. Bradbury, 1987. ISBN 0–02–737830–6. Folk Art. Watercolors. Legends, Indians of North America. Cheyenne Indians. Railroads.

A fictional account of the Cheyenne Indian attack on an "Iron Horse." As Paul Goble explains in his introduction, Hollywood made millions inserting random Indian attacks of trains in movies. Actually only one train was derailed by Indians, and it was a protest to the encroachment of white men on Indian land. As with all his books, Goble's research is dependable and worthy of inclusion in any curriculum. His folk art illustrations are meticulously researched.

334 Goble, Paul. *Her Seven Brothers.* Illus. by author. Bradbury, 1988. ISBN 0–02–737960–4. Folk Art. Watercolors. Legends, Indians of North America. Cheyenne Indians. Stars.

A young Cheyenne girl, with no brothers or sisters, lives with her parents. With porcupine quills she skillfully stitches beautiful clothing and blankets from buffalo skins. One day she begins to work on seven pairs of shoes and shirts for men because the spirits tell her that she will seek her heart and at last find the brothers she longs for. When the chief of the buffaloes demands the girl, the brothers refuse, and all eight flee for their lives to avoid his anger. They climb up a tree and get so high that they become stars in the night sky. This Cheyenne pourquoi tale explains the often overlooked eighth star in the Big Dipper constellation.

335 Goble, Paul. *The Return of the Buffaloes.* Illus. by author. National Geographic Society, 1996. ISBN 0–7922–2714–X. Folk Art. Watercolors. Legends, Indians of North America. Great Plains Indians. Buffaloes—Folklore.

In his eminent style Paul Goble brings a tale of profound beauty and a timeless message about natural resources. Little or no part of the buffalo killed by Plains Indians was thrown away, but even though they honored and worshipped the buffalo, sometimes the herds would wander and could not be found by warriors. This Plains Indian legend tells of a mysterious woman who brings buffalo back to the Plains Indians when the people are near starvation. Paul Goble includes source notes, a bibliography, and detailed sketches of a way of life nearly forgotten. Also included is a pattern for a parfleche [par-flesh], which is envelope-shaped rawhide container thrown over horses and used to carry home meat from a good hunt. *Buffalo Dance: A Blackfoot Legend* (Little, Brown, 1993) by Nancy Van Laan and *Crow Chief: A Plain Indian Story* (Orchard, 1992) by Paul Goble are two companion titles about North American buffalo folklore.

336   Golenbeck, Peter. *Teammates.* Illus. by Paul Bacon. Harcourt Brace, 1990. ISBN 0-15-200603-6. Impressionism. Watercolors. Fiction. Prejudice. Athletes. Baseball.

Chronicles the careers and friendship of Jackie Robinson and Pee Wee Reese. Robinson was the first black man to play on a major league baseball team. The abuse and hostility Robinson suffered was abated when white Pee Wee Reese stood up to the fans and publicly declared his support and admiration for Robinson. The illustrations are a combination of watercolor illustrations and rare photographs from private collections. The story is an affirming tale about the barriers of prejudice. Some other illustrated baseball books include *Baseball Saved Us* (Lee & Low, 1993) by Ken Mochizuki, *Take Me Out to the Ball Game* (Four Winds, 1993) by Jack Norworth and *Casey at the Bat* (Atheneum, 1988) by Ernest Lawrence Thayer with illustrations by Barry Moser. *The Great Ball Game: A Muskogee Story* (Dial, 1994) by Joseph Bruchac is a pourquoi tale about the invention of baseball.

337   Hamanaka, Sheila. *The Journey: Japanese Americans, Racism, and Renewal.* Illus. by author. Orchard, 1990. ISBN 0-531-05849-2. Representational. Oils. Nonfiction. Japanese Americans. Internment Camps—United States. World War II.

Illustrated book of Sheila Hamanaka's five-panel mural of the triumphs of Japanese Americans who have experienced joy and pain in their struggle to find a place in American society. Hamanaka, a third-generation Japanese American, tells of the admonitions and cruelty her people suffered at American hands by relating the personal account of her family's imprisonment in interment camps during World War II. Until recently this shameful chapter of American history was glossed over in schools and textbooks if it was included at all. The American "concentration camps," though not as horrifying as Hitler's, were nonetheless a shameful injustice against an innocent group of people. *The Bracelet* (Philomel, 1993) by Yoshiko Uchida, *Bluejay in the Desert* (Polychrome, 1993) by Marlene Shigekawa, and *Baseball Saved Us* (Lee & Low) by Ken Mochizuki are accounts of Japanese Americans placed in internment camps. Use this title with *Child of the Warsaw Ghetto* (Holiday House) by David A. Adler and *Let the Celebrations Begin!* (Orchard, 1991) by Margaret Wild, *Light from a Yellow Star: A Lesson of Love from the Holocaust* (University of Minnesota, 1994) by Robert O. Fisch, and *Rose Blanche* (Creative Education, 1985) by Christophe Gallaz, titles about the hideous treatment of Jews during World War II.

338 Harvey, Brett. *Cassie's Journey: Going West in the 1860s.* Illus. by Deborah Kogan Ray. Holiday House, 1988. ISBN 0-8234-0684-9. Impressionism. Pencil. Fiction. Frontier and Pioneer Life. Westward Expansion.

Moving account of one family's travels from Illinois to the promise of a better life in the west. Told from the perspective of a young girl, this personal narrative captures the strength and determination of families who forged across unknown territory to build better lives. Impressionistic pencil drawings capture the enduring spirit of a typical family in the 1800s. Brett Harvey based this story on the journals of actual women who completed the difficult journey from the Eastern Coast to the western United States. Introduce young people to frontier life with this book and encourage further exploration of pioneer diaries with Lillian Schliffel's *Women's Diaries of the Westward Journey* (Schocker Books, 1982), one of the sources the author used to develop this book. Other companion titles include *Only Opal: Diary of a Young Girl* (Philomel, 1994) by Opal Whiteley, from her diary, *Along the Santa Fe Trail: Marion Russell's Own Story* (Whitman, 1993) by Marion Russell, and *My Prairie Year: Based on the Diary of Elenore Plaisted* (Holiday House, 1986) by Brett Harvey.

339 Harvey, Brett. *My Prairie Christmas.* Illus. by Deborah Kogan Ray. Holiday House, 1990. ISBN 0-8234-0827-2. Impressionism. Watercolors. Fiction. Frontier and Pioneer Life. Westward Expansion.

An historical account of a family's first year in the harsh prairie environment of the Midwest. From Maine, the Plaisted family endure climate changes and a sense of loneliness and isolation in a midwestern frozen wasteland. Back home, Christmas was celebrated with an pine tree adorned with candles and fresh berries. After trimming the tree, the family would feast on an abundance of freshly baked pies and cakes. Brett Harvey's moving narration is balanced with thorough research and draws upon the actual diaries of Elenore Plaisted, her grandmother. Told in the first-person by the daughter, Elenore, this title is appropriate to augment a study of personal narratives. Deborah Kogan Ray's warm watercolor illustrations of a family's struggle to survive in a harsh, icy world are worthy of Harvey's strong storyline. Use this title to supplement a unit on western expansion and pioneer lifestyles.

340 Harvey, Brett. *My Prairie Year: Based on the Diary of Elenore Plaisted.*
Illus. by Deborah Kogan Ray. Holiday House, 1986. ISBN 0-8234-0604-0.
Impressionism. Charcoal. Fiction. Frontier and Pioneer Life. Westward Ex-
pansion. Personal Narratives.

Brett Harvey, granddaughter of Elenore Plaisted, adapted this touching
story from her grandmother's diary. Harvey manages to capture the details of
pioneer life—complete with the heartbreak and drudgery of forging a new
land—while maintaining an exciting narrative. Detailed pencil illustrations
reveal the endurance and strength of the pioneers who forged the vast expanse
of the prairies. Harvey wrote another book about Elenore Plaisted, *My Prairie
Christmas* (Holiday House, 1994), which explores the Plaisteds' first Christmas
in their new prairie home. Use this title to supplement a unit on western
expansion and pioneer lifestyles or personal narratives by pioneers. Companion
picture book titles are Jean Van Leeuwen's *Going West* (Dial, 1992) and
Courtni C. Wright's *Wagon Train: A Family Goes West in 1865* (Holiday
House, 1994).

341 Herold, Maggie Rugg. *A Very Important Day.* Illus. by Catherine Stock.
Morrow Junior, 1995. ISBN 0-688-13065-8. Representational. Watercolors.
Fiction. Immigration. Citizenship.

As snowflakes fall gently to blanket the earth, 219 people from thirty-two
different countries make their way through a snowstorm in New York City to
take part in a very important ceremony. After fulfilling the necessary re-
quirements, filling out official papers, and taking special tests, these 219 will be
sworn in as American citizens. Catherine Stock captures the excitement and
importance of this special day with soft watercolor illustrations flecked with
snowflakes and happy faces. Maggie Rugg Herold and Catherine Stock
participated in an actual naturalization ceremony to make this book reliable and
extra special. There is a pronunciation guide at the end of book and information
about becoming a U. S. citizen. Most young readers in the United States are
born here and fail to comprehend the importance of citizenship; this book will
help them better understand the privilege and importance of being a citizen of
the United States of America.

342 Hoestlandt, Jo (English translation by Mark Polizzotti). *Star of Fear, Star
of Hope.* Illus. by Johanna Kang. Walker and Company, 1995. ISBN 0-8027-
8373-2. Expressionism. Pastels. Fiction. Holocaust. Jews. World War II. Children and War.

A haunting story of the madness of war made more powerful by the
innocent voice of the narrator. Young Helen has a difficult time understanding

why her friend Lydia must wear a yellow star on her clothes. On the night of Helen's birthday party, Lydia leaves Helen's party to warn her family of the impending danger: Nazi soldiers have been hunting through the streets to round up Jews. Helen, confused by the abandonment, yells out to Lydia as she leaves, "You're not my friend anymore!" Helen lives to regret her words because she never sees or hears from Lydia again. Johanna Kang's haunting illustrations are rendered with dismal hues that make the pictures as evocative and powerful as the story itself. This book will make a perfect introduction to the topic of war and the innocent victims who are sacrificed to it.

343   Hong, Lily Toy. *The Empress and the Silkworm*. Illus. by author. Whitman, 1995. ISBN 0-8075-2009-8. Fiction. Acrylics/Gouache. China. Silk. Silkworms.

Five thousand years ago a Chinese empress was having tea in the garden when something fell from the tree—plop!—right into her teacup. The heat from Si Ling-Chi's tea made the cocoon unravel, and to her delight a fine silken thread was all that was left. After a dream the young empress realizes that the cocoon was made by a silkworm and that the fine thread can be woven into beautiful cloth. This tale is a fictionalized account of the discovery that the cocoons of silkworms are made of fine, silken threads can be used to make the finest fabric in the world—silk. Source notes detail the actual facts about the history of silk and silkworms. *The Silk Route: 7000 Miles of History* (HarperCollins, 1995) by John S. Major is an ideal companion title.

344   Hopkinson, Deborah. *Sweet Clara and the Freedom Quilt*. Illus. by James Ransome. Knopf, 1993. ISBN 0-679-82311-5. Representational. Acrylics. Fiction. Slaves. Quilts. Slavery.

Moving story of one girl's determination to escape from the bonds of slavery and make a new life in the north. Sweet Clara aims to leave Home Plantation, where she has been sent, to return to her mother at North Farm and then escape to freedom via the Underground Railroad. Sweet Clara spends years collecting scraps and bits of information that she uses to stitch together a quilt with squares resembling landmarks that will serve as a map to the northern United States. Sweet Clara leaves the quilt when she makes her journey so that other slaves may follow her to freedom. The author does not provide source notes or reveal the inspiration for the story, which leaves the reader wondering if there is any truth to the freedom quilt. James Ransome's exhilarating acrylic paintings are stunning, but they paint a bright picture of slavery that seems contrary to the horrors that really occurred.

345 Jakes, John. *Susanna of the Alamo: A True Story.* Illus. by Paul Bacon. Harcourt Brace, 1986. ISBN 0–15–200592–7. Impressionism. Watercolors. Biography. Dickenson, Susanna. Alamo (San Antonio, Texas). Pioneers.

Of all of the deeds sung about the brave soldiers who fought and died at the siege at San Antonio, Texas, one has been forgotten—until now. "Remember the Alamo" resounds through time to remind people of the heroic men. Now Susanna Dickenson's story can be told as well. Spared by the general of the Mexican Army, Susanna refused to be his emissary and instead carried the true tale of the brutality to Sam Houston. Somber tones dominate the illustrations in an appropriate display capturing the sadness and grief of the people who were spared a cruel death but forced to live with horrible memories of the massacre. Use this book with a unit on famous battles or frontier and pioneer life during the early 1800s.

346 Jakobsen, Kathy. *My New York.* Illus. by author. Little, Brown, 1993. ISBN 0–316–45653–5. Representational. Oils. Fiction. New York City. Cities.

A girl living in New York City writes a letter to her friend living in the Midwest to tell him about some of the wonderful things to see in New York. The text, though simple and told in letter form, is an exciting introduction to the Big Apple. The entire experience is a rich, detailed journey of one of the most exciting cities in the world—New York City. The design of the book includes foldout pages of the Empire State Building and endpapers decorated with a map of New York City. Judging from the details, the author spent numerous hours researching and developing her paintings. Other books exploring the vibrant life of New York City include *Tar Beach* (Crown, 1991) by Faith Ringgold, *Abuela* (Dutton, 1991) by Arthur Dorros, and *Peppe the Lamplighter* (Lothrop, Lee & Shepard, 1993) by Elisa Bartone.

347 Katz, William Loren. *Black Women of the Old West.* Photographs. Atheneum, 1995. ISBN 0–689–31944–4. Representational. Photographs. Nonfiction. Frontier and Pioneer Life. African American Women. African Americans—Biography. Women—Biography.

An inspiring book about a formative population who helped forge the wild west: African-American women. Rarely figured in other books or films, African-American women were as prominent in the shaping of the western frontier as white men or women. With determination and a gritty view of the possibilities of the frontier, these women opened and ran laundries, restaurants, hotels, and stores. From dawn till dusk African-American women worked with one goal in mind: keeping the budding communities above water. A stunning

series of rare photographs and newspaper articles capture the spirit and pride of
a group of people too long left unsung.

348 Key, Francis Scott. *The Star-Spangled Banner.* Illus. by Peter Spier.
Doubleday, 1973. ISBN 0–385–09458–2. Cartoon Art. Watercolors. Songs.
Key, Francis Scott (1779–1843). Illustrated Classics.

On September 14, 1814, in a Baltimore hotel room Francis Scott Key
(1779–1843) wrote a song after witnessing the bombardment of Fort McHenry.
That song would later be known as the "The Star-Spangled Banner." Key made
three copies of the poem, of which only two are in existence. Each line of the
song was illustrated by Peter Spier with a scene form American life and symbols
that represent America to the world. This essential addition to the classroom
library includes guitar chords, a replication of Francis Scott Key's original
manuscript, and endpapers decorated with flags from the American Revolution.
Use this title to introduce discussion about America's attempt to establish itself
as a free and independent nation or to preface the events of the War of 1812.
Augment by using Stephen Kroll's *By the Dawn's Early Light: The Story of the
Star-Spangled Banner* (Scholastic 1994). Peter Spier also wrote and illustrated
We the People: The Constitution of the United States of America (Doubleday,
1987), which is as visually pleasing and thoroughly researched as *The Star-
Spangled Banner.*

349 Knight, Margy Burns. *Talking Walls.* Illus. by Anne Sibley O'Brien. Tilbury Press, 1992. ISBN 0–88448–102–6. Representational. Pastels. Nonfiction.
Walls.

An introduction to various cultures around the world via a tour of fourteen
famous walls, including the Vietnam Memorial in Washington, D. C., which
millions of people visit every year to pay homage to Americans who died
fighting for world peace, and the Berlin Wall in Germany, erected in 1961,
which separated East Berlin and West Berlin. Other walls visited are the
Western Wall in Jerusalem, the prison wall of Nelson Mandela, and the Great
Zimbabwe in southeast Africa. Anne Sibley O'Brien's soft pastel illustrations
catch children—a promise for a better world—dancing upon walls that once
held people in and upon other walls that were destroyed to set them free. Pair
with *The Wall* (Clarion, 1990) by Eve Bunting, *The Great Wall of China*
(Macmillan, 1986) by Leonard Everett Fisher, and *The Wailing Wall*
(Macmillan, 1989) by Leonard Everett Fisher, titles that explore three walls
featured in *Talking Walls* in greater depth. A compendium at the end of the
book has further information about each wall and contains a map to help young
readers pinpoint the location of each wall. Anne Sibley O'Brien and Margy

Burns Knight reunited for a sequel *Talking Walls: The Stories Continue* (Tilbury House, 1996).

350 Kodama, Tatsuhara (Text translated by Kazuko Hokumen-Jones). *Shin's Tricycle*. Illus. by Noriyuki Ando. Walker & Company, 1992. ISBN 0–8027–8376–7. Representational. Oils. Personal Narratives. World War II—Japan. Hiroshima, Japan. Atomic Bomb. Children and War.

Tatsuhara Kodama recounts the true story of his son, Shin, whose young life was cut short by the atomic bomb dropped on Hiroshima. The moving words of a father's loss will touch readers and bring the horror of nuclear war full circle. The cover illustration of an innocent child in the foreground with a mushroom cloud in the distance is heartbreaking, as are all of Noriyuki Ando's paintings in *Shin's Tricycle*. The tricycle was discovered years after the blast and placed in Shin's memory in the Hiroshima Peace Museum to remind people of the brutality of war and the loss of innocence. Pair with *My Hiroshima* (Viking, 1987) by Junko Morimoto, *Faithful Elephants: A True Story of Animals, People, and War* (Houghton Mifflin, 1988) by Yukio Tsuchiya, and *Hiroshima No Pika* (Lothrop, Lee & Shepard, 1980) by Toshi Maruki for a revealing exploration of the horror experienced by the citizens of Japan that fateful day—August 6, 1945.

351 Kroll, Steven. *Lewis and Clark: Explorers of the American West*. Illus. by Richard Williams. Holiday House, 1994. ISBN 0–8234–1034–X. Representational. Watercolors. Fiction. Lewis, Meriwether (1774–1809). Clark, William (1770–1838). Westward Expansion. Explorers.

Overview of Meriwether Lewis and William Clark's two-and-a-half-year expedition to from the Louisiana Territory to the Pacific coast to determine the worth of the Louisiana Purchase. Stephen Kroll includes fascinating details about provisions, gear, and weapons selected by the forty-three men who joined Lewis and Clark on the journey. Richard Williams's lush oil paintings effortlessly transport readers back in time to the world of the 1800s. The afterword, maps, list of important dates, and bibliography will encourage further exploration of the achievements of Lewis and Clark's expedition. This title is appropriate as an introduction to several topics: famous explorers, the Louisiana Purchase or relations with Native Americans during the western expansion of the United States.

352 Kroll, Steven. *Pony Express!* Illus. by Dan Andreasen. Scholastic, 1996. ISBN 0–590–20239–1. Representational. Oils. Nonfiction. Pony Express. Postal Service. Western Expansion.

A historically accurate portrayal of the Pony Express, the fastest way to send a letter—in 1860! Although the Pony Express was defunct after only eighteen months, the intent for faster mail service spurred people then as it does now to deliver mail and packages as quickly as possible. Dan Andreasen's exquisite oil paintings capture the essence and romance of an era in American history that still fascinates people. Use this book with students to juxtapose with the speed of electronic mail and overnight postal service available today to highlight the fascinating achievement of the Pony Express at a time when animals were the main source of transport for people as well as for mail. The author includes a map with a route of the Pony Express, a bibliography of titles for further reading, an index, and photographs from the U. S. Postal Service archives.

353 Kroll, Steven. *By the Dawn's Early Light: The Story of The Star-Spangled Banner.* Illus. by Dan Andreasen. Scholastic, 1994. ISBN 0–590–45054–9. Representational. Oils. Biography. Key, Frances Scott (1799–1843). National Anthem. "Star Spangled Banner."

Historically accurate account of the life of the man responsible for writing "The Star-Spangled Banner." Intimate details about Francis Scott Key's life glossed over in other sources make this book an essential starting point when studying America's fight for freedom from Great Britain. This book approaches the creation of the national anthem from the perspective of Key's relationship with Dr. William Beanes, a close personal friend of Key's held captive by the British ship. Evocative oil paintings relate the proud spirit that made America the great nation it is today. Teachers will appreciate the inclusion of maps, music chords, a bibliography, and a reproduction of the original manuscript drafted by Key. Use this title in conjunction with Peter Spier's illustrated version of the song.

354 Kunhardt, Edith. *Honest Abe.* Illus. by Malcah Zeldis. Greenwillow, 1993. ISBN 0–688–11190–8. Naive. Gouache. Biography. Lincoln, Abraham (1809–1865). Presidents—United States.

A biography of Abraham Lincoln with simple text that easily opens up discussion about the Lincoln's presidency. This book makes an ideal introduction to the study Lincoln's life and his achievements as sixteenth president of the United States. Kunhardt covers the major events in Lincoln's life from his humble boyhood in Kentucky to his turbulent presidential years in Washington. Malcah Zeldis used bold colors to illustrate the incredible life of a legendary man. Each rich illustration will allow students to make many interpretations of the life of Abraham Lincoln. Along with Michael McCurdy's illustrated *Gettysburg Address* (Harcourt Brace, 1995). *Honest Abe* will excite students to explore the familiar life of Abraham Lincoln with new eyes. Other companion titles include *Abraham Lincoln: A Man for All the People* (Holiday House, 1993) by Myra Cohn Livingston, *Young Abe Lincoln: The Frontier Days, 1809–1837* (National Geographic Society, 1996) by Cheryl Harness, and *Lincoln: A Photobiography* (Clarion, 1987) by Russell Freedman, which won the Newbery Award in 1988.

355 Lattimore, Deborah Nourse. *The Flame of Peace: A Tale of the Aztecs.* Illus. by author. Harper & Row, 1989. ISBN 0–06–023708–2. Folk Art. Watercolors. Fiction. Aztecs. Indians of Mexico.

A fictional account of the Aztec people based on Aztec mythology, art, and legend. A boy named Two Flint watches his father leave home to dissuade an approaching army from attacking. When his father does not return, the warriors gather for war. Two Flint, striving to avoid war and bring his father home safely, heads to the sun to seek the council of Lord Morning Star. The illustrations, inspired by Aztec art, successfully bring the story from the mists of time and make it appealing for modern readers. The vitality and courage of a lost race of people is brought to startling life in this book. The endpapers are an excellent example of the use of design in picture book illustration. Use with *Pyramid of the Sun, Pyramid of the Moon* (Macmillan, 1988) by Leonard Everett Fisher and *The Sad Night: The Story of an Aztec Victory and a Spanish Loss* (Clarion, 1994) by Sally Schofer Mathews to explore Aztec culture.

356 Lawlor, Veronica. *I Was Dreaming to Come to America.* Illus. by author. Viking. ISBN 0–670–86164–2. Impressionism. Collage. Information. Immigrants. Naturalization.

Veronica Lawlor interviewed people who passed through Ellis Island as children as part of an oral history project. In *I Was Dreaming to Come to America* Lawlor has taken the recollections of adults and paired them with startling collage illustrations to recount the images of a child's first view of America. The author included biographies of the people whose memories are used in the book. She chose immigrant representatives from countries all across Europe who entered America between 1900 and 1925. Through the words of the people who immigrated to America for a better life, the text captures the powerful vision of a country that symbolizes freedom. Other inspiring titles about immigration include *An Ellis Island Christmas* (Viking, 1992) by Maxine Rhea Leighton, *The Lotus Seed* (Harcourt, 1993) by Sherry Garland, *Klara's New World* (Knopf, 1992) by Jeanette Winter, and *The Butterfly Seeds* (Tambourine, 1995) Mary Watson.

357 Lawrence, Jacob. *Harriet and the Promised Land.* Illus. by author. Simon & Schuster, 1993. ISBN 0–671–86673–7. Expressionism. Gouache. Poetry. Harriet Tubman (1815?–1913). Slavery. African American Women. Women— Biography.

A biography in spirited verse about the brave heart and achievements of Harriet Tubman and her efforts on the Underground Railroad. Jacob Lawrence celebrates Harriet Tubman's mission with compassion and depth in a splendid picture book format. His expressionistic paintings provide insight to the spirit and passion of Harriet's continued efforts to assist escaped slaves from the South to the "promised land" in the North. The brief, rhythmic text makes this book an ideal introduction to a unit of study about prominent women, slavery, or African American heritage. Jacob Lawrence's extensive body of work includes narrative paintings about the abolitionist John Brown and Troussaint L'Ouverture, liberator of Haiti. Use Lawrence's books to study the influence of this prominent African American Artist. *Minty: A Story of Young Harriet Tubman* (Dial, 1996) by Alan Schroeder is a fictional account of Harriet's childhood.

358 Lawrence, Jacob. *The Great Migration.* Illus. by author. HarperCollins, 1993. ISBN 0–06–023037–1. Naive. Tempera. Personal Accounts. Lawrence, Jacob (1917–). African Americans. Urban Migration.

A magnificent artistic journey about the African American great migration as rendered by famed African American artist Jacob Lawrence. Lawrence created a series of paintings chronicling the migration of African Americans from the southern United States to the northern United States. Thousands of people left the bitter memories of the South to find new strength in the industrious northern United States during and after World War I. The haunting images and painful journey are captured in bold tempera paintings that are now housed in the Museum of Modern Art in New York City and the in Phillips Collection in Washington, D.C., The sixty paintings created in the 1940s are given a new dimension in picture book format along with a moving poem by celebrated children's writer Walter Dean Myers. An elegant introduction to a chapter of history not found in textbooks.

359 Leigh, Nila K. *Learning to Swim in Swaziland: A Child's-Eye View of a Southern African Country.* Illus. by author. Scholastic, 1993. ISBN 0–590–45938–4. Naive. Photographs/Crayola. Nonfiction. Authors—Children. South Africa. Children's Writings.

Eight-year-old Nila spent a year in Swaziland with her parents. Nila, in a world different from the one she was accustomed to, drew pictures, took photographs, and wrote letters to ease her transition into the foreign country. She enclosed her pictures with her letters describing Swaziland to her friends in the United States. When Nila was ten, her pictures, photographs, and letters were compiled into the collection that makes up the text and illustrations in this book. Educators could use this as an introduction to social life in Swaziland or as an example of a young person's creative writing skills.

360   Levine, Arthur A. *All the Lights in the Night.* Illus. by James E. Ransome. Tambourine, 1991. ISBN 0–688–10107–0. Representational. Oils. Fiction. Hanukkah. Jews. Immigration.

A memorable tale of family devotion and religious pride set in nineteenth-century Russia. Young Moses and his smaller brother, Benjamin, flee their family farm when an opportunity arises for passage to Palestine. The tsar has made life unbearable for Jews in Russia, and it is with heavy hearts that the boys kiss their parents goodbye and set out on dangerous journey to freedom. Before the journey ends, the boys will face many obstacles. A highpoint in the narrative is the history of Hanukkah that the boys share with each other to keep the light burning during their journey even in the dead of night. Companion titles include Leonard Everett Fisher's *The Wailing Wall* (Macmillan, 1989), which is about the struggle of the Jewish people throughout history. The title also fits nicely to include with Holocaust titles such as Margaret Wild's *Let the Celebrations Begin!* (Orchard, 1991) and David Adler's *Child of the Warsaw Ghetto* (Holiday House, 1995).

361   Lewin, Ted. *Market!* Illus. by author. Lothrop, Lee & Shepard, 1996. ISBN 0–688–12161–6. Impressionism. Watercolors. Markets.

A vibrant array of marketplaces from countries around the world. From the waterfront in New York City to the lush green hills of Ireland there are stalls, tables, and baskets of wares sold by local folk dependent on the profit from the market for their livelihood. Lewin's bold watercolors capture the excitement of market day in a series of paintings of folk traveling miles barefoot in Morocco to sell dates or by taxi to the harbor in New York City to sell hand-crafted jewelry. This is an ideal title to explore the old world ways still prevalent in the modern world. Other titles about markets include Eve Bunting's *Market Day* (HarperCollins, 1996), Karen Lynn Williams's *Tap-Tap* (Clarion, 1994), Leyla Torres's *Saturday Sancocho* (Farrar, Straus & Giroux, 1995), and Anita Lobel's *On Market Street* (Greenwillow, 1981).

362 Lincoln, Abraham. *The Gettysburg Address.* Illus. by Michael McCurdy. Harcourt Brace, 1995. ISBN 0-395-699824-3. Expressionism. Scratchboard. Speeches. Lincoln, Abraham (1809-1865). Gettysburg Address.

A stunning picture book with scratchboard illustrations that captures the nuances and power of Abraham Lincoln's most famous speech. This book will seize the attention of students who would scan but fail to absorb the message of the Gettysburg Address. At once powerful and encompassing, the illustrations add depth and dimension to a speech of great historic significance. Librarians and teachers will eagerly await other artists who attempt to capture the power of historical documents in a format as magnificent as that used by Michael McCurdy. Companion titles *Abraham Lincoln: A Man for All the People* (Holiday House, 1993) by Myra Cohn Livingston, *Young Abe Lincoln: The Frontier Days, 1809-1837* (National Geographic Society, 1996) by Cheryl Harness, and *Lincoln: A Photobiography* (Clarion, 1987) by Russell Freedman.

363 Maruki, Toshi. *Hiroshima No Pika.* Illus. by author. Lothrop, Lee & Shepard, 1980. ISBN 0-688-01297-3. Impressionism. Watercolors. Nonfiction. World War II. Hiroshima, Japan. Atomic Bomb.

An account of the horror and destruction caused by the atomic bomb dropped on Hiroshima August 6, 1945. This story, based on the memories of a woman who was seven years old at the time of the blast, is striking in its intensity. Even more startling are the impressionistic paintings, which seize the reader, making them relive the horror and anguish of the innocent citizens of Hiroshima. This book will grab the attention of students and put a jolt into any discussion because of the raw, emotional appeal of the illustrations. Use in conjunction with a unit about World War II or the history of Japan and her people. Some companion titles include *Faithful Elephants: A True Story of Animal, People, and War* (Houghton Mifflin, 1988) by Yukio Tsuchiya and *Shin's Tricycle* (Walker & Company, 1992) by Tatsuhara Kodama.

364 Mathews, Sally Schofer. *The Sad Night: The Story of an Aztec Victory and a Spanish Loss.* Illus. by author. Clarion, 1994. ISBN 0-395-63035-5. Folk Art. Watercolors/Black Ink. Nonfiction. Aztecs. Indians of Mexico. Mexico. Cortés, Hernán (1485-1547?).

A journey through the mythic origins of Aztec history. The year 1519 was a pivotal year for the Aztec people when Spaniard Hernán Cortés arrived in the city of Tenochtitlán seeking treasure. What ensued was a battle that devastated the Aztec nation and led to the eventual conquest of Mexico by the Spaniards. A stunning example of the possibilities of historical events presented in picture book format. The illustrations, reminiscent of Aztec art, enhance the story. Use with *Pyramid of the Sun, Pyramid of the Moon* (Macmillan, 1988) by Leonard Everett Fisher, *How Music Came to the World* (Houghton Mifflin, 1994) by Hal Ober, and *The Flame of Peace: A Tale of the Aztecs* (Harper & Row, 1989) by Deborah Nourse Lattimore, three titles about the Indians of Mexico.

365 McCully, Emily Arnold. *The Pirate Queen*. Illus. by author. G. P. Putnam's, 1995. ISBN 0-399-22657-5. Expressionism. Watercolors. Biography. O'Malley, Grace (1530?-1603?). Ireland—History. Women Pirates. Women—Biography.

Thrilling tale of a daring woman pirate, Grace O'Malley, based on historical fact and colorful legend. A woman ahead of her time, Grace led a life of intrigue, espionage, and daring deeds on the water and on the land. During a tumultuous period in Irish history when many Irish chieftains succumbed to "Submit and Regrant" policy established by Henry VIII, Grace would fight on land and sea to retain her Irish heritage. Emily Arnold McCully's exquisite illustrations in *The Pirate Queen*, as with her other books *Mirette on the High Wire* (G. P. Putnam's, 1992) and *The Amazing Felix* (G. P. Putnam's, 1993), are the product of meticulous research.

366 McDonough, Yona Zeldis. *Eve and Her Sisters*. Illus. by Malcah Zeldis. Greenwillow, 1994. ISBN 0-688-12512-3. Naive. Gouache. Nonfiction. Biblical Women. Religion.

Fourteen short segments featuring women from the Bible. From Eve and her banishment from Eden to the sacrifice of Yokheved, mother of Moses, this title explores the feminine aspects of these brave and courageous women who were more than just mothers and wives. Their deeds and achievements echo through the centuries, making their stories some of the most well known in literature. These stories act as windows though time by allowing glimpses of women who figured prominently in the evolution of the Christian and Jewish faiths. Malcah Zeldis captures the essence of their contribution in a series of bold illustrations that will attract younger readers because of their bright color and majesty. Use this title in a women's studies unit to explore women who are often overlooked as liberated females because of the patriarchal representations in the Bible. *But God Remembered: Stories of Women from Creation to the Promised Land* (Jewish Lights, 1995) by Sandy Eisenberg Sasso is another collection of stories about biblical women.

367 Miller, Robert H. *The Story of Nat Love*. Illus. by Michael Bryant. Silver Press, 1995. ISBN 0-382-24389-7. Representational. Pastels. Biography. Frontier and Pioneer Life. Western Expansion. African Americans—Biography.

A title from Robert H. Miller's Stories from the Forgotten West celebrating the achievements of African Americans who were instrumental in carving out the land in the nineteenth-century. Nat Love, an African American, was a formative figure during the shaping of the wild and unknown western territories. Born a slave, Nat earns his freedom after the war and heads out to conquer the West with only a horse and his formative roping and shooting skills. His exploits soon earn him a reputation that eventually leads to his gaining legendary status. Miller captures the essence of the man who led an adventurous and daring life and whose exploits have become embedded in American folklore. The tone of the narrative has a tall tale feel because of the spirit and gumption of Nat Love and his readiness to tackle any situation, anytime. Michael Bryant's impressionistic watercolor paintings capture the vitality of a man who lives on in the imagination of people who dream about the Old West.

368 Miller, Robert H. *The Story of Stagecoach Mary Fields.* Illus. by Cheryl Hanna. Silver Press, 1995. ISBN 0-382-24399-4. Representational. Pastels. Biography. African Americans—Biography. African Americans Women. Postal Service, Frontier and Pioneer Life. Women—Biography.

An account of the life of Mary Fields, the first woman postal carrier in the United States. In addition to being a woman, Mary was also black and sixty years old at the time of her appointment. Her achievements as a female and a minority were heroic during her lifetime and left a legacy for future women. Robert H. Miller created this titles as part of a series exploring the unsung African American men and women who were instrumental in forging the unknown territories of the West during the nineteenth-century. Cheryl Hanna's soft pastel illustrations capture the effervescence of a truly exceptional woman. The title is suitable to include in a study of African American heritage. Pair with Steven Kroll's *Pony Express!* (Scholastic, 1996) for a look at mail delivery before the advent of trains, planes, and electronic mail.

369 Miller, William. *Frederick Douglass: The Last Day of Slavery.* Illus. by Cedric Lucas. Lee & Low, 1995. ISBN 1-880000-17-2. Impressionism. Pastels. Biography. Douglass, Frederick (1817?-1895). Slavery. African Americans—Biography.

Captivating glimpse at the early life of Frederick Douglass. Born a slave, Frederick dreams of one day being free. His only escape is in books given to him by the woman who encouraged his learning: the master's wife. As a slave, his ability to read is rare and an impetus for a new overseer to break down the learned black man. The conflict between the men comes to head one day when the overseer attempts to beat Frederick for a minor infraction. Frederick, tired of the cruelty, stands up to the white man in an unprecedented fight that gives courage and hope to all slaves, for this is Frederick's last day of slavery. The impressionistic pastel illustrations convey the strength and determination of one of history's greatest freedom fighters.

370   Mochizuki, Ken. *Baseball Saved Us.* Illus. by Dom Lee. Lee & Low, 1993. ISBN 1-880000-01-6. Impressionism. Mixed Media. Fiction. World War II. Japanese Americans. Internment Camps. Children and War.

A heartrending tale of the unfair treatment of innocent Japanese Americans during World War II. Shorty and his family, as well as thousands of other Japanese Americans, were forced from their homes and relocated to internment camps after the Japanese attack on Pearl Harbor. To abate the loneliness and isolation, Shorty's father builds a baseball diamond. The treatment of the Japanese Americans was a disgrace and not renounced by the government as wrong until 1988. Discuss the "forgotten" treatment of these people with your class and the rash actions inspired by war. Two companions titles are based on actual events *Journey: Japanese Americans, Racism, and Renewal* (Orchard, 1990) by Sheila Hamanaka and *The Bracelet* (Philomel, 1993) by Yoshiko Uchida.

371   Mühlberger, Richard. *The Story of Christmas: Told through Paintings.* Illus. by Reproductions. Harcourt Brace, 1990. ISBN 0-15-200426-2. Reproductions. Nonfiction. Christmas. Nativity.

An exquisite illustrated book that couples paintings from the collection at the Metropolitan Museum of Art and excerpts from the King James version of the Bible to tell the story of Jesus Christ's birth through art. Among the paintings included in this book are *The Adoration of the Magi* by Quentin Massys and *Madonna and Child Enthroned with Two Angels* by Fra Filippo Lippi. Commentary by Richard Mühlberger aids the reader through the background of both the story and the works of art in a spirited verse that enlightens us. The text is replete with interesting tidbits of information that makes this book useful beyond the Christmas season. Included are subjects ranging from the identity of the Magi to the origins of the nativity scene. Celebrate the Christmas holidays with *Joy to the World: The Story of the First Christmas* (Platt & Munch, 1992) by Dina Anastasio, *The First Christmas* (Simon & Schuster, 1992), featuring paintings from the National Gallery in London, and *The Christmas Story* (Holiday House, 1996) by Kay Chorao.

372   Musgrove, Margaret. *Ashanti to Zulu.* Illus. by Leo and Diane Dillon. Dial, 1976. ISBN 0-8037-0357-0. Expressionism. Mixed Media. Fiction. Alphabet Books. Africa. African Tribes. Africa—Social Life and Customs.

Introduces twenty-six cultures that make up the diverse population of Africa. Each illustration contains a man, a woman, a child, an artifact, housing, and a local animal to give the reader a thorough glimpse of each culture represented. Underneath each illustration is a pronunciation of the tribe's name and interesting facts to encourage further exploration. Leo and Diane Dillon, two-time winners of the prestigious Caldecott Award, succeeded in capturing the essence of each culture in brilliant full-color paintings. A map in the back shows the geographic locations of each of the tribes represented in the book. In a note the author explains that her intention was to bring the cultures of Africa to American children. Exemplary research matches the author's attempt to bring the rich traditions of Africa to readers everywhere.

373 Myers, Walter Dean. *Toussaint L'Ouverture.* Illus. by Jacob Lawrence. Simon & Schuster, 1996. ISBN 0-689-80126-2. Naive. Tempera. Biography. Lawrence, Jacob (1917-). Haiti. Toussaint L'Ouverture (1743?-1803). Haitian Revolution (1791-1804).

Walter Dean Myers creates a fascinating biography of Toussaint L'Ouverture, Haitian liberator, to accompany a narrative series of paintings by famed artist Jacob Lawrence. The series, first displayed at the 1940 Chicago Negro Exposition, is currently part of the collection at the Armistad Research Center in New Orleans. Both the artist and the author do an exemplar job of honoring a man responsible for setting in motion a revolution that led to the first black republic. Toussaint L'Ouverture died in November 1803, just months before a document declaring his Haiti an independent country, but his spirit and yearning for freedom live on in others who fight against oppression.

374 Oppenheim, Shulamith Levey. *Iblis.* Illus. by Ed Young. Harcourt Brace, 1994. ISBN 0-15-238016-7. Impressionism. Pastels. Fiction. Adam (biblical figure). Eve (biblical figure). Islamic Religion.

An Islamic version of the Adam and Eve story. Oppenheim's retelling is gripping and powerful, drawing upon Islamic sources, including the research of respected scholar Jarir at-Taburi. In this version, the serpent becomes the vehicle the Iblis (devil) uses to gain entry into paradise. By hiding in the space between the serpent's teeth, the Iblis enters paradise and marks the teeth of the serpent as poisonous for eternity. Ed Young, famed for his impressionistic illustrations, culls details from the story and presents them in powerful images that explode in a splash of color on the pages. *Iblis* is useful for a comparative study of creation myths. Professionals cautious of promoting one religion over another may want to review the title prior to using it in comparison with the Christian story of Adam and Eve. Another Islamic version of Adam and Eve is *And the Earth Trembled: The Creation of Adam and Eve* (Harcourt Brace, 1996) also by Shulamith Levey Oppenheim. *Ramadan* (Holiday House, 1996) by Suhaib Hamid Ghazi explores the Islamic holiday, Ramadan. Warwick Hutton's *Adam and Eve: The Bible Story* (Macmillan, 1987) presents the Christian version of the inhabitants of the Garden of Eden.

375 Oppenheim, Shulamith Levey. *The Lily Cupboard.* Illus. by Ronald Himler. HarperCollins, 1992. ISBN 0–06–024670–7. Impressionism. Watercolors/Gouache. Historical Fiction. Jews. World War II. German Occupation. Children and War.

An affecting tale of the devastation of the German occupation throughout Europe during World War II. The story is told from the perspective of Miriam, a young Jewish girl, who is sent from her home in the city to live with a compassionate family in the country following invasion by German soldiers. Protected from the harsh reality of the German occupation, Miriam fails to grasp the meaning of the war and all its implications until the day she is forced to hide in the designated hiding place when soldiers pass through the village. Ronald Himler, noted for his realistic watercolors illustrations, adds spirit to Shulamith Levey Oppenheim's tribute to the heroism of Dutch people who risked their own lives hiding Jewish families during the war. The title is effective to open discussion about the brave deeds of ordinary people risking their lives to help heal a wound that will fester for generations to come.

376 Parker, Nancy Winslow. *Locks, Crocs and Skeeters: The Story of the Panama Canal.* Illus. by author. Greenwillow, 1996. ISBN 0–688–12241–8. Cartoon Art. Mixed Media. Nonfiction. Panama Canal—History.

A informational title about the inspiration, development, and building of the Panama Canal. Nancy Winslow Parker combines the poetry, historical facts, and maps together in an illustrated book with concise, dependable information about "the eighth wonder of the world." The magnificent splendor of the canal is overshadowed by the staggering loss of human lives from its inception to its completion in 1914. The book in is two parts: The poem "Beyond the Chagres" by James Stanley Gilbert, which was inspired by life in Panama. The second part has detailed information about key figures in the development and building of the Panama Canal, including Theodore Roosevelt, the American president who promoted financial backing of the canal, John Stevens, chief engineer, and William Crawford Gorgas, who helped rid the Panama area of mosquitoes.

377 Paul, Ann Whitford. *The Seasons Sewn: A Year in Patchwork.* Illus. by Michael McCurdy. Harcourt Brace, 1996. ISBN 0–15–276918–8. Express-

ionism. Scratchboard. Nonfiction. Seasons. Quilts and Quilting. Frontier and Pioneer Life.

An illustrated collection of patchwork quilt designs from the nineteenth century. Ann Whitford Paul's text involves snippets of information about frontier and pioneer life and suggests that certain practices of people during the nineteenth century, which may have inspired the quilt pattern designs. This titles in beneficial for its imaginative suggestions of the origin of the names of the quilt designs and the plethora of information about frontier life. The author uses second-person narration, which is seldom employed by writers. Michael McCurdy's detailed scratchboard illustrations bring the nineteenth-century frontier family to life. *Sweet Clara and the Freedom Quilt* (Knopf, 1993) by Deborah Hopkinson, *Luka's Quilt* (Greenwillow, 1994) by Georgia Guback, and *The Patchwork Quilt* (Dial, 1985) by Valerie Flournoy are fictional books that would make ideal companion books. *Sewing Quilts* (Macmillan, 1994) by Ann Turner is a companion quilt title with a pioneer setting.

378 Paxton, Tom. *The Story of Santa Claus.* Illus. by Michael Dooling. Morrow Junior, 1995. ISBN 0-688-11365-6. Expressionism. Oils. Fiction. Santa Claus (legendary character). Holidays. Christmas.

A jolly tale of Santa Claus relating the traditional practices, including the climb down the chimney and Santa's helpers, the elves. Students will enjoy sharing stories of personal visits from Santa Claus because no one ever really stops believing in the legendary figure of the white-bearded man in the red suit. This book would have been more beneficial with a historical view of Santa Claus telling how he evolved as a legendary figure rather than exploring the traditional and well-known aspects of the story. Have students research other cultures for traces of a Santa Claus figure, including England's Father Christmas and Russia's Grandfather Frost. Pair with Clement C. Moore's classic poem "A Visit from St. Nicholas," which is in picture book format (Holiday House, 1980) with illustrations by Tomie dePaola. Students could also explore the cartoons of Thomas Nast (1840–1902), who is attributed with creating the modern attire worn by Santa Claus. *Twas the Night B'fore Christmas* (Scholastic, 1996) by Melodye Rosales is an African American version set in rural North Carolina at the turn of the century and based on Clement C. Moore's poem.

379 Pinkney, Andrea. *Dear Benjamin Banneker.* Illus. by Brian Pinkney. Harcourt Brace, 1994. ISBN 0-15-200417-3. Expressionism. Scratchboard. Biography. Banneker, Benjamin (1731–1806). Astronomers. African Americans—Biography.

An heartening biography about the first black astronomer in the United States. Benjamin Banneker, born free, struggled with the concept of slavery all his life. Eventually his confusion led him to write to Thomas Jefferson, then secretary of state, to challenge his double standards for declaring freedom for all men while at the same time owning slaves. The animated correspondence was the inspiration for this book. Andrea Pinkney's vivacious writing style captures both the passion of a free man and his desire for freedom for everyone. The illustrations by Brian Pinkney are vigorous, capturing the dedication and resolve of a man who would make history by becoming the first black man to write an almanac. Use along with other titles about lesser-known African Americans whose achievements are largely left unsung. Some titles include *The Story of Nat Love* (Silver Press, 1995) by Robert H. Miller, *Bill Pickett: Rodeo-Ridin' Cowboy* (Harcourt Brace, 1996) by Andrea D. Pinkney, and *The Real McCoy: The Life of an African American Inventor* (Scholastic, 1993) by Wendy Towle.

380 Presilla, Maricel E., and Gloria Soto. *Life Around the Lake.* Illus. by Embroideries by the Women of Lake Pátzcuaro. Holt, 1996. ISBN 0–8050–3800–0. Expressionism. Embroidery. Nonfiction. Indians of Mexico. Tarasco Indians. Mexico—Social Life and Customs.

Life Around the Lake is a spirited account of the people and traditions of the Tarascan Indians of Mexico. Pronunciation guide. Text is interspersed with Spanish word making the effect astonishing. Lake Pátzcuaro, a source of life to the Tarascan Indians, is slowly dying and the effects are felt by all. The intricate needlepoint art recalls a way of life way long abandoned. Compare the embroidery illustrations with Dia Cha's *Dia's Story Cloth: The Hmong People's Journey of Freedom* (Lee & Low, 1996) and Pegi Deitz Shea's *Whispering Cloth: A Refugee's Story* (Boyds Mills, 1995). Other books about the Indians of Mexico include Emery Bernhard's *The Tree That Rains* (Holiday House, 1994), Leonard Everett Fisher's *Pyramid of the Sun, Pyramid of the Moon* (Macmillan, 1988), Deborah Nourse Lattimore's *The Flame of Peace: A Tale of the Aztecs* (Harper & Row, 1989), and Sally Schofer Mathews's *The Sad Night: The Story of an Aztec Victory and a Spanish Loss* (Clarion, 1994).

381 Provensen, Alice. *My Fellow Americans: A Family Album.* Illus. by author. Harcourt Brace, 1995. ISBN 0–15–276642–1. Representational. Oils. Nonfiction. United States.

A fascinating illustrated history of the diverse population that makes America the great country it is. Details about the achievements of people such as Susan B. Anthony, Cesar Chavez, Thomas Paine, and Mother Jones—to name just a few. The text consists of famous remarks by the featured Americans that accompany Alice Provensen's finely detailed portraits of the painters, writers, fighters, politicians, inventors, and reformers who made this land great. Each illustration is carefully labeled with events that mark the significance of each individual. This book has many uses because of its wide subject content. Ideally, a copy should be placed on a table in the classroom or library for student to browse through at their leisure.

382 Provensen, Alice. *The Buck Stops Here: The Presidents of the United States.* Illus. by author. Harper & Row, 1990. ISBN 0-06-024786-X. Representational. Watercolors. Biography. Presidents—United States.

A journey through time with stops along the way to meet the most formidable men in American history: the Presidents of the United States. Each president from George Washington to George Bush is introduced in a silly, rhymed text and associated with his accomplishments (and mistakes) in a series of detailed paintings replete with symbols and hidden pictures of major events that occurred during each presidency. This exhilarating biographical book will inspire students to explore the illustrations to find information "hidden" within the pictures. As an overview, this book will serve nicely to open a unit about the American presidency. Simply by exploring the illustrations, students will discover which president was in office when the Pony Express delivered mail and who was in office when the Kansas–Nebraska Act allowed states to choose between slavery and a free state. Pair with *The President's Cabinet and How it Grew* (HarperCollins, 1978, 1991) by Nancy Winslow Parker, which explores the creation and evolution of the presidential cabinet. Betsy and Giulio Maestro's *The Voice of the People: American Democracy in Action* (Lothrop, Lee & Shepard, 1996) features more information about American government.

383 Ritter, Lawrence S. *Leagues Apart: The Men and Times of the Negro Baseball League.* Illus. by Richard Merkin. Morrow Junior, 1995. ISBN 0-688-13316-9. Expressionism. Oil Pastels. Nonfiction. African Americans—Biography. Baseball—History. Negro Leagues.

A glowing tribute to the men who played their best despite segregation laws that prevented them from playing in white baseball leagues. Lawrence Ritter's fascinating exploration of the history of Negro Leagues is engaging for its unusual approach, using short vignettes to introduce each player. Equally engaging are Richard Merkin's oil pastels, which capture the agility and brilliance of the men who broke ground for African American athletes even before 1947, when Jackie Robinson would break the color barrier and play on a white team. Use this book with *Wilma Unlimited* (Harcourt Brace, 1996) by Kathleen Krull and *Teammates* (Harcourt Brace, 1990) by Peter Golenbeck to explore other black athletes. Some other illustrated baseball books include *Baseball Saved Us* (Lee & Low, 1993) by Ken Mochizuki, *Take Me Out to the*

Ball Game (Four Winds, 1993) by Jack Norworth, and *Casey at the Bat* (Atheneum, 1988) by Ernest Lawrence Thayer. Joseph Bruchac's *The Great Ball Game: A Muskogee Story* (Dial, 1994) is a pourquoi tale about the invention of baseball.

384   Roth, Susan L. *Buddha.* Illus. by author. Doubleday, 1994. ISBN 0–385–31072–2. Expressionism. Collage. Fiction. Gautama Buddha (B.C. 563?–483?). Buddhism.

A lyrical rendition of the life of a man who left a legacy that affects the lives of millions of people 2000 years after his death. Siddhartha, born a prince and raised in luxurious surroundings, casts aside the trappings of wealth after he witnesses the poverty and agony of people less fortunate than himself. His struggle for understanding and enlightenment lead him to isolate himself for six years. When he emerges, he delivers his famous Deer Park sermon, which includes his Noble Eightfold Path and Doctrine of Four Truths—the cornerstone of Buddhist teachings. Susan L. Roth carefully researched her topic and accented her information with abstract collage illustrations that enhance the mystery and power of a man whose wisdom reaches across the centuries to influence 250 million followers in the modern world. Historic in presentation, the text should not offend anyone sensitive to religions not their own.

385   Rounds, Glen. *Sod Houses on the Great Plains.* Illus. by author. Holiday House, 1995. ISBN 0–8234–1162–1. Naive. Black Marker/Pastels. Fiction. Frontier and Pioneer Life. Sod Houses. Great Plains.

Glen Rounds once again delights with an offering for Great Plains enthusiasts. *Sod Hoses of the Great Plains* is also a perfect introduction to Great Plains history for younger readers. Rounds, who was himself born in a sod house, describes the building of a prairie dwelling in the area of the United States now known as Nebraska. In his distinctive style, Rounds accompanies his text with trademark illustrations. The soft watercolors are a perfect compliment to this reminiscent story of the Great Plains. For a closer look at the midwest, use this title with *Dakota Dugout* (Macmillan, 1985) by Ann Turner and *Heartland* (Crowell, 1989) by Diane Siebert. The title is also appropriate for a unit about frontier and pioneer life.

386   Rylant, Cynthia. *Appalachia: Voices of Sleeping Birds.* Illus. by Barry Moser. Harcourt Brace, 1991. ISBN 0–15–201605–8. Representational. Watercolors. Fiction. Appalachian Region—Social Life and Customs. Mountains—Appalachia.

A touching tribute to the people who call an area of the United States stretching from Quebec, Canada, to Alabama home. With lyrical prose Cynthia Rylant pays homage to a place where dogs are named Prince and people live in towns called Sally's Backbone. Barry Moser's watercolors draw upon the common folk and sights of the Appalachian region to create a picture book of quiet dignity with powerful impact. Both the author and the illustrator were born in the Appalachian region of the United States, and the connection they feel for their birthplace has been transformed into picture book format to share their poignant and memorable experiences. Use the book to introduce an aspect of the southern United States often glossed over in standard text books.

387 Sabuda, Robert. *Saint Valentine*. Illus. by author. Atheneum, 1992. ISBN 0–689–31762–X. Expressionism. Mosaic Collage. Biography. Valentine, Saint (3rd century). Christian Saints. Martyrs.

Recounts the life and death of Valentine, a physician and Christian priest, who lived approximately two hundred years after Christ. Saint Valentine was a humble, generous man who gave unselfishly of his time and knowledge. Use this book to discuss the self-absorbed behavior versus selfless behavior. Robert Sabuda's exquisite mosaic illustrations are worthy of examination distinct from the text. Art teachers will find this picture book intriguing because of the author's original choice of medium. Sabuda gives a detailed explanation of the process in the title page. Includes author's note with further information about Saint Valentine. Saint Valentine is ideal to explore the origins of the popular holiday. *Lives and Legends of the Saints* (Simon & Schuster, 1995) by Carole Armstrong is another picture book that explores the powerful effect of religion in art. Other books about saints include *Patrick: Patron Saint of Ireland* (Holiday House, 1992) and *Francis: The Man of the Poor* (Holiday House, 1982), both by Tomie dePaola. Other books about saints include *Saint Patrick and the Peddler* (Orchard, 1993) and *St. Jerome and the Lion* (Orchard, 1991), both by Margaret Hodges.

388 Saint James, Synthia. *The Gifts of Kwanzaa*. Illus. by author. Whitman, 1994. ISBN 0–8075–2907–9. Naive. Acrylics. Nonfiction. Kwanzaa. African-Americans.

Dr. Maulana Karenga was inspired to create the African-American holiday Kwanzaa in 1966 to reaffirm the rich heritage of people of African descent. Kwanzaa, which is celebrated from December 26 to January 1, is celebrated by millions of people around the world. *Nguzo saba* [en-GOO-zoh SAH-bah]—the seven principles of Kwanzaa—are from the Swahili language because it is spoken widely throughout Africa. Other titles about Kwanzaa include *The Story of Kwanzaa* (HarperCollins, 1996) by Donna L. Washington and *Seven Candles*

for Kwanzaa (Dial, 1993) by Andrea Davis Pinkney. Camille Yarbrough's
Cornrows (Coward, McCann, 1979) is a rich history about the stories
represented by the coils and braids in cornrow hairstyles. *Moja Means One*
(Dial, 1971) and *Jambo Means Hello* (Dial, 1974), both by Muriel Feelings with
illustrations by Tom Feelings, are titles about the Swahili language.

389 San Souci, Robert D. *Kate Shelley: Bound For Legend.* Illus. by Max
Ginsburg. Dial, 1995. ISBN 0-8037-1290-1. Representational. Oils. Bio-
graphy. Kate Shelley. United States—Iowa. Railroads—Accidents. Women—
Biography.

A fast-paced biography of the heroic circumstances surrounding a young
girl's valiant behavior during a storm in 1881. Kate Shelley loves trains and is
familiar with the times they pass her farm as well as the whistles that herald
their arrival. One night Kate sense something amiss and braves thunder and
torrential rains to warn a coming train of impending disaster. Kate Shelley is
still celebrated in Iowa today for a deed of common sense so unexpected that it
made her a heroine. Max Ginsberg's lush oil paintings transport readers back
100 years to stand beside Kate Shelley during her courageous and unselfish act.
Use *Kate Shelley: Bound for Legend* to explore other women whose courage
and determination inspire us.

390 Seattle, Chief. *Brother Eagle, Sister Sky.* Illus. by Susan Jeffers. Dial,
1991. ISBN 0-8037-0963-3. Representational. Mixed Media. Speech. Seattle,
Chief (1790-1866). Indians of North America. Environmental Protection.
Illustrated Classics.

A haunting message from Chief Seattle, leader of the Suquamish Indians,
concerning the preservation of the precious resources provided by the earth.
Although the speech was delivered in the 1850s, the timely message is as
pertinent to society today as it was to the white settlers who laid waste to Chief
Seattle's land as they moved west. Susan Jeffers's detailed illustrations enhance
Chief Seattle's vision, and together they reinforce the importance of
environmental protection. Jeffers provides source notes that make this book a
reliable source for teachers. *Brother Eagle, Sister Sky* is a suitable addition to a
unit on American Indians or a study of famous speeches. Pair with Michael
McCurdy's illustrated *The Gettysburg Address* (Harcourt Brace, 1995) to
explore the possibilities of other famous speeches that would be suitable for
illustration. What speech or essay would your class select? What illustrator
would be best suited to tackle the project? For example, *I Have a Dream* by
Martin Luther King Jr. Which African American illustrator would be ideal to
capture the essence and passion of Dr. Martin's vision?

391 Sewall, Marcia. *People of the Breaking Day.* Illus. by author. Atheneum, 1990. ISBN 0-689-31407-8. Expressionism. Gouache. Fiction. Wampanoag Indians. Indians of North America.

A lyrical prose of the Wampanoag Indians who lived in the area of America that would later be claimed by the Pilgrims on The *Mayflower.* This title is second in a trilogy by Marcia Sewall that explores the relationship between two different groups of people at a very crucial time in American history. Sewall's delicate words and paintings interweave to create a book of outstanding quality. Sewall's focus is the innocence and natural attributes of the Wampanoag Indians prior to their meeting with settlers from England. *Tapenum's Day: A Wampanoag Indian Boy in Pilgrim Times* (Scholastic, 1996) by Kate Waters is an ideal companion title. Use this book with Jane Yolen's *Encounter* (Harcourt Brace, 1992), which relates Christopher Columbus's meeting with another Indian tribe—the Taino Indians.

392 Sewall, Marcia. *Thunder From a Clear Sky.* Illus. by author. Atheneum, 1995. ISBN 0-689-31775-1. Naive. Gouache. Fiction. Wampanoag Indians. Indians of North America. Pilgrims.

Thunder from a Clear Sky is the third in a series of books that explores the early settlement of America. *People of the Breaking Day* (Atheneum, 1990) and *The Pilgrims of Plimoth* (Atheneum, 1986) are companion books that can be read conjointly with *Thunder from a Clear Sky*, or they can be read separately as individual titles because they deal with events earlier in history. Sewall narrates from two points of view: that of a Wampanoag youth and that of a Pilgrim boy. The decision to tell about history in this manner makes the time period appealing. Sewall's skill as a writer shines through as she is able to keep the two narrators, observations distinct without drawing the story down. *Thunder from a Clear Sky* would be ideal for a history class, but English teachers would also find the split narrative useful for creative writing courses.

393 Shea, Pegi Deitz. *The Whispering Cloth: A Refugee's Story.* Illus. by Anita Riggio. Boyds Mills, 1995. ISBN 1-56397-134-8. Representational. Watercolors/Embroidery. Fiction. Hmong (Asian People). Thailand. Refugee Camps.

A heartening story of a child's hope in the midst of a ravaging war. Little Mai loves to sit with the elder women as they chat and stitch *pa'ndaus*—story cloths to sell to traders. At the feet of the women gathered at Widow's store, Mai watches patiently, eager to begin her own stitches. Mai longs for the day she will have the skill and know the history required to stitch the story cloths. After listening to so many stories, Mai is able to look within herself to find a story to stitch on her own *pa'ndau*. When the time comes to sell her cloth to traders, Mai learns to listen to her own story and must make a brave decision. The subtle watercolor paintings and reproductions of an original *pa'ndau* combine to create illustrations with visual impact as memorable as the story.

394   Sis, Peter. *A Small Tall Tale from the Far Far North*. Illus. by author. Knopf, 1993. ISBN 0-679-84345-0. Expressionism. Mixed Media. Fiction. Welzl, Jan (1868-1951). Explorers. Arctic Region.

An elaborately illustrated picture book about the extraordinary life of Czechoslovakian explorer Jan Welzl. Welzl left his native Moravia and was not seen or heard from for more than thirty years. Despite dispute about the authenticity of Welzl's adventures, the tales are nonetheless exciting and worthy of a listen. Although Jan Welzl's life is exciting, it is the design and invention of the author-illustrator that makes this book so appealing. Peter Sis includes maps, panoramas, and a pictograph about an Eskimo myth. Include this book in a study of explorers or in a tall tale unit because many scholars many believe Welzl's adventures were just that. Sis includes an author and source notes that combine with his extensive research to make this title an impressive book.

395   Sisulu, Elinor Batezat. *The Day Gogo Went to Vote: South Africa, April 1994*. Illus. by Sharon Wilson. Little, Brown, 1996. ISBN 0-316-70267-6. Impressionism. Pastels. Fiction. South Africa. Voting.

A fictional account of the momentous occasion when black South Africans are allowed to vote in a government election for the first time. Young Thembi and her Gogo, grandmother, are inseparable and together travel to the polls to cast Gogo's vote for elected official. Brisk, impressionistic images capture the immense feeling and excitement of the eventful day. The protagonist is an eight-year-old girl, and the tone of the story may seem simple, but the topic of white South African oppression and the fight to earn the right to vote is timely and appropriate for older readers. In America, barely half of the people eligible to vote do so. Use this book to discuss government elections and the precious freedom of voting denied to many people throughout the world. Pair with Floyd Cooper's *Mandela: From the Life of the South African Statesman* (Philomel, 1996) for exploration of South Africa's fight for freedom.

396   Stanley, Diane. *The True Adventures of Daniel Hall*. Illus. by author. Dial, 1995. ISBN 0-8037-1469-6. Representational. Pastels. Fiction. Hall, Daniel Weston, b. 1841. Whaling. Adventurers and Adventures.

An adaptation of *Arctic Rovings, or, The Adventures of a New Bedford Boy on Sea and Land*, which relates the treatment of crew members who left America to make their fortunes at sea in the whaling trade. Young Daniel set sail from his home in Massachusetts in 1836 aboard the ship *The Condor*, ready for a life of adventure and riches. What he did not expect was a violent and cruel captain. After two years of abuse, Daniel abandons the ship and eventually finds his way home to Massachusetts from the Siberian wastelands against all odds. Diane Stanley's captivating narrative follows Daniel from New Bedford to the isolated expanse of Siberia in a thrilling adventure story based on Daniel Hall's actual diaries. Stanley's detailed watercolor paintings capture an era long past and revive the excitement that people experienced when travel was still a dangerous journey.

397 Stanley, Diane, and Peter Vennema. *Good Queen Bess: The Story of Elizabeth I of England*. Illus. by Diane Stanley. Four Winds Press, 1990. ISBN 0–02–786810–9. Expressionism. Gouache. Biography. Elizabeth I, Queen of England (1533–1603). Kings, Queens, Rulers. England.

Illustrated biography about one of history's most famous rulers. With grace and dignity, Elizabeth I ruled a country during a time of religious strife. Twenty years before her birth, a religious movement tore the Christians in western Europe into two opposing fractions, a legacy to her reign handed to her by Henry the VIII. As with all their other collaborations, Diane Stanley and Peter Vennema have created a reliable source with dependent information spanning the years between Bess's birth and death with acute sensitivity. Use this in a study of remarkable women who succeeded despite enormous odds. Some additional titles to use include *Cleopatra* (Morrow, 1994) by Diane Stanley and Peter Vennema, *Wilma Unlimited: How Wilma Rudolph Became the World's Fastest Woman* (Harcourt Brace, 1996) by Kathleen Krull, *Ruth Law Thrills a Nation* (Ticknor & Fields, 1993) by Don Brown, and *The True Story of Stagecoach Mary Fields* (Silver Press, 1995) by Robert H. Miller.

398 Stanley, Diane, and Peter Vennema. *Cleopatra*. Illus. by Diane Stanley. Morrow, 1994. ISBN 0–688–10413–4. Expressionism. Gouache. Biography. Cleopatra (d. 30 B.C.). Egypt. Kings, Queens, Rulers. Women—Biography.

An outstanding illustrated biography about the life and brief, uncertain reign of Cleopatra, Queen of Egypt. The text is thorough and dependable. Diane Stanley and Peter Vennema are renowned for their picture book biographies, which include sources, maps, and background information. Stanley and Vennema reach across time and bring the opulence and glory of Cleopatra's court to glorious life. Diane Stanley's sparkling paintings on a tile background are astounding, capturing both the legend and the passion of one of history's most fascinating women. Cleopatra is often portrayed as a selfish and immoral woman who placed pleasure above rule. Dependent on sources written by Cleopatra's enemies (the only records to survive), the authors manage to create a compassionate and exiting biography without stooping to sensationalism. Use this book to explore women who affected the history and fate of the world.

399   Stanley, Diane, and Peter Vennema. *Shaka: King of the Zulus.* Illus. by Diane Stanley. Morrow, 1988. ISBN 0–688–07342–5. Expressionism. Gouache. Biography. Chaka, Zulu Chief (1787?–1828). Zulus. Kings, Queens, Rulers.

An enticing and thoroughly researched biography of a great nineteenth-century ruler. As a child Shaka was banished along with his mother for a minor infraction. It was his disgrace that afforded Shaka the desire and will to rise from a tormented childhood to become one of history's greatest rulers. His prowess as a leader and his skill in managing his army had reached legendary status by the time the Europeans arrived to colonize South Africa. The authors chose to highlight major events in the life of Shaka but emphasized the significance his childhood played in his rise to power. By the time he was assassinated in 1828, Shaka had created one of the most formidable fighting forces in the world. Today 6 million descendants of the Zulus proudly tell of the great warrior Shaka, King of the Zulus. Pair this book with *The King's Day: Louis XIV of France* (Crowell, 1989) by Aliki, *Cleopatra* (Morrow, 1994) by Diane Stanley and Peter Vennema, *Gilgamesh the King* (Tundra Books, 1992) by Ludmila Zeman, and *Chingis Khan* (Holt, 1991) by Demi for a look at a few prominent rulers.

400   Stewart, Dianne. *The Dove.* Illus. by Jude Daly. Greenwillow, 1993. ISBN 0–688–1164–1. Folk Art. Watercolors. Fiction. South Africa.

After heavy rains destroy their crops, Lindi and her grandma must find another way to earn money to pay for food. They spend days creating beautiful bead necklaces, but so many other people also make bead creations that none of the shops will buy what Lindi and her grandma make. To honor the dove that signaled the end of the rains, Lindi and her grandma make a bead bird that catches the attention of the shop owners and brings them the income they need. *The Day Gogo Went to Vote: South Africa April 1994 (*Little, Brown, 1996) by Elinor Batezat Sisulu is a celebration of the black South African's struggle for the right to vote in elections. *At The Crossroads* (Greenwillow, 1991) and *Over the Green Hills* (Greenwillow, 1992) by Rachel Isadora are set in South Africa.

401   Stolz, Mary. *Zekmet the Stone Carver: A Tale of Ancient Egypt.* Illus. by Deborah Nourse Lattimore. Harcourt Brace, 1988. ISBN 0–15–299961–2. Representational. Watercolors. Fiction. Egypt.

A fictional account of the inception and creation of one of Egypt's greatest monuments: the Sphinx. Zekmet is a stone carver, a creation of the author's imagination, based on the mystery surrounding the man responsible for the gargantuan half man, half lion monument that still guards the arid sands today. The original tale, based on ancient folklore, is spirited and fresh. Deborah Nourse Lattimore incorporated hieroglyphics in the borders around the illustrations, which tell the story in pictures. The muted tones perfectly suit the desert setting of the book. A guide to the hieroglyphics is found in the decorated endpapers. Companion titles include *Egyptian Cinderella* (Crowell, 1989) by Shirley Climo, *Cleopatra* (Morrow,1994) by Diane Stanley, and *Aïda* (Harcourt Brace, 1990) by Leontyne Price. *The Golden Flower: A Story from Egypt* (Troll, 1995) by Janet Palazzo-Craig and *The Winged Cat: A Tale of Ancient Egypt* (HarperCollins, 1992) by Deborah Nourse Lattimore are other Egyptian legends. Leonard Everett Fisher, in his signature style, has created *The Gods and Goddesses of Egypt* (Holiday House, 1997).

402 Stroud, Virginia. *The Path of the Quiet Elk.* Illus. by author. Dial, 1996. ISBN 0-8037-1718-0. Naive. Acrylics. Alphabet Book. Indians of North America. Religion. Indian Philosophy.

An alphabet picture book based upon the teachings of Indian philosophies. Each letter of the alphabet presents a lesson that teaches about the connection between all human beings and nature. The two central characters, Wisdom Keeper and Looks Within, begin their journey along the Path of the Quiet Elk by calling for the assistance of Animal Helper. To summon Animal Helper they sing an ancient song passed from generation to generation. The text, though set up in an alphabet book format, reads smoothly as any storybook. Virginia Stroud, a respected artist, draws upon her experiences as a medicine woman to create a book unique for its illustrations as well as its subject.

403 Towle, Wendy. *The Real McCoy: The Life of an African American Inventor.* Illus. by Will Clay. Scholastic, 1993. ISBN 0-590-43596-5. Representational. Acrylics. Biography. McCoy, Elijah (1844-1929). Inventors. African Americans—Biography.

A biography about one of the first African-American inventors. Elijah McCoy, the son of fugitive slaves, was born in Canada and from an early age displayed an avid interest in machinery. By the time of his death in 1929, Elijah had invented lawn sprinklers and ironing boards—common household appliances used today. Despite his formal training as an engineer, Elijah was unable to get work in his field. This inspiring story about one man's efforts to tackle prejudice in a society with double standards is well rounded and thoroughly researched. Although his achievements were as outstanding as those of Frederick Douglass or W. E. B. Dubois, Elijah McCoy remains relatively unknown. Use this book to explore other great African Americans whose achievements are shrouded by the mists of time.

404   Tsuchiya, Yukio. *Faithful Elephants: A True Story of Animals People and War.* Illus. by Ted Lewin. Houghton Mifflin, 1988. ISBN 0-395-46555-9. Representational. Watercolors. Nonfiction. World War II. Animals, Zoo. Elephants.

A moving tale of the devastating effects of war. Bombs fall on the city of Tokyo day and night. Fearing that the animals in the zoo will escape as war ravishes the country, a painful decision is made by the keepers at the Ueno Zoo. All the animals are to be killed to prevent their escape in the event a bomb destroys the cages and sets the animals free. Most of the animals die quickly and painlessly by poison in their food. The three elephants are smarter, though, and refuse to eat the poison food and their hides are too thick for a needle to pierce. The only option is death by starvation. This true tale will touch students and open discussion about aspects of war seldom thought of. Ted Lewin's touching paintings capture the heartbreak of the zookeepers and the proud death of the elephants.

405   Tunnell, Michael O. *The Joke's on George.* Illus. by Kathy Osborne. Tambourine, 1993. ISBN 0-688-11759-7. Naive. Acrylics. Historical Fiction. Peale, George Willson (1741-1827) and Washington, George (1732-1799). Presidents—United States. Painters.

Humorous account of the polite first president of the United States, George Washington. Washington was known for his unfailing politeness. This book relates the friendship between the early American painter Charles Willson Peake (1741-1827) and George Washington. Washington's courteous bow to a painting by Peale of his two sons climbing a staircase is the central incident in the book. With a tip of his hat, George waits for the children to return his greeting and is astounded by the rudeness of no reply. The bold illustrations are as playful as the storyline. Read this book aloud to introduce a unit on George Washington and to illustrate that not all aspects of history are merely facts. *The Ingenious Mr. Peale* (Atheneum, 1996) by Janet Wilson is an illustrated biography of George Willson Peale, which reveals more details about a fascinating man seldom discussed in history or art classes.

406   Turner, Ann. *Dakota Dugout.* Illus. by Ronald Himler. Macmillan, 1985. ISBN 0-02-789700-1. Representational. Pencil. Fiction. Frontier and Pioneer Life. Great Plains.

A grandmother describes the hardships and loneliness of life on the Great Plains during the westward expansion. As a young bride, the woman was heartbroken to see the harsh land that would be her home for the rest of her life. But time and patience yielded a homestead that brought joy and happiness to the woman made evident in her tale to her granddaughter. The first-person narration is effective with the authentic details that bring the barren stretch of the eighteenth-century Dakota prairie to unforgettable life. Ronald Himler's pencil drawings are especially effective for this lyrical text of pioneer life. Brett Harvey is the author of three ideal companion titles *Cassie's Journey: Going West in the 1860s* (Holiday House, 1988), *My Prairie Christmas* (Holiday House, 1990), and *My Prairie Year: Based on the Diary of Elenore Plaisted* (Holiday House, 1986). Glen Rounds's *Sod Houses on the Great Plains* (Holiday House, 1995) will give students another look at housing during the 1800s.

407 Turner, Ann. *Nettie's Trip South.* Illus. by Ronald Himler. Macmillan, 1987. ISBN 0–02–789240–9. Representational. Pencil. Historical Fiction. Slavery. Civil War.

Dramatic account of a northern girl's trip South during the Civil War. Nettie had heard of the horrors of slavery, but when she sees with her own eyes the abominable practices and cruelty of slavery, she vows to fight for the freedom of the slaves. The first-person narration pulls the reader into the story and will make a powerful read aloud. With a child's keen awareness, Nettie easily sees the world from the view of a slave and realizes how drastically her life would change if her skin were black. Ronald Himler's haunting pencil illustrations are spare and strike the heart with the horrors of slavery. Vivid images of slave quarters and auction blocks make the harsh realities of slavery real. Based on the diary of the author's great-grandmother, this account of slavery will capture students attention. Use this book to open a unit on slavery in America or as part of a study of African American history. Stunning!

408 Uchida, Yoshiko. *The Bracelet.* Illus. by Joanna Yardley. Philomel, 1993. ISBN 0–399–22503–X. Representational. Watercolors. Fiction. Japanese Americans. Internment Camps. World War II. Children and War.

Two girls find their friendship threatened when the United States declares war on Japan in 1942. Because of war hysteria and prejudice, all Japanese Americans are shipped to internment camps because "Americans" feel they are a threat to the safety and security of the nation. The girls exchange bracelets to remind each other of their bond. The uprooting and imprisonment of 120 thousand Japanese Americans during World War II in the United States is an ugly black mark on American history. This powerful story by Yoshiko Uchida, a Japanese American woman who spent her childhood in an internment camp, draws upon memory to remind Americans the true meaning of freedom. Include this book in a study of World War II by looking at the Japanese American experience. Other titles concerning this topic are *The Journey: Japanese Americans, Racism, and Renewal* (Orchard, 1990) by Sheila Hamanaka, *Bluejay in the Desert (*Polychrome, 1993) by Marlene Shigekawa, and *Baseball Saved Us* (Lee & Low, 1993) by Ken Mochizuki.

409 Van Allsburg, Chris. *The Sweetest Fig.* Illus. by author. Houghton Mifflin, 1993. ISBN 0–395–67346–1. Representational. Pastels. Fiction. Dreams. Magic.

Monsieur Bibot is a selfish dentist without thought or compassion for his patients. After a payment of figs from an old woman without money, Bibot refuses her medication to ease the pain after he pulls a tooth. "But they are magic figs," she says. Before long Bibot realizes she is right. When he discovers that his dreams are coming true, he tempts fate to alter his destiny. In a fantastic twist of fate, which could only come from the magnificent mind of Chris Van Allsburg, Bibot learns that it is better if some dreams never come true. Other titles by Van Allsburg that feature dreams as a means of discovery include *Ben's Dream* (Houghton Mifflin, 1982) and *Just a Dream* (Houghton Mifflin, 1990).

410 Van Allsburg, Chris. *The Wretched Stone.* Illus. by author. Houghton Mifflin, 1991. ISBN 0–395–53307–4. Representational. Pastels. Fiction. Television. Evolution.

Something odd is happening to the crew of the *Rita Anne.* After the men discover a roughly hewn stone, two feet across with a smooth surface, on a desert island, nothing is the same. Within a few days, the crew begins to act strangely, staring at the stone all day. Duties and responsibilities fall to the wayside. The captain is mystified because the stone doesn't seem to have any special features that he can see—except for the strange glow emanating from it. The metaphor for television is cleverly told in this eerie tale and will generate lively discussion. Van Allsburg's illustrations evoke powerful questions about evolution. Another Van Allsburg book about another strange ship voyage is *The Wreck of the Zephyr* (Houghton Mifflin, 1983).

411 Van Leeuwen, Jean. *Across the Wide Dark Sea:* The Mayflower *Journey.* Illus. by Thomas B. Allen. Dial, 1995. ISBN 0–8037–1167–0. Representational. Mixed Media. Fiction. Pilgrims. New Plymouth Colony. The *Mayflower.*

A fictionalized account of The Mayflower journey. In 1620 100 people, thirty of them children, sailed from England in search of religious freedom. Through the eyes of a young boy, Van Leeuwen captures the danger the voyagers faced crossing the bitter cold waters of the Atlantic Ocean and the hardships of the first harsh winter. The authentic text is based on primary resources researched at Plimoth Plantation in Massachusetts. What is interesting is Van Leeuwen's decision to refrain from using personal names, instead using an anonymous cast of characters to tell her tale. Thomas B. Allen's artistic grasp encompasses the courage and grace of the first settlers in a series of evocative illustrations. Use this book to springboard discussion of America as a land of opportunity for people in the 1600s and today.

412 Waldman, Neil. *The Golden City: Jerusalem's 3,000 Years.* Illus. by author. Atheneum, 1995. ISBN 0-689-80080-0. Representational. Watercolors. Nonfiction. Jerusalem. Cities.

An illustrated journey through time to a city that has figured prominently in many religions for over 3,000 years. The author-illustrator has traveled throughout the land of Israel many times and the effects of his journeys are evident in his soft watercolor scenes of the city of Jerusalem as it must have looked over the centuries. The bloody and violent history of this grand city is carefully researched, complete with the dates of significant events that have formed the Jerusalem standing today. Pair with *The Wailing Wall* (Macmillan, 1989) by Leonard Everett Fisher, a history of the one remaining piece of the First and Second Temples built by Solomon and restored by Herod during the evolution of the Jewish faith. This title is also effective to use with other titles about the Jewish faith (see index). *Next Year in Jerusalem: 3,000 Years of Jewish Stories* (Viking, 1996) by Howard Schwartz was also illustrated by Neil Waldman and is a perfect companion to *The Golden City.*

413 Wallner, Alexandra. *Betsy Ross.* Illus. by author. Holiday House, 1994. ISBN 0-8234-1071-4. Naive. Acrylics. Historical Fiction. Betsy Ross. American Revolution. American Flag.

A biographical account of Betsy Ross, the seamstress credited with sewing the first American flag. Brief but informative, the prose makes this a worthy addition book to include with study of the American Revolution or the achievements of women. Bright illustrations are loaded with detail despite the naive style. No absolute proof exists as to the historical accuracy concerning Betsy Ross's part in the creation of the flag. Read this book aloud to your class and then have students research other sources to discover "the truth" behind the legend of the U.S. flag and the woman responsible for the world's greatest symbol of freedom. Pair with Leonard Everett Fisher's *Stars and Stripes: Our National Flag* (Holiday House, 1993).

414　Wells, Ruth. *A to Zen: A Book of Japanese Culture.* Illus. by Yoshi. Picture Book Studio, 1992. ISBN 0–88708–175–4. Representational. Dyes on Silk Cloth. Fiction. Alphabet Books. Japanese Culture.

An alphabetical tour of Japanese culture. The author reveals dozens of aspects of Japanese culture, and since the Japanese language has no sounds for L, Q, V, X, there are no topics to represent those letters. The book is designed Japanese style—back to front—and it reads from left to right. Wells introduces words such as *bunraku* (Japanese puppets) and *aikido* (a form of martial arts). Yoshi's rich illustrations were rendered on silk using dyes in the manner that kimonos are created. Many alphabet books designed in the last decade are very sophisticated; have students explore some of these books to develop their own alphabet book. Some alphabet books to explore include *Animalia* (Abrams, 1986) by Graeme Base and *Ashanti to Zulu* (Dial, 1976) by Margaret Musgrove.

415　Whiteley, Opal Stanley (Selected by Jane Boulton). *Only Opal: The Diary of a Young Girl.* Illus. by Barbara Cooney. Philomel, 1994. ISBN 0–399–21990–0. Naive. Watercolors. Personal Narratives. Whiteley, Opal Stanley. United States—Oregon. Frontier and Pioneer Life.

Excerpts from the diary of Opal Stanley Whiteley, a girl born circa 1900 in Oregon. The text in the book consists of pages from Opal's fifth and sixth years. Opal's strong impression of the life in Oregon at the turn of the nineteenth-century is innocent and refreshing. The narrative is from Opal's point of view and was not tampered with by editors. The diary was almost lost when Opal's stepsister found the dairy and tore it into "a million pieces." When an editor was captured by Opal's writing and requested more of her work, she spent nine months piecing the torn pages of her diary together again. Some people may take exception to the references to spankings and the negative images of stepparents in Opal's records; but taken in context, this book is a delightful tool to use when exploring late-nineteenth-century or personal narratives. Jane Boulton, who selected the excerpts for this book, is also the editor of Opal Stanley Whiteley's full diary.

416　Wild, Margaret. *Let the Celebrations Begin!* Illus. by Julie Vivas. Orchard, 1991. ISBN 0–531–08537–6. Cartoon Art. Watercolors. Fiction. Jews. Concentration Camps. Holocaust. World War II.

A poignant story of the bravery of the innocent Jewish people held captive in Nazi concentration camps during World War II. This book's unusual focus is the first-person story of a little girl who remembers life at home before life in a concentration camp. Exciting news has reached the camp—liberators are coming soon to free the people. The women gather together stray buttons and bits of cloth to make toys for children for the moment when they celebrate the end of their incarceration. When they run short, they use their scant clothing to finish the toys in time for the party. Julie Vivas's expressionistic watercolors are oddly charming despite the harsh subject. This book is based on actual events, and the toys discussed in the story are part of a collection in Poland. Wrap up a unit discussing World War II with this book celebrating the liberation of the Jews.

417 Williams, Sherley Ann. *Working Cotton.* Illus. by Carole Byard. Harcourt Brace, 1992. ISBN 0-15-299624-9. Impressionism. Acrylics. Fiction. African Americans. United States—California. Migrant labor.

A story with an unusual topic based on the author's experiences as a child working the migrant circuit in California. The text is simple, but the topic is timely and will easily generate discussion of an aspect of American culture seldom written about or spoken of. In her author's note, Williams discusses the dignity of people who are forced to travel the migrant route picking cotton and fruits in order to make a living; she also shows what society can do improve conditions for a sector of the population who bring the produce to the markets. Carole Byard's striking acrylic illustrations earned her a Caldecott Honor in 1993 for this book. The harsh realities of the life of a migrant family are captured in a series of paintings balanced with the love and devotion that help these strong people endure the migrant circuit. Companion titles with glimpses of African American culture include *Tar Beach* (Crown, 1991) by Faith Ringgold, *The Great Migration: An American Story.* (Museum of Modern Art, 1993) by Jacob Lawrence, *Carolina Shout!* (Dial, 1995) by Alan Schroeder, *Jumping the Broom* (Holiday House, 1994) by Courtni Wright, and *Cornrows* (Coward, McCann, 1979) by Camille Yarbrough.

418 Winter, Jeanette. *Cowboy Charlie.* Illus. by author. Harcourt Brace, 1995. ISBN 0-15-200857-8. Expressionism. Acrylics. Biography. Russell, Charles Marion (1864–1926). Artists. West (U.S.).

An unusual subject for a picture book biography, the story of Charles Marion Russell nevertheless makes for an exciting exploration. Young Charles, born in St. Louis, dreams of becoming a cowboy, of traveling across vast expanses of prairie and meeting the heroes who made the West tame: Davy Crockett, Daniel Boone, and Kit Carson, to name a few. To pass time on cold winter nights, Charlie would draw pictures of the West as he envisioned it. His relocation to Montana gave him an opportunity to be a cowboy and supplied him with the inspiration to create beautiful western art. After retiring in 1892, Charlie took up painting full time until his death in 1926. Include this book in a unit about frontier and pioneer life for an exciting glimpse at one of the West's unsung heroes.

419   Winter, Jeanette. *Follow the Drinking Gourd.* Illus. by author. Knopf, 1988. ISBN 0–394–99694–1. Expressionism. Acrylics. Fiction. Slavery. Underground Railroad.

A fictional account of Peg Leg Joe, a conductor on the Underground Railroad. Like Harriet Tubman, he led slaves across the southern states to freedom in Canada. Peg Leg Joe hired himself out as a handyman to slave owners. In the evenings, he would teach the slaves lines to a song that held clues to travel the Underground Railroad safely. The drinking gourd in the song is the Big Dipper, which points to the North Star and freedom in the north. Jeanette Winter's unique style marks her illustrations with an intensity that radiates through the entire book. The simple text is as rhythmic as the song that inspired the story. An author's note with details about the background of the story and the music for the song are included. Use with other titles about the Civil War, slavery, or Underground Railroad.

420   Winter, Jeanette. *Shaker Boy.* Illus. by author. Harcourt Brace, 1994. ISBN 0–15–276921–8. Expressionism. Acrylics. Fiction. Shakers.

A brief look at the simple, devout life of the Shaker people as seen through the eyes of a small boy. The Shaker people were a group of generous men and women who believed in a quiet life surrounded by their faith. The Shaker experiment, begun in England, was brought to America in 1774 by the founder, Ann Lee (1736–1784). Today only one Shaker village—located in Sabbathday Lake, Maine—survives. The text, which includes seven songs culled from Shaker collections, is carefully researched. Jeanette Winter's bright paintings celebrate the simplicity and devotion that was the basis for Shaker beliefs. Supplement a unit about colonial England with this title. Supplement *Shaker Boy* with *A Peaceable Kingdom: Shaker Abecedarius* (Viking, 1978) by Alice and Martin Provensen, *Shaker Home* (Houghton Mifflin, 1994) by Raymond Bial, *Shaker Hearts* (HarperCollins, 1997) by Ann Turner, and *Shaker Villages* (Walker, 1993) by Nancy O'Keefe and Sallie G. Randolph to thoroughly explore the Shaker movement.

421   Wright, Courtni C. *Wagon Train: A Family Goes West in 1865.* Illus. by Gershom Griffith. Holiday House, 1995. ISBN 0-8234-1152-4. Representational. Watercolors. Fiction. Frontier and Pioneer Life. America. Westward Expansion.

A fictional account of the hardships and triumphs of an African American family during their journey from the war-torn South to the promise of freedom in the West. Thousands of African Americans made the journey in the same fashion as the white people, but their experiences where seldom recorded because of their illiteracy and the tendency for history to be recorded from a white perspective. Courtni C. Wright's depiction is based on the scant journals and records to be found, but she nonetheless manages to vividly recreate a slice of history that has been overlooked for a century. Gershom Griffith's realistic watercolor paintings are historically accurate and complement the story nicely. This book is ideal for a unit exploring westward expansion or African-American heritage.

422   Yolen, Jane. *Encounter.* Illus. by David Shannon. Harcourt Brace, 1992. ISBN 0-15-225962-7. Acrylics. Historical Fiction. Taino Indians. West Indies. Columbus, Christopher (1446?-1506). Explorers. Discovery of the Americas.

The story of Christopher Columbus's landing in the New World is often told from the European point of view. Jane Yolen, author of more than 100 titles for children, has taken the history of the Taino people, who inhabited the islands where Columbus first landed, and created a tale from a different perspective. Columbus did not find a barren land, but instead a civilization of people with an established culture and entrenched beliefs. Yolen combined a storyteller's imagination with her research of the Taino culture to tell a tale of the arrival of the Spaniards through the eyes of a Taino youth. The young boy dreams of winged birds with voices like thunder. In the morning he sees the ships of Columbus on the horizon. "Beware," he tells his people. But he is only a child, and his dreams are paid no heed. The Taino people are fascinated with the pale men who cover their bodies with cloth. They want the gifts the strangers offer: glass beads and woven things to cover the head and ears of a boy. "Do not welcome them," the boy cries. It is too late. The welcome has begun. Today there are no full-blooded Taino Indians in the world. The few artifacts left are made of stone because the Spanish people took their gold and melted it down. Illustrator David Shannon was faced with many challenges because there are few historical records of the Taino people and their culture.

423   Zelver, Patricia. *The Wonderful Tower of Watts.* Illus. by Frané Lessac. Tambourine, 1994. ISBN 0-688-12649-9. Expressionism. Gouache. Fiction. Simon Rodia's Towers. Watts Towers.

An amazing story of one man's dream to improve the scenery in his poverty-stricken neighborhood. Simon Rodia, an immigrant from Italy, had no training but this did not stop him from building three towers in the backyard of his house in a poor area of Los Angeles known as Watts. To the amazement of the world, Simon did as he said he would and spent the next thirty-three years developing his structure. Simon's accomplishment is outstanding because he never gave up on his dream despite the odds against him. Most students will be unfamiliar with Simon and his architectural achievement, so it will be beneficial to gather photographs or film footage of Simon and the Watts Towers. Use this book to introduce students to less familiar aspects of California. Companion titles include *Working Cotton* (Harcourt Brace, 1992) by Sherley Ann Williams and *Sierra* (HarperCollins, 1991) by Diane Siebert.

424 Zeman, Ludmila. *Gilgamesh the King.* Illus. by author. Tundra Books, 1992. ISBN 0-88776-283-2. Folk Art. Watercolors. Fiction. Gilgamesh (legendary character). Mesopotamia.

A richly illustrated account of a half-god and half-man, Gilgamesh, who ruled over the ancient land of Mesopotamia. The story of Gilgamesh is one of the earliest recorded tales and the basis for many myths and tales prevalent today. Clay tablets discovered during the nineteenth century held the mystical stories of the great ruler, Gilgamesh. Resounding applause for Ludmila Zeman for creating an evocative series of books about an amazing period in history. The author wrote two other titles about the ancient ruler *Revenge of Ishtar* (Tundra Books, 1993) and *The Last Quest of Gilgamesh* (Tundra Books, 1995), which continue the saga of Gilgamesh the king.

Appendix I

Exploring Picture Books with Adolescents: A Checklist

To help your students use a picture book to the full potential, use the following checklist. Help students develop a vocabulary using terms specific to book design and picture book illustration. The glossary following Appendix II may be useful for this purpose.

1. Is there text on every page? How does this affect the flow of the narrative?
2. Does the typeface affect the mood of the story?
3. Does the placement of the text add to the story?
4. Is the story enhanced by the illustrations, or did you enjoy the story without paying much attention to the pictures?
5. Are the illustrations single-page, double-page, or vignettes?
6. What type of cover does the book have? Wrap-around? Single image? The illustrator chose the type of cover for a specific reason. Discuss.
7. Illustrators have specific reasons for choosing the colors they use. Are the effects of their choices in sync with the story?
8. Are the endpapers illustrated or simply in a color that blends with the illustrations?
9. Where does the first illustration appear? Does it reveal something about the story?
10. Do any of the illustrations disappear into the gutter? Does this affect the illustrations?
11. What medium was used to create the illustrations?
12. What style are the illustrations? Realistic, impressionistic, cartoon-style, expressionistic, or naive?
13. Are there borders on any of the pages? Do they add to the story?

14. Is there an author's or illustrator's note with information about the story or illustrations?
15. What information is gleaned from the illustrations that add to the story?
16. Size varies in picture books. Would a different size have affected the outcome of the book?
17. Is the information on the cover and inside flaps important to the entire book?
18. What literary form is your book. For example, if it was a fairy tale, could the information be adapted into a poem or tall tale?
19. If your book was folk literature (a fairy tale, folktale, or tall-tale), did the illustrations create a specific atmosphere as you read?
20. If possible, cover the text and attempt to discover the story from the illustrations.
21. Photographs are frequently used in picture books. Discuss how they compare with other media.
22. Consider the entire design of the book. Would you have used another medium or chosen different colors for the illustrations? What about the shape of the book? Number of pages?
23. Examine three picture books with the same style of illustrations (e.g., cartoon art or representational) or medium (e.g., watercolors or oils) and discuss how the style or medium of the illustrations affected the book.
24. Select three books with a similar type (i.e., folktales or tall tales) and evaluate how the author or illustrator utilized the format to tell the story.
25. Select three books about a particular subject (i.e., World War II or ecology) and then discuss how using the books together helped you better understand a topic.

Appendix II

Professional Resources

The professional resources have been arranged in eight categories to assist educators and librarians in locating a resource for a specific topic. They are: artists, awards, bibliographies, content area, creation, criticism, history and survey.

ARTISTS

Collier, Laurie, and Joyce Nakamura. *Major Authors and Illustrators for Children and Young Adults: A Selection of Sketches from "Something about the Author."* 6 Volumes. Detroit, Michigan: Gale, 1993.

Eight hundred updated biographical sketches of authors and illustrators of children's literature. Suitable for background information of a particular writer or artist.

Commire, Anne, et al. eds. *Something about the Author: Facts and Pictures about Authors and Illustrators of Books for Young People.* Detroit, Michigan: Gale, published annually.

Series published annually devoted to gathering biographical information of creators of children's literature. Includes authors of novels and nonfiction as well as picture books, authors and illustrators. Cumulative index in each volume refers user to previous volumes and individuals with previous sketches.

Cummings, Pat. *Talking with Artists, Vol. 1.* New York: Bradbury, 1992.

Prominent illustrators gave illustrators the eight most sought after answers to her questions about picture book illustration. Includes full-color and b/w reproductions of each illustrator's work. A research tool intended for young readers.

Cummings, Pat. *Talking with Artists, Vol. 2.* New York: Simon & Schuster, 1995.

More interviews with prominent illustrators about the eight most sought after answers of picture book illustration. Includes full-color and b/w reproductions of each illustrator's work. Intended for young readers to use when researching.

Cummins, Julie. *Children's Book Illustration and Design.* New York: Rizzoli, 1992.

Full-color and b/w reproductions of over 100 illustrators noted for their unique contributions to the field. Each illustrator is represented with a brief sketch of the artist and quotations concerning his or her methods and inspiration.

McElmeel, Sharon M. *Bookpeople: A First Album.* Englewood, Colorado: Libraries Unlimited, 1990.

An introduction to forty-one authors and illustrators of children's literature. Includes biographical information and critique of published works about each writer or artist. A section of related activities and further reading for teachers interested in using picture books in the classroom.

McElmeel, Sharon M. *Bookpeople: A Multicultural Album.* Englewood, Colorado: Libraries Unlimited, 1992.

An introduction to multicultural authors and illustrators of children's literature. Includes biographical information and critique of published works about each writer or artist. A section of related activities and further reading for teachers interested in using picture book in the classroom.

Roginski, James W. *Behind the Covers: Interviews with Authors and Illustrators of Books for Children and Young Adults.* Englewood, Colorado: Libraries Unlimited, 1985.

A collection of interviews with prominent children's book writers and illustrators, including Demi, Ellen Raskin, and Donald Crews. In addition to personal insight from the authors and artists, each interview includes a selected bibliography, awards and honors bestowed, and sources for further research. Roginski introduces the subjects in turn with a brief overview of their body of work and tells how they came to create children's books.

Roginski, James W. *Behind the Covers: Interviews with Authors and Illustrators of Books for Children and Young Adults, Vol. 2.* Englewood, Colorado: Libraries Unlimited, 1989.

A second collection of interviews with prominent children's book writers and illustrators. The subject are introduced in turn in a brief sketch of their body of work with an explanation of how they came to create children's books. The featured artists include Chris Van Allsburg, Margot Tomes, Pat Cummings, and Ann Jonas. In addition to personal insight from the authors and artists, each interview includes a selected bibliography, awards and honors bestowed, and sources for further research.

AWARDS

Children's Book Council. *Children's Books: Awards and Prizes.* New York: Children's Book Council, 1992.

A source for international and national awards for illustrators and writers of children's literature. Particularly useful for teachers interested in applying critical study to international authors and illustrators. Updated periodically.

Staerkle, Kathleen, Nancy Hackett, and Linda Ward-Callaghan. *Newbery and Caldecott Mock Election Kit: Choosing Champions in Children's Books.* Chicago: American Library Association, 1994

Outstanding source of ways to present and promote Newbery- and Caldecott-winning titles to children. Unique for the approach in illustrating the process used by selections committees to help children appreciate quality literature.

BIBLIOGRAPHIES

Brown, Muriel W., and Rita Schuch Foudray. *Newbery and Caldecott Medalists and Honor Book Winners: Bibliographies and Resource Material through 1991.* New York: Neal-Schuman, 1992.

Competent source for information about Caldecott and Newbery winners and honorees to 1991. Each entry includes other awards received, a bibliography of work and sources for further research on the author or artist in question.

Ivy, Barbara. *Children's Books about Art: An Annotated Bibliography with Classroom Activities.* Palo Alto, California: Dale Seymour, 1992.

A guide to over 100 picture books about art, artists, and museums. Intended for teachers introducing elements of art to students. Includes classroom activities.

Peterson, Linda Kauffman, and Marilyn Leathers Solt. *Newbery and Caldecott Medal and Honor Books: An Annotated Bibliography.* Boston: G. K. Hall, 1982.

A guide to the unique aspects and artistic accomplishments of the authors and illustrators who have been bestowed with the distinguished Caldecott or

Newbery award presented annually by the American Library Association. Includes honor winners.

Richey, Virginia H., and Kathryn E. Puckett. *Wordless/Almost Wordless Picture Books.* Englewood, Colorado: Libraries Unlimited, 1992.

An annotated bibliography of over 600 wordless or almost wordless picture books. Indexed by titles, subject, author, type, and series. Wordless picture books are particularly useful for studying the effect of illustration in story evolution and character development.

CONTENT AREA

Bosma, Bette. *Fairy Tales, Fables, Legends, and Myths: Using Folk Literature in Your Classroom, second ed.* New York: Teachers College Press, 1992.

Ideas for using folk literature in the classroom, with limited emphasis on the contribution of illustration. Intended to explore adapting the literary form of folk literature into the curriculum.

Bourne, Barbara, and Wendy Saul. *Exploring Space: Using Seymour Simon's Astrology Books in the Classroom.* New York: Morrow Junior Books, 1994.

Seymour Simon's photographic science picture books are excellent resources for teachers working with students of all ages. This book offers insightful ideas and programs to get full benefit from Simon's extensive body of work.

Butzow, John, and Carol Butzow. *Science through Children's Literature.* Englewood, Colorado: Libraries Unlimited, 1989.

Practical application of children's literature for science classrooms. Specific activities for thirty-three children's books noted for their themes in earth sciences, astronomy, and life sciences.

Carroll, Joyce Armstrong. *Picture Books: Integrated Teaching of Reading, Writing, Listening, Speaking, Viewing, and Thinking, Vol. 1.* Englewood, Colorado: Libraries Unlimited, 1991.

Focus on twenty-eight picture books appropriate for integrated curriculum from grades 1 through grade 12. The focus on subject matter rather that artistic contribution mars the overall effect of the discussion of picture books in the classroom. An annotated bibliography of over 100 other books appropriate for the classroom.

Carroll, Joyce Armstrong. *Story Books: Integrated Teaching of Reading, Writing, Listening, Speaking, Viewing, and Thinking, Vol. 2.* Englewood, Colorado: Libraries Unlimited, 1992.

More picture books appropriate for integrated curriculum from grades 1 through grade 12. The focus on subject matter rather that artistic contribution mars the overall effect of the discussion of picture books in the classroom. Includes an annotated bibliography of over 100 other books appropriate for the classroom.

Considine, David M., and Gail E. Haley, and Lyn Ellen Lacy. *Imagine That: Developing Critical Thinking and Critical Viewing through Children's Literature.* Englewood, Colorado: Teacher Ideas Press, 1994.

Useful exploration of the terminology and applications associated with children's book illustration. The overuse of Gail Haley's body of work limits the effectiveness of the title.

Griffiths, Rachel, and Margaret Clyne. *Books You Can Count On.* Portsmouth, New Hampshire: Heinemann, 1991.

A guide to forty picture books with strong math ties to introduce or review math skills with young people. Suitable for inclusion in math content areas.

Hall, Susan. *Using Picture Storybooks to Teach Literary Devices.* Phoenix, Arizona: Oryx Press, 1994.

An annotated bibliography of 300 picture books that demonstrate literary elements such as alliteration, irony, onomatopoeia, parody, and analogy. Excellent resource for English and creative writing teachers who want to ignite interest in the art of the English language.

McElmeel, Sharon L. *Adventuring with Social Studies through Literature.* Englewood, Colorado: Libraries Unlimited, 1991.

A guide to children's books on community, national, and regional issues, with related activities. Useful for social studies teachers who are unfamiliar with children's literature.

Norton, Donna. *The Impact of a Literature-Based Classroom.* Columbus, Ohio: Merrill, 1992.

Intensive exploration of the effect and benefits of a literature-based curriculum. Powerful and thoroughly researched. This title will make converts of people who hesitate to use literature in science and social studies areas.

Polette, Nancy. *Brain Power through Picture Books: Help Children Develop with Books that Stimulate Specific Parts of their Minds.* Jefferson, North Carolina: McFarland, 1992.

Booklists and activities developed to enhance learning and induce creativity by stimulating the four quadrants of the brain: intellectual, contextual, affective, and creative.

Rothlein, Liz, and Anita M. Meinbach. *The Literature Connection: Using Children's Books in the Classroom.* Glenview, Illinois: Scott, Foresman, 1991.

Strategies and discussion concerning the integration of children's literature into the classroom. Particularly useful for teachers who have not yet taken advantage of the opportunities offered by quality literature.

Saul, Wendy, and Sybille A. Jagusch. *Vital Connections—Children, Science and Books*. Portsmouth, New Hampshire: Heinemann, 1992.

An introduction to incorporating children's literature into a science classroom or unit. Includes a selected list of outstanding children's books appropriate for teaching science in the classroom.

Spillman, Carolyn V., and Frances S. Goforth. *Using Folk Literature in the Classroom*. Phoenix, Arizona: Oryx Press, 1994.

An array of activities and ideas for incorporating folk literature in the classroom, with emphasis on the text rather than the illustrations. However, the title could be easily adapted to explore artistic elements. Intended to explore adapting the literary form of folk literature into the curriculum.

Whitin, David J., and Sandra Wilde. *Read Any Good Math Lately? Children's Books for Mathematical Learning*. Portsmouth, New Hampshire: Heinemann, 1992.

Offers picture book titles teachers can incorporate into the curriculum to extend math concepts from the chalkboard to the application. Arranged into chapters by concepts, among them classification, operations, fractions, and geometry.

CREATION

Bang, Molly. *Picture This: Perception and Composition*. Boston: Little, Brown, 1991.

A beneficial source for anyone who wants insight to the approaches illustrators employ when designing a picture book. Bang is noted for her collage illustrations, which figure prominently in the title.

Hands, Nancy. *Illustrating Children's Books: A Guide to Drawing, Printing, and Publishing*. Englewood Cliffs, New Jersey: Prentice-Hall, 1986.

An overview of children's book illustration for people interested in creating a picture book. Includes a glossary of terms and a brief history of illustration. Useful for teachers to use with students interested in illustrating their creative writing.

Martin, Douglas. *Book Design: A Practical Introduction*. New York: Van Nostrand Reinhold, 1991.

An introduction to children's book design. Covers layout, text, typeface, medium, size, and materials. Includes an extensive glossary of terms and an annotated bibliography.

CRITICISM

Benedict, Susan, and Lenore Carlisle. *Beyond Words: Picture Books for Older Readers and Writers.* Portsmouth, New Hampshire: Heinemann, 1992.

A compilation of essays by noted librarians, teachers, and illustrators exploring the use of picture books with older students.

Brown, Marcia. *Lotus Seeds: Children, Pictures, and Books.* New York: Scribner's, 1985.

A compilation of articles and essays by picture book illustrator Marcia Brown. Offers an insider's view of the people who design and create illustrated books for children.

Lacy, Lyn Ellen. *Art and Design in Children's Picture Books.* Chicago: American Library Association, 1986.

The Caldecott Medal is a prestigious honor bestowed upon the most outstanding illustrated books for children. Ms. Lacy explores the elements of thirteen Caldecott winners and the art, layout, and design that set these books apart.

Lehr, Susan. *Battling Dragons: Issues and Controversy in Children's Literature.* Portsmouth, New Hampshire: Heinemann, 1995.

A collection of articles on topics such as gender, censorship, and race, which affect the publication, purchase, and application of children's literature in the library and on a private level.

Schwarcz, Joseph H., and Chava Schwarcz. *The Picture Book Comes of Age: Looking at Childhood through the Art of Illustration.* Chicago, Illinois: American Library Association, 1991.

A collection of essays selected and arranged by social and psychological themes with focus on the visual elements, including media, style, and page design. Unique for the analysis of internationally recognized picture books commonly not explored in most critical surveys.

Smith, Lillian. *The Unreluctant Years: A Critical Approach to Children's Literature.* Chicago: American Library Association, 1991.

An authoritative source for educators interested in the impact and development of children's literature in a critical aspect. Focus on the effect of literature in the development of children.

HISTORY

Alderson, Brian. *Sing A Song for Sixpence.* London: Cambridge University Press, 1986.

Prepared to accompany an exhibition at the British Library of Randolph Caldecott's contribution to the field of children's illustration. Rounded resource included the "English style" of illustration and other influential illustrators who followed him.

Bader, Barbara. *American Picture Books from* Noah's Ark *to* The Beast Within. New York: MacMillan, 1976.

A critical study of illustrated books for children from the early years to the 1970s. Extensive in scope and outstanding for its readability. Includes over 600 illustrations (130 in color). A classic.

Cott, Jonathon, gen. ed. *Masterworks of Children's Literature, 8 Volumes.* New York: Stonehill/Chelsea House, 1983.

Eight volumes of historical information on all aspects of children's literature. Series includes *The Early Years, 1550–1739*; *The Middle Period, 1740–1836*; *The Victorian Age, 1837–1900*; *Victorian Color Picture Books*; *The Twentieth Century*.

Mahony Bertha E. *Illustrators of Children's Books, 1744–1945.* Boston: Horn Book, 1947. Supplements published 1958, 1968, and 1978.

A guide to illustrators of children's books from 1744, the year John Newbery's *Goody Two Shoes* appeared, through 1945. Useful as a tool when researching the history of children's book illustration.

Meyer, Susan. *A Treasury of Great Children's Illustrators.* New York: Abrams Inc. 1983.

A lavish introduction to the nineteenth-century artists who broke ground in the field of children's book illustration. Includes Randolph Caldecott, Walter Crane, W. W. Denslow, Edmund Dulac, Kate Greenaway, Beatrix Potter, Howard Pyle, Arthur Rackham, Ernest H. Sheperd, John Tenniel, and N. C. Wyeth.

Whalley, Joyce, and Tessa Chester. *A History of Children's Book Illustration.* London: John Murray, Ltd. 1988.

A critical look at the development of literature for children. The emphasis is placed on English authors since the development of the genre started in England. Over 200 illustrations, most of them in full color.

SURVEY

Day, Frances Ann. *Multicultural Voices in Contemporary Literature.* Portsmouth, New Hampshire: Heinemann, 1994.

An introduction to thirty-nine authors from different ethnic backgrounds. Includes brief biographical sketch, selected bibliography, photograph of each author or illustrator, and ideas for using each literature in the classroom.

Edwards, Margaret A. *The Fair Garden and the Swarm of Beasts.* Chicago: American Library Association, 1994.

Practical handbook explores elements of program development for young adults. Includes excellent advice on conducting booktalks with young adults.

Lukens, Rebecca J. *A Critical Handbook of Children's Literature, fourth ed.* Glenview, Illinois: Scott, Foresman, 1990.

A guide to evaluating children's literature in terms of genre, characterization, plot, setting, theme, point of view, tone, and style. Easy-to-follow format useful for professionals and parents.

Nodelman, Perry. *Words about Pictures: The Narrative Art of Children's Picture Books.* Athens, Georgia: University of Georgia, 1988.

A critical survey of the effect of combining narration with illustrations to tell a story.

Nodelman, Perry. *The Pleasures of Children's Literature.* White Plains, New York: Longman, 1992.

A survey of children's literature aimed at adults with limited background on literature or children. Chapter 10, "Picture Books," gives attention to terms and design.

Norton, Donna F. *Through the Eyes of a Child: An Introduction to Children's Literature,* third ed. New York: Macmillan, 1991.

A comprehensive overview of the broad field of children's literature from its beginnings to the present day. Numerous reading lists and suggestions for use highlight this title. Intended for children's literature courses.

Russell, David L. *Literature for Children: A Short Introduction.* New York: Longman Publishing Group, 1991.

Simple, straightforward narrative makes this title ideal for people with little or no background in children's literature. Covers genres, literary types, formats, and creators of children's books.

Glossary

Many terms applied to picture books are specific to the format. Develop picture book vocabulary by copying the list below and distributing it to your students. For further exploration of illustration and picture book design, I recommend the following titles: *Art and Design in Children's Picture Books* (American Library Association, 1986) by Lyn Ellen Lacy offers extensive examination of thirteen Caldecott winners by exploring the elements of artistic style, layout, and design that set these books apart; *The Picture Book Comes of Age: Looking at Childhood through the Art of Illustration* (American Library Association, 1991) by Joseph H Schwarcz and Chava Schwarcz, a collection of essays selected and arranged by social and psychological themes with focus on the visual elements, including media, style, and page design, found in picture books; *Picture This: Perception and Composition* (Little, Brown, 1991) by Molly Bang is a invaluable source for anyone interested in the approach an illustrator employs when designing a picture book. Bang is noted for her collage illustrations, which figure prominently in the title.

Acrylics: Paint with a synthetic base that dissolves in water. Colored pigments are added for an opaque finish. Acrylic paint dries faster than oil paint and has a different texture. Compare with OILS.

Adventure Story: A type of story where action, sometimes violent, is the predominant characteristic. Survival stories where the protagonist is pursued and evades a dangerous element, human or animal. Adventure stories are plot based rather than character driven, making setting more important than character development.

Afterimage: Phenomenon which occurs after the eye is exposed to an image in an intense color. When the eye looks at a neutral background, the image appears in the opposite color.

Alphabet Books: Usually fall into three categories: theme, potpourri, and sequential story patterns. Theme alphabet books follow thematic or topical focus. Potpourri alphabet books offer the author the greatest freedom but are also the reason for so many "A is for" titles. The sequential story alphabet book relies on a continuous storyline.

Anamorphic Images: Images that have been distorted to create an optical illusion. When viewed from a special angle, the image appears normal.

Anthropomorphic Stories: Realistic stories that have animal or inanimate objects as the main character. There is usually little or no magic because the animals or objects have human characteristics that render them capable of extraordinary feats.

Artist or Author Notes: Background information about the origins or process involved in creating the story or illustrations. Often found in books with a historical setting or an adaptation of a folk or fairy tale. In a quality picture book with significant historical background, teachers and librarians should depend on finding source notes.

Assemblage: A variety of materials are used to express a need to use natural, or "ready made" resources. Assemblage can be two-dimensional but is usually three-dimensional. Compare with COLLAGE.

Beast Tales: A short tale that features animal characters with human characteristics. See also ANTHROPOMORPHIC STORIES.

Biography: A written account of a person's life, with emphasis on achievement. Quality biographies are thoroughly researched and dependable resources. Biographies are written by someone other than the subject of the work.

Book Jacket: The cover of the book. There are several types of covers to consider. Contains a brief synopsis of the story on the inside flap and author and illustrator information on the back flap. See also WRAPAROUND, SINGLE IMAGE, and DUAL IMAGE COVERS.

Borders: Frames used to enclose text or illustrations. Borders can be simple lines or elaborate and detailed artwork that provides additional information about the story. Borders are common in the artwork of Leo and Diane Dillon, Jan Brett, and Paul Goble. Borders, as with panels and vignettes, provide balance and variety in picture books.

Canvas: Canvas is one of the most commonly used supports for painting. Tightly stretched strong unbleached cloth, usually of hemp or flax, is fixed over a wooden framework, on which acrylic or oil paint is applied.

Cartoon Art: Art representative of Saturday morning cartoons. Pictures are silly, goofy, and the artist makes no attempt to make the art appear realistic. Tomie dePaola, Gail Gibbons, and Marcia Williams have very distinctive styles and are renowned for their cartoon-style art.

Chalk: The term chalk, when applied to drawing, is used to describe various natural substances formed into sticks for the purpose of drawing. White chalk is limestone-based.

Charcoal: Charcoal is what happens to wood before it burns to ash. Using charcoal allows the artist to sketch with the edge for a fine line or to use the broad side, which produces thick strokes.

Collage: Two-dimensional form of assemblage achieved by gluing paper, fabric, wood, and other materials to a flat surface. Compare with ASSEMBLAGE.

Color: Result of pigments' ability to absorb, transmit, and reflect light. The primary colors are red, yellow, and blue. Primary colors are used to create secondary colors are green, orange, and violet. Primary colors are also used to create tertiary colors red-orange, yellow-orange, yellow-green, blue-green, blue-violet, and red violet.

Concept Books: Well-developed and illustrated concept books are recommended in helping children understand easy concepts, such as shapes and colors, and more difficult concepts, such as principles of grammar.

Copyright Page: Found in the beginning of the book, usually opposite the title page. Includes ISBN number, brief summary of story, Library of Congress subjects designations, publisher, copyright date, and details of illustration medium.

Counting Books: Counting books, like alphabet books, are used in an instructional manner to introduce children to numbers and other math concepts, including fractions and measurements.

Crayon: A medium in which the dry color is mixed with wax. It is similar to pastel but greasier and cannot be easily rubbed or altered for effect.

Cumulative Tales: Tales that have a repetitive, sing-song text. The words are easy to follow and read along with. The verses build on each other, lengthening the story as more characters are added. "The Gingerbread Boy," "Henny Penny," and "The House That Jack Built" are cumulative tales.

Design: The visual effect the artwork has in presentation. Composition and artistic style are factors when deciding on design. Text placement, front matter, shape, and illustrations are also considerations when determining the overall visual effect a book will have.

Double-Page Spread: Illustrations that spread across both sides of an open book. The effect of a double-page illustration is ideal for landscape views or scenes.

Drawing: Involves marking lines on a paper. A drawing can be an initial sketch or a completed illustration.

Dual Image Covers: Illustrations appear on the front and back of the book that depict images different from the story. Often by studying these different illustrations, clues to the story reveal themselves.

Endpapers: The glued pages inside the cover of the book are the endpapers. Because endpapers are intended to enhance the mood or setting of a book, planning and design are important. Endpapers are often decorated with a design or motif that complements the story or with one color that is dominant in the illustrations.

Expressionism: A style of art that emphasizes the emotion experienced by the subject. Expressionistic art has the appearance of reality, but facial expressions or structural lines may be exaggerated.

Fables: Brief tales that teach a short lesson. The moral is always stated at the end of a fable. Animals are characteristically featured as the protagonists. Aesop's fables are the most recognized fables in the world.

Fairy Tale: A tale or story relating the mysterious intervention of enchanted forces who aid humans in achieving a goal or fulfilling a desire. Fairy tales often feature royalty and always have a "happily ever after" ending.

Fantasy: Fantasy literature requires a willingness to suspend disbelief on the part of the reader. The setting of a fantasy novel is a nonexistent world or altered version of our world. Magic and characters capable of magical feats are commonplace in fantasy literature. See also MODERN FANTASY.

Folk Art: A style that is passed from generation to generation that reflects commonly held beliefs, values, and customs. The artist spends a lot of time researching costumes, mood, and spirit.

Folktale: A short tale that is handed down from generation to generation through the oral tradition. Folktales are gradually altered through various tellings and then recorded in written form. Folktales feature common people, such as peasants, and commonplace events.

Format: The physical make up of a book. Includes size and shape (square, rectangular, horizontal, or vertical) of a book. Nontraditional formats include pop-up books, books with partial pages, flap books, board books, and bathtub books.

Front Matter: The pages after the endpapers and before the first page of the story. The half-title page, title page, copyright page, and dedications are found in the front matter. Author or source notes, pronunciation guides, and glossaries are sometimes included in the front matter. The front matter is part of the overall design of the book and includes important information about the book.

Genre: A term used in literature to designate a type—for example: mystery, adventure, romance, history, folklore, fairy tales, and biographies.

Gouache: A French term used to describe a type of watercolor paint. The word is derived from the Italian *guazzo*, which means a watering place. Pigments used are ground in water and mixed with gum. The finish of gouache is opaque. The appearance of gouache is quite different from the finish of watercolor. Compare with WATERCOLORS and TEMPERA.

Gutter: The open space between the pages where the pages form the spine. Gutters are a special point for discussion because improper design will lead to some illustrations "disappearing" into the gutter.

Historical Fiction: Fiction set in a era before the story was written. Historical books also include personal accounts and fiction written during the period in which the story is set. Historical fiction is thoroughly researched and allows young people to better comprehend history. Titles concerning World War II can be considered historical.

Hue: The exact shade of a color.

Illustrated Book: A book with more text than illustrations. Small illustrations are used to add to or emphasize the story.

Impressionism: A style that captures the moment as it happens. Bright colors and swift brush strokes often mark impressionist art.

ISBN: International Standard Book Number. Each edition—library, trade, paperback, and book club—of a title has a separate ISBN number. The number is unique allowing title to be tracked by libraries, bookstores, and educational institutions with ease.

Jataka Tales: Jataka tales, or birth stories, are tales of Buddha's birth and are believed to be the inspiration for Aesop's fables and the Arabian Nights stories. Jataka tales relate the origin and teachings of Buddha.

Layout: The overall design of a picture book, including the text, illustrations, book jacket, and trim size. Book design and layout are important processes that should be explored when considering a book.

Legends: Legends are based in history and embellish the acts of a real person. The facts and adventures of the person are exaggerated, making the individual legendary for his or her deeds. Compare with MYTHS.

Library Edition: A special edition reinforced to stand up to multiple uses. Library editions have a reinforced spine that make them popular with librarians and media specialists. Library editions have separate ISBN numbers. See TRADE EDITION and ISBN.

Linoleum Cuts: Similar to woodcut illustrations except that linoleum is made by humans and allows artists to create their own patterns because linoleum does not have the natural grains of wood. See also PRINTMAKING and WOODCUTS.

Literary Fairy Tale: Similar to traditional fairy tales except that literary fairy tales are envisioned in the imagination of the author. Hans Christian Andersen wrote literary fairy tales. Many children's writers today are writing fairy tales based on thorough research. Compare with TRADITIONAL FAIRY TALE.

Medium: The type of materials used to create the illustrations. Information about medium can often be found in the copyright page. Books with elaborate preparations sometimes provide an illustrator's explanation of the techniques used for a particular title.

Modern Fantasy: Tales with modern settings and strong magical associations. *Charlie and the Chocolate Factory* is a modern fantasy. Appealing to people who fancy make-believe. See also FANTASY.

Mother Goose Rhymes: Mother Goose rhymes are among a child's first introduction to books and traditional literature. Numerous illustrated versions are available, but many sacrifice the authenticity of the original rhymes.

Myths: Anonymous stories based on primitive beliefs that explain natural events. Greek and Roman myths are the most commonly known tales, although other cultures have myths. Compare with LEGENDS.

Naive Art: Naive paintings often have a very childlike quality and are identifiable by the flat, two-dimensional quality they possess. There is little detail and no regard for anatomy.

Nonfiction (Informational): Books that are thoroughly researched and fact based. Categories include how-to books, cookbooks, and craft books as well as books about sports, health, science, history, social studies, and math. Accuracy is very important in informational books. The term informational is sometimes applied to nonfiction books.

Noodlehead Tales: These tales are distinctive by the foolish character who is always doing the right thing at the wrong time. The character in a noodlehead tale is a hero by result rather than intent.

Oils: Paint from mixing colored pigments with an oil base. The thickness of oil paint can vary. It dries slowly and must be added to the painting in layers. Painting with oil paint allows previous layers to show through as more are applied. Compare with ACRYLICS.

Panels: Illustrations that are broken apart for effect. Panels add to the story by allowing the illustrator to achieve artistic statements not possible in a single- or double-page spread. Panels, as with vignettes and borders, provide balance and variety in picture books.

Parable: A story that answers a question or points to a moral conclusion. Parables are known for the obvious moral lessons contained in the text.

Pastels: Pastels consist of pigments that are formed into manageable sticks. Pastels can be either soft or hard, which will affect the final images. Simliar to crayon but not as greasy. Pastels can be rubbed and altered for effect.

Pen and Ink: Pen and ink is a medium that can stand alone or be used with other mediums to create detail. Pen and ink is often mixed with water to create what is known as "wash" drawing. Using pen and ink allows the artist to create shadows and light with a process known as crosshatching.

Picture Book: A book that depends on illustrations to help relate the story. The amount of text is equal to or less than the number of illustrations. Compare with PICTURE STORY BOOK and WORDLESS BOOKS.

Picture Story Book: A book with illustrations that complement the text but are not relied upon to relate the story. Anthologies and longer texts are often illustrated with single-page illustrations. Compare with PICTURE BOOK and WORDLESS BOOKS.

Pigment: The pigment is the element in paint that provides its color. Pigments can be made of a wide variety of materials, including minerals, natural, and synthetic dyes.

Poetry: Rhythmic form that depends on imagination and perception to relate or express an idea. There are several types of poetry, including free verse (unrhymed), rhymed verse, and haiku.

Pourquoi Tales: Explanation of why or how an object or event came to be. Pourquoi tales use stories to explain nature, seasons, and animal characteristics. For example, many cultures have versions of how fire came to earth. Among the fire tales is the Greek myth of Prometheus.

Prequel: A story that relates events prior to a book that has already been published. Serves as explanation of events in a narrative. In "The Chronicles of Narnia" by C. S. Lewis *The Magician's Nephew*, although sixth in the series, serves to give the reader background on the creation of Narnia.

Printmaking: An image is created on a original source and transferred to another, usually paper. Prints are made on metal, stones, or woodblocks. The process is time consuming, but the effect is fresh and original. See also WOODCUTS and LINOLEUM CUTS.

Realistic Fiction: Realistic stories with sympathetic characters that children identify and empathize with. Realistic fiction can have a contemporary or historical setting.

Render: The way an artist uses his or her tools and medium to achieve the desired result. Illustrators often include explanation of their method in the verso page of picture books.

Representational: Subjects are portrayed with accuracy, shown as they would be in real life. Subjects and objects in realistic paintings are recognizable, and pictures have a lot of detail.

Scratchboard: A process that includes scratching the illustration in the black paint covering a white board. Colors may be underneath the black paint.

Sequel: A story or tale that features characters and places developed in an earlier work.

Shade: A color to which black has been added.

Shape: Picture books generally have four shapes: square, rectangular, horizontal, and vertical. The illustrator's intentions often have a direct effect on the shape of the book.

Single-Image Covers: One image appears on the front of this type of cover. The back of the book may contain another small illustration or a solid color that blends with the cover.

Single-Page Illustration: An illustration confined to one page. Text is often opposite a single-page illustration.

Surrealism: Surrealistic art is represented by imaginative details and startling or bizarre images. The picture books by Graeme Base and Audrey and Don Wood are surreal.

Symbolism: Figures and symbols are purposely distorted to express an idea. In picture books, symbols are often imbedded in the illustrations and are not hinted at in the story.

Tall Tales: A humorous tale usually set in the American frontier. Realistic detail and common speech are distorted and exaggerated to recount unusual happenings.

Tempera: Similar to watercolors, except colored pigments are mixed with a sticky base. Tempera paint dries very quickly. Compare with GOUACHE and WATERCOLORS.

Text: The words in the book. When used in discussion, usually refers to the story. Distribution and organization of the text are very important elements of the overall effect of any picture book.

Theme: The overall idea of the story; a common thread running through the story. In picture books, the illustrations, book design, and story are integral parts of the theme.

Tint: A color to which white has been added.

Title Page: Contains the title, author, illustrator, and name of publisher. The title page is usually illustrated with a vignette illustration that hints at a theme in the plot.

Toy Books: Toy books are board books, pull-tab books, flap books, pop-up books, cloth books, and plastic books (bathtub books). They are a wonderful introduction to children's literature.

Trade Edition: Edition for private use purchased in bookstores. Distinct from library editions, which are reinforced for numerous uses. Trade editions have separate ISBN numbers. See also LIBRARY EDITION and ISBN.

Traditional Fairy Tale: Fairy tales passed down through generations in an oral tradition and have majestic plots and royal settings. Fairy tales are more fantastic than opposed to folktales. The Brothers Grimm's fairy tales are traditional. Compare with LITERARY FAIRY TALE.

Traditional Literature: Based in the oral tradition, these tales are of unknown origin. Many tales have different versions representing different cultures. The Cinderella tale, with over 1,000 recorded versions is an example. Elements of the relevant culture are evident in each of the versions. Traditional literature includes fairy tales, folktales, tall tales, legends, and myths.

Trickster Tales: All cultures have an animal trickster figure that often achieves success through cunning and swiftness. Some trickster figures include Ananse the Spider from Africa, Coyote and Raven from Native American legends, and Rabbit from African American cultures.

Trim Size: The overall size of a book; the size of the pages, book jacket, and cover. Because size is very important to the overall design of the book, attention and consideration are given to the trim size of a picture book. Horizontal or vertical page orientation contributes to the size considerations.

Typeface: The type or lettering used for the text. Typeface is an integral part of the design of the book, and much consideration is given to which typeface is used in a picture book. The choice of typeface may reflect the setting of a book or simply the need for legibility.

Vignettes: Small inset illustrations that can be integrated into double-page illustrations or isolated and balanced against text. Vignettes, as with panels and borders, provide balance and variety in picture books.

Watercolors: Finely ground-up pigments with natural or chemical base that are mixed with water. Watercolors come in pans, tubes, or bottles. Compare with GOUACHE and TEMPERA.

Woodcuts: Illustrations carved into the wood with chisels and knives. The natural grain of the wood is allowed to enhance and contribute to the illustration. The blocks are then covered with paint and pressed to another surface, usually paper. See also PRINTMAKING and LINOLELUM CUTS.

Wordless Books: A format that has few words or no text. Wordless books are excellent tools for developing oral and written skills because text is usually absent. Well-illustrated wordless books will offer a degree of detail and plot complexity. Wordless formats are excellent to encourage students to explore the details and attributes of picture books.

Wraparound Cover: Art in a wraparound cover begins on the front and wraps around to the back. When removed, the jacket can be laid flat and examined for details about the story and clues to the characters.

Annotated Title Index

Numbers following main entries in the index refer to entry numbers in the text.

Companion Title Index

Numbers following main entries in the index refer to entry numbers in the text.

Author Index

Numbers following main entries in the index refer to entry numbers in the text.

Illustrator Index

Numbers following main entries in the index refer to entry numbers in the text.

Subject Index

Numbers following main entries in the index refer to entry numbers in the text.

About the Author

DENISE I. MATULKA is a freelance writer who has dedicated her education and professional interests to the field of children's literature. She holds a degree in English and Children's Literature from the University of Nebraska and is a candidate for a Master of Library Science degree. She has worked for Reading Rainbow, the Emmy-award winning PBS television series for children, and is currently writing a novel and collection of short stories for children.